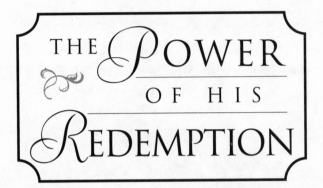

THE POWER OF HIS

OF HIS

REDEMPTION

Other volumes in the BYU Women's Conference series

The Rock of Our Redeemer

Ye Shall Bear Record of Me

Arise and Shine Forth

The Arms of His Love

May Christ Lift Thee Up

Every Good Thing

Clothed with Charity

Hearts Knit Together

To Rejoice as Women

Women in the Covenant of Grace

Women and Christ

Women Steadfast in Christ

Women and the Power Within

Women of Wisdom and Knowledge

As Women of Faith

A Heritage of Faith

Woman to Woman

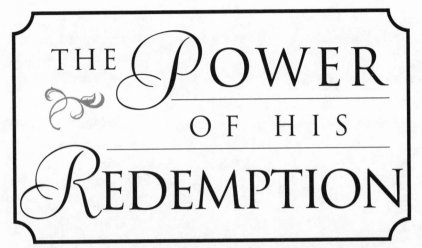

THE POWER OF HIS REDEMPTION

TALKS FROM THE 2003 BYU WOMEN'S CONFERENCE

DESERET
BOOK

SALT LAKE CITY, UTAH

Library of Congress Cataloging-in-Publication Data

Women's Conference (2003 : Brigham Young University)
    The power of His redemption : talks from the 2003 BYU Women's Conference.
      p.   cm.
    Includes bibliographical references and index.
    ISBN 1-59038-238-2 (alk. paper)
      1. Mormon women—Religious life—Congresses.   I. Title.

BX8641.W73 2003
289.3'32'082—dc22   2003026297

Printed in the United States of America   18961-7184
R. R. Donnelley and Sons, Crawfordsville, IN

10   9   8   7   6   5   4   3   2   1

CONTENTS

CROWNING PRINCIPLES

REWRITING OUR DREAMS

PRACTICAL SAINTS

PREFACE

꒰ ꒱

This volume, the eighteenth in the series, is a compilation of selected addresses from the 2003 BYU Women's Conference. We are grateful for the time, energy, and prayer the authors put into preparing their presentations at the conference, and we are pleased to share in this volume a sampling of their ideas and feelings on subjects that will appeal to sisters throughout our worldwide Church.

Here you will find uplifting and insightful commentary on the power of the Savior's redemption, the strength of covenants, the importance of unity in Church and family councils, the need for true discipleship, and a host of other topics that will benefit women of God.

We are grateful for the efforts of the conference planning committee, who made both the conference and this volume possible. We acknowledge the dedication and skill of our editorial team—Dawn Hall Anderson, Suzanne Brady, Rebecca Chambers, Dlora Dalton, and Susette Green—who compiled this work.

As you read this volume, may you receive strength and encouragement from Amaleki's words in Omni 1:26, "And now, my beloved brethren, I would that ye should come unto Christ, who is the Holy One of Israel, and partake of his salvation, and the power of his redemption. Yea, come unto him, and offer your whole souls as an offering unto him, and continue in fasting and praying, and endure to the end; and as the Lord liveth ye will be saved."

—Sandra Rogers
Chair, 2003 BYU Women's Conference

CARRIED BY OUR COVENANTS

Sandra Rogers

Nearly twenty-five years ago, in the first Women's Fireside of The Church of Jesus Christ of Latter-day Saints, President Spencer W. Kimball said: "To be a righteous woman is a glorious thing in any age. To be a righteous woman during the winding-up scenes on this earth, before the second coming of our Savior, is an especially noble calling. The righteous woman's strength and influence today can be tenfold what it might be in more tranquil times."[1]

We are not living in tranquil times. Around us we see war, death, contention, dishonesty, greed, immorality, infidelity, economic instability, new diseases, and natural disasters. Our homes are challenged by pornography, immodesty, selfishness, and worldly philosophies. As Primary children sing, "Now we have a world where people are confused. If you don't believe it, go and watch the news."[2]

But, as President Kimball stressed, these uncertain times give us the opportunity to "arise and shine forth, that [our] light may be a standard for the nations" (D&C 115:5). In a darkening world, there has never been a better time to "walk in the light" and to draw others to know and love the Savior because they see, through us, that knowing him and loving him make a difference.

In the midst of contention, chaos, and turbulence, we can, as the Lord instructs in the Doctrine and Covenants, "Lift up an ensign of

---

Sandra Rogers served as chair for the 2003 BYU Women's Conference. Former dean of the College of Nursing, she now works as the international vice president of Brigham Young University. She served as a Welfare Services missionary in the Philippines and has taught in her ward Relief Society.

peace, and make a proclamation of peace unto the ends of the earth" (D&C 105:39). Making and keeping covenants will bring a peace of mind and peace of community that truly makes us distinct and different—in happy ways.[3] We can do this, not because of our politics or our governments, but because "the chastisement of our peace was upon him; and with his stripes we are healed" (Isaiah 53:5).

I have prayed and reflected often in the past few months about my assignment over the international activities at Brigham Young University. I have joined in counsel with faculty, staff, and administrators about the effects on our faculty and student programs of war, conflict, demonstrations, potential terrorist actions, civil disobedience, and disease. We have prayed for the safety of our faculty, students, and friends abroad.

As much as I have longed for peace, however, I have learned yet again this year that the requisites for peace—individual, family, community, and international—are agency, righteousness, and obedience to two great commandments: love God and love our neighbors as ourselves (see Matthew 22:37, 39). We have to walk in His ways to turn swords into plowshares. The prophet Isaiah wrote, "And the work of righteousness shall be peace" (Isaiah 32:17). Elder Dallin H. Oaks observed, "For over fifty years, I have heard the leaders of this Church preach that peace can only come through the gospel of Jesus Christ. I am coming to understand why," he said. "The peace the gospel brings is not just the *absence* of war. It is the *opposite* of war. Gospel peace is the opposite of any conflict."[4]

During World War II, President David O. McKay taught that "peace will come and be maintained only through the triumph of the principles of peace, and by the consequent subjection of the enemies of peace, which are hatred, envy, ill-gotten gain, [and] the exercise of unrighteous dominion over men. Yielding to these evils brings misery to the individual, unhappiness to the home, war among nations."[5]

Elder Marion G. Romney maintained that "the price of peace is victory over Satan." He reminded us that "as a prelude to peace . . . the influence of Satan must be completely subjugated. Even in heaven there could be no peace with him [that is, Satan] after his rebellion. There, in the world of spirits, the Father and the Son could find no ground upon which they could cooperate with him. He had to be cast out—not compromised with, but cast out."[6]

Peace never comes from compromising with the devil, because his every snare is designed to draw us into captivity. Lehi taught this great truth when he said, "Men are . . . free to choose liberty and eternal life, through the great Mediator of all men, or to choose captivity and death, according to the . . . power of the devil; for he seeketh that all men might be miserable like unto himself " (2 Nephi 2:27). The peace the Savior promises is a peace born of agency and righteousness. Our covenants help us to use our agency to choose righteously and establish peace within ourselves, and with our friends, families, and others. We earn victories in the war for peace by winning daily battles for personal righteousness.

There can be no true peace when there is no agency. The war in heaven was fought because Lucifer wanted to take away our agency. Agency was so important that the Prince of Peace went to war to assure that we would have it. Agency was so vital to the plan of salvation that our Heavenly Father was willing to wage war and lose one-third of His children to preserve it. Agency is sacred: Without it we cannot progress. We cannot be rewarded for righteousness if we do not use our agency to choose it. Satan's terrible plan would not have guaranteed us all eternal life with the Father. Instead, his plan guaranteed that none of us would be exalted, despite our obedience, because compelled obedience without agency could not put us in the celestial kingdom.

Just as uncompelled righteousness is the only path to exaltation in the hereafter, so it is the only path to true peace among the peoples of the world today. Elder John A. Widtsoe said: "The only way to build a peaceful community is to build men and women who are lovers and makers of peace. Each individual . . . holds in his own hands the peace of the world. That makes me responsible for the peace of the world, and makes you individually responsible for the peace of the world. The responsibility cannot be shifted to someone else. It cannot be placed upon the shoulders of Congress or Parliament, or any other organization of men with governing authority."[7]

We hold peace in our hands, perhaps even more than others, because we have the truths of the gospel. We teach peace in our homes to our children when we behave with charity, kindness, honesty, and forgiveness. We practice peace when we pray, serve, humble ourselves, admit our failings, and repent of actions and thoughts not appropriate for a follower of Christ. We practice peace when we forgive those who may have been unkind to us or unkind to those we love. We practice peace when we reach out to others and build bridges of respect and understanding. We also recognize that the practice of peace often requires sacrifice to defend and uphold it. Many of us have loved ones who have given their lives for peace. We honor their memory and are grateful for them. Nothing is more courageous and valiant than practicing peace. Never, perhaps, do we practice peace more fervently and deeply than when we keep our sacred covenants.

I have too often disregarded the little book of Omni, hidden in between the books of Jacob and Mosiah. It contains only thirty verses written by five authors whose lives were surrounded by war, contention, and bloodshed. Amaleki was the last of these five warrior scribes. Before giving the records to King Benjamin, this soldier took the time to write this year's women's conference theme: "And now, my beloved brethren, I would that ye should come unto Christ, who is the Holy One of Israel, and partake of his salvation, and the power of his redemption. Yea, come unto him, and offer your whole souls as an offering unto him, and continue in fasting and praying, and endure to the end; and as the Lord liveth ye will be saved" (Omni 1:26).

Peace in this life and eternal life hereafter come when we use our precious gift of agency and offer our whole souls—body, mind, and spirit—to the Lord. There is no other way. And no compromise is possible.

My memories of home are suffused with the aromas of bread, pies, cinnamon rolls, cookies, and brownies, all baked by my mother. Once Mom was asked to give a Relief Society Homemaking miniclass on her spectacular brownies. She taught the class, made the brownies, and shared the recipe. A few days later, a sister in the ward telephoned to lodge a complaint. She had tried my mother's recipe, and her brownies, she said, didn't taste anything like my mother's. She was sure that my mother had given the sisters an incomplete recipe, holding back her secret ingredients so that no one in the ward could duplicate those brownies.

My mother asked a few questions. Had the sister used real butter as listed on the recipe card? No, she had not because shortening worked just as well. Had she used baker's chocolate melted carefully in a double boiler? No, cocoa powder was much cheaper and faster. All the "secret ingredients" were right there on the recipe card; the sister had just chosen to make substitutions.

You can't get real-butter, baker's-chocolate brownies from shortening and cocoa, and you can't get real peace without offering your whole soul to God. There are no substitutions, no matter what other voices may say. Nephi explained it this way: "O then, my beloved brethren, come unto the Lord, the Holy One. Remember that his paths are righteous. Behold, the way for a man is narrow, but it lieth in a straight course before him, and the keeper of the gate is the Holy One of Israel; and he employeth no servant there; and there is none other way save it be by the gate; for he cannot be deceived, for the Lord God is his name" (2 Nephi 9:41).

When we offer our souls to the Lord, we become the peacemakers who are His sons and daughters (see Matthew 5:9). We proclaim peace in the little things we do in our own homes as we keep sacred covenants. When I was in the fifth grade, my mother agreed to celebrate my birthday by inviting all my classmates to our home for a lunch of homemade hamburgers. (This was pre-Happy Meal.) I toiled several days making the invitations, drawing a red-checkered tablecloth with, I'm sure, a very enticing hamburger on the front. On my birthday everyone at school was excited about the party, except Rebecca Gladstone. New to our little town that year, Rebecca was the only Catholic in my mostly Mormon class. "I can't come to your party, " she said, "because it's on Friday and you're having hamburgers." That made no sense to me, but I didn't want Rebecca to be the only one in the class who couldn't come. She finally consented to come when I told her confidently, "My mother will know what to do."

When we all arrived at home, I told my mother about Rebecca's problem. She asked me to go downstairs for a can of tuna fish. I still remember standing in front of the pantry shelves holding a can of Starkist™ tuna and wondering how it was going to solve anything. Mom quickly whipped up a tuna sandwich on a hamburger bun, and Rebecca enjoyed the party that Friday without anyone even noticing she was eating something different. I loved my mother, who had worked her magic to make Rebecca feel comfortable and welcome.

I doubt that my mother would ever define that tuna fish moment as keeping a baptismal covenant she had made in an irrigation ditch in Woodruff, Arizona. But she was sensitive to Rebecca's faith, and that day she certainly had borne another's burden and made it light. Her kindness was a sermon to me on the practice of peace.

Covenants can carry us through the very worst of times. During World War II, Holland suffered greatly under German occupation. During the last months, as Allied forces advanced, the Nazis confiscated supplies, robbing the Dutch of food, fuel, and clothing.[8] That winter, people froze and starved to death. After the war, the Dutch harbored great bitterness toward the Germans, and members of the Church were not immune from these feelings.

The Church sent many tons of relief supplies to hungry Holland, but mission president Cornelius Zappey worried deeply about the bitter and scarred souls of his people. When Elder Ezra Taft Benson suggested that the Dutch Latter-day Saints be welfare producers as well as consumers, they began to grow potatoes. They worked hard planting, weeding, and watering the potatoes—and expected to use the bountiful harvest themselves. President Zappey, however, had learned of the even more desperate conditions in Germany. Clothing was still not available, food was being rationed on a subsistence basis, and the crisis was severe. As harvest time came, President Zappey knew the Lord wanted the Dutch welfare potatoes sent to Germany, but he worried about the reaction of the Saints who had worked so hard. How could he ask them to send their potatoes to the very people who had caused so much death and suffering in Holland?

He called the Dutch Latter-day Saint leaders together and said, "Some of the most bitter enemies you people have encountered as a result of this war are the German people. We know what intense feelings of dislike you have for them. But those people are now much worse off than you, and we are asking you to send your entire potato harvest to the German Saints. Will you do it?"[9]

Touched by the spirit of peace, and perhaps reminded of their baptismal covenants, the Saints in Holland voted to ship fifteen tons of potatoes to Germany that year. President David O. McKay called it "one of the greatest acts of true Christian conduct ever brought to my attention."[10] President Zappey recognized that the true miracle was the healing of Dutch souls. That outcome alone would be a glorious tribute to offering whole souls to God, keeping covenants, and being peacemakers.

But the story doesn't end there. German members of the Church in Berlin saved some of the Dutch potatoes to use for seed and planted a four-acre section of a city park with them. Soon after the potatoes were planted, Berlin was encircled by a Russian blockade. The famous Berlin Airlift kept Berliners alive for nearly a year, but the Saints had the extra insurance of their Dutch potato field.

In Holland a new spirit of unity and love grew among the Saints. The next year, Dutch members asked if they could again aid the German Saints. One Church leader observed, "The hate was simply out of [our] branches for the Germans."[11] (Imagine how the Book of Mormon would have changed if the Lamanites decided to send potatoes to the Nephites instead of fostering other "traditions" that held back their posterity for generations.)

In Berlin, the Hilbert family was also keeping their covenants in the terrible postwar occupation.[12] Karola Hilbert Reece recalled her mother's faith and prayers helping them locate a large amount of food,

enough to last perhaps six months if hoarded and rationed. But aware
that others were also desperate, the mother then prayed, "Lord, Thou
hast blessed us so bounteously. Surely there are people in our branch
who are starving. I fear to send [my] girls to find them. Thou knowest
those in need. Please send them to us."[13] An hour later the acting
branch president came to the door and helped distribute food to other
members who were starving.

Over the next year, food remained scarce. By the fall of 1946,
Sister Hilbert had had so little to eat that she had become too weak to
move. She prayed one morning, expressing her desire to stay and care
for her family and her utter faith in the Lord, but she said, "I can do no
more. I know Thou canst send help if it be Thy will."[14] At noon that
day, the doorbell rang, and she dragged herself to the door to open it.
There stood a complete stranger, a major in the American army, with a
huge box of food in his arms. In broken German, he greeted Sister
Hilbert by name and put the food on the table. He didn't know why
he had come but said that that morning he had felt literally pushed
into the Army PX to buy food. Though he had heard the Hilberts'
name mentioned only once at a branch meeting, he felt impressed to
call Church leaders in Berlin to get their name and address. The soldier returned with food and medicine every week for nine months. He
would not accept any payment offered by the Hilberts. He explained
on his last visit, "This war has been so terrible that I could not believe
God still loved us. When I found you, Sister Hilbert, I had lost my
faith. Now I know that he pushed me into that PX so that I could
know again the feeling of serving Him. And so I could meet a family
whose faith has not wavered even through horrors worse than I have
yet encountered. It is I who am indebted to you."[15]

Think of the chain of covenant-keeping peacemakers in these two
stories. American Saints kept their covenants and sent relief supplies
to Holland. Dutch Saints kept their covenants, repented of their bitterness toward the Germans, and sent their potatoes to Germany.
German Saints, including the Hilbert family in Berlin, kept their
covenants and offered what little they had to others, and they received,

like the widow of Zarephath (1 Kings 17:8–16), food to sustain them when there seemed to be no food to be had. An American army officer, stung to doubting by the inhumanity of war, followed the promptings of the Spirit to keep a covenant to serve and found his faith in God restored. Can we have any doubt that the influence of the righteous is magnified ten-fold in times of turmoil?

A faithful young man approached the Savior with an earnest question. "Good Master," he said, "what good thing shall I do, that I may have eternal life?" Jesus answered, "If thou wilt enter into life, keep the commandments." The young man responded, "Which?" and the Savior repeated the ten commandments. The young man then said, "All these things have I kept from my youth up: what lack I yet?" Then "Jesus said unto him, If thou wilt be perfect, go and sell that thou hast, and give to the poor, and thou shalt have treasure in heaven: and come and follow me. But when the young man heard that saying, he went away sorrowful: for he had great possessions" (Matthew 19:16–22).

Elder James E. Talmage explains that the young man was probably looking for one special observance by which he would achieve excellence. He was being asked to do more than be charitable: He was being asked to give up everything he thought important in the world to follow Jesus. To give up wealth, social position, and official distinction was too great a sacrifice and the self-denial was a cross too heavy for him to bear.[16] The man probably did give alms to the poor as part of his regular obedience; he just wasn't ready to give his "whole soul."

The covenant of obedience must be followed by the covenants of sacrifice and consecration if we are to give our whole souls. We sometimes view sacrifice as an odious effort. We may spiritually shrug our shoulders, roll our eyes, and sigh in the same way teenagers do when they ultimately "give in" and finally do the dishes. I learned the true meaning of sacrifice from Elder Neal A. Maxwell in the Language Training Mission many years ago. It was Christmas Eve. Knowing that we were thinking about home and all the sacrifices we were making to serve our missions, Elder Maxwell acknowledged our feelings. Then he told us that sacrifice was giving up something good for something better. He said, "Because of your sacrifice in giving up Christmas with your families, you have the opportunity to bring the gospel to others, making all their future Christmases more meaningful."[17] When "sacrifice brings forth the blessings of heaven,"[18] we always get more than we could possibly give. The Lord taught the early Saints that those whose "hearts are honest, and are broken, and their spirits contrite, and are willing to observe their covenants by sacrifice—yea, every sacrifice which I, the Lord, shall command—they are accepted of me" (D&C 97:8).

Our sacred covenants, made with the Lord over all the earth and kept by giving our whole souls to Him, will be an anchor in turmoil, a compass in chaos, a light in darkness, and a comfort in the sorrows that mortality may bring. They offer peace that surpasseth all understanding, a peace that comes from being accepted by the Lord. When we feel uncertain, may we remember these words: "This mighty God is ours, Our Father and our Love. He will send down his heavn'ly pow'rs to carry us above."[19] Let us lay aside the things that easily beset or distract us and be carried by our covenants to do His will, to feel His love, to be guided by His Spirit, and to enjoy His peace.

Notes

1. Spencer W. Kimball, "Privileges and Responsibilities of Sisters," Ensign, November 1978, 103.
2. "Follow the Prophet," Children's Songbook of The Church of Jesus Christ of Latter-day Saints (Salt Lake City: The Church of Jesus Christ of Latter-day Saints, 1989), 110.
3. In 1979, President Kimball's message at the second Women's Fireside Address was this: "Much of the major growth that is coming to the Church in the last days will come because many of the good women of the world . . . will be drawn to the Church in large numbers. This will happen to the degree that the women of the Church reflect righteousness and articulateness in their lives and to the degree that the women of the Church are seen as distinct and different—in happy ways—from the women of the world" ("The Role of Righteous Women," Ensign, November 1979, 104).
4. Dallin H. Oaks, "World Peace," Ensign, May 1990, 71; emphasis in original.

5. David O. McKay, *Gospel Ideals* (Salt Lake City: Deseret Book, 1953), 280.
6. Marion G. Romney, "The Price of Peace," *Ensign*, October 1983, 4–5.
7. John A. Widtsoe, Conference Report, October 1943, 113; see also "The Nature of Peace," in *Peace* (Salt Lake City: Deseret Book, 1998), 56.
8. William G. Hartley, "War and Peace and Dutch Potatoes," *Ensign*, July 1978, 19–23.
9. Hartley, "Dutch Potatoes," 20–21.
10. Hartley, "Dutch Potatoes," 23.
11. Hartley, "Dutch Potatoes," 22.
12. Karola Hilbert Reece and Dora Flack, "Berlin Miracle," *Ensign*, October 1978, 18–21. See also Patricia R. Roper and Karola Hilbert Reece, *We Were Not Alone: How an LDS Family Survived World War II Berlin* (Salt Lake City: Deseret Book, 2003).
13. Reece and Flack, "Berlin Miracle," 20.
14. Reece and Flack, "Berlin Miracle," 21.
15. Reece and Flack, "Berlin Miracle," 21.
16. James E. Talmage, *Jesus the Christ* (Salt Lake City: Deseret Book, 1975), 477–78.
17. Personal recollection of author.
18. "Praise to the Man," *Hymns of The Church of Jesus Christ of Latter-day Saints* (Salt Lake City: The Church of Jesus Christ of Latter-day Saints, 1985), no. 27.
19. "Come, We that Love the Lord," *Hymns*, no. 119; line breaks omitted.

WE WERE BORN
TO BUILD THE KINGDOM

Sheri Dew

Recently, a young woman gave me a compliment that I didn't deserve but that made me laugh right out loud. She said, "Sister Dew, every morning when you wake up I'll bet the adversary says to himself, 'Oh heck, she's awake again.'" Her comment not only gave me a new daily goal, but prompted me to again ponder the fact that we who are here now, in the last wave of laborers in the Lord's vineyard (see D&C 33:3), have been born now for very specific reasons. Yes, we are here to receive bodies and ordinances and to be tested. But I am certain that, for us, it goes even further.

Joseph Smith's translation of the verse "Seek ye first the kingdom of God, and his righteousness" adds five words that spell out our mission: "Seek ye first *to build up* the kingdom of God and *to establish* his righteousness" (JST Matthew 6:38; emphasis added).

Sisters, here is the simple, sobering, spine-tingling truth: By virtue of who we are, what we know, the covenants we have made, and the fact that we are here now, we were born to help build up the kingdom of God—as mothers and grandmothers, sisters and friends who will defend truth in every setting. We were born to be a light and a "standard for the nations" (D&C 115:5). We were born to open our mouths and declare the gospel "with the sound of rejoicing" (D&C 28:16).

Sheri Dew is president and CEO of Deseret Book Company. She grew up in Ulysses, Kansas, and graduated from Brigham Young University with a degree in history. She is a popular speaker and author and has served as second counselor in the general Relief Society presidency.

And yes, like the Prophet Joseph, we were born to be disturbers and annoyers of the adversary's kingdom (see Joseph Smith–History 1:20).

Because of the complex, convoluted, confounded time in which we live, our assignment is not easy. So, how will we do what we agreed long ago to do?

The Savior has shown us the way. In addition, valiant women have proven that mortality can be mastered. I refer specifically to two glorious women upon whom the entire plan of salvation depended: Eve, whose choice in Eden initiated the Fall, and Mary, who was worthy to bear the Messiah. Both were firsts, elected to go where no woman had gone before. According to our Father's plan, we had to fall and we had to have a redeemer. Mary and Eve were pivotal to both. Yet, it is not the drama of their duties that inspires me; it is the simple fact that under staggering circumstances and with the fate of the human family hanging in the balance they did what they were sent here to do.

We do not worship Mary or Eve. They were mortals, not gods. But we may safely look to them to see where they looked, to see how they dealt with the impossible, and to identify God-given attributes we need to awaken within ourselves if we are going to do what we have been sent here to do.

Attribute number 1: Faith. Mary and Eve had unwavering faith in God the Father and His Son Jesus Christ.

Consider Adam and Eve's challenge. Prior to being introduced into mortality, they were commanded to "multiply, and replenish the earth" (Moses 2:28). Yet they were placed in the Garden in a state in which they could not have children, hence the imperative need for a Fall that would result in posterity as well as mortality and death. Our eternal destiny hung on Adam and Eve's faith in the Plan and their willingness to obey the command to multiply. President Joseph Fielding Smith said: "I never speak of the part Eve took in [the] fall as a sin. . . . This was a transgression of the law, but not a sin . . . for it was something that Adam and Eve had to do!"[1] Further, he later added, "Adam and Eve could have remained in the Garden . . . to this day, if Eve hadn't done [what she did]."[2] Elder John A. Widtsoe added that their choice "raises Adam and Eve to pre-eminence among all who have come on earth."³ What monumental faith by the mother of all living!

Mary's faith was equally remarkable. She was stunned when Gabriel announced that she would bear the Christ child. But her response, "Behold the handmaid of the Lord; be it unto me according to thy word" (Luke 1:38), compares in terms of submission to that which her Son would utter later in Gethsemane: "Not my will, but thine, be done" (Luke 22:42). Imagine also the faith required to mother the Son of God. Surely at times Mary felt a crushing sense of inadequacy that could be managed only with faith.

Faith is the first principle of the gospel for good reason. It is our faith—our fervent trust that the Father and the Son will do for us what they have promised to do—that unlocks the power of the Atonement in our lives. There is nothing we need more than an increase of faith. Few of us doubt the Lord can help us; our question is usually, But will He help me?—which is why, even if we only "desire to believe" (Alma 32:27), we may experiment upon His words, meaning, put His promises to the test.

Recently, I faced a baffling challenge that tested my faith all over again. I worked and fasted and pleaded for help. But the answers didn't come easily or quickly. At times things looked hopeless, until I ask myself one question: "Sheri, do you believe the Lord is going to help you, or don't you?" That question always stops me short, because I do believe. I believe He will help because He always has. And every time I undergo another divine tutorial, it increases my reservoir of faith for the next challenge. As hard as it is, I am grateful every time my faith is stretched, because only if our testimonies of Jesus Christ penetrates every aspect of our lives will we be able to do what we have come here to do.

Attribute number 2: Knowledge. Mary and Eve understood the doctrine. There is no finer sentence-sermon on the plan of happiness than Eve's: "Were it not for our transgression we never should have had seed, and never should have known good and evil, and the joy of our redemption, and the eternal life which God giveth unto all the obedient" (Moses 5:11). Likewise, Mary's sublime doctrinal soliloquy beginning with the words, "My soul doth magnify the Lord, And my spirit hath rejoiced in God my Saviour" (Luke 1:47), revealed that she clearly understood the work, character, love, and mission of the Son she was carrying.

These women knew the doctrine. They had to. Adam and Eve were the only ones who could make "all things known unto their sons and their daughters" (Moses 5:12), and Mary was entrusted with nurturing the boy Jesus. Both Mary and Eve taught, testified, and prophesied. Their knowledge undergirded their faith, because in order to produce results, faith must be based upon truth.

Not long ago, I was racing through security in a major airport when I was pulled aside for an extra search. The officer opened my briefcase, pulled out my scriptures, replaced them, handed me my bag, and said with a charming accent, "I do not worry about the people who have this book." I don't worry either about those who have allowed the truths in these books to penetrate their hearts and minds and lives, because they know who they are and why they are here. They know how to detect even subtle distortions of truth. They know where and how to turn for peace, strength, and guidance. They cannot resist repenting. And they not only know what the Lord has promised He will do but they know that He will do it for them.

The word of God has a "more powerful effect upon [our] minds . . . than . . . anything else" (Alma 31:5). So, do we know the doctrine? Joseph Smith declared that he could teach us "a hundredfold more" about the "glories of the kingdoms," if we were "prepared to receive them."[4] A hundredfold more than the truths revealed in section 76, for example? But do we know what's in section 76? We know that whatever "intelligence we attain . . . in this life . . . will rise with us in the resurrection" (D&C 130:18), but I'd like to suggest that it also helps while we are here.

Recently a friend lamented that she can't remember half of the scriptures she studies. "But I've decided it's my job to put them in," she said, "and the Holy Ghost's job to pull them out when I need them."

Keep in mind that the greatest source of knowledge is the temple. The more we know, the more our faith will increase, and the more useful we will be in building the kingdom.

Attribute number 3: Obedience. Mary and Eve were models of obedience. At Gabriel's dramatic announcement, Mary asked in wonder, "How shall this be?" (Luke 1:34) But after angelic reassurance, she doubted no more and demonstrated total obedience. Likewise, after being banished from the presence of God, Adam and Eve were "obedient unto the commandments of the Lord" (Moses 5:5), "ceased not to call upon God" (Moses 5:16), and taught their children to obey (see Moses 5:12). What obedience!

Satan makes sin look liberating and obedience look restrictive and unreasonable, but sin is never the easier way. A poignant experience reinforced this for me when one evening I accompanied a dear friend, who asked for support, to a disciplinary council and there witnessed the unconsolable remorse of someone fully aware of the consequences of sin. I saw the anguish that accompanies the loss of membership in the Church and all of those attendant gifts. Greater agony I have not seen. Unrepented sin enslaves us to anguish.

If you had a video of that experience, you'd never have to give another morality talk at a Standards Night. The anguish of that evening would speak for itself, for it is not possible to sin enough to be happy. Happiness comes only from honoring covenants and keeping commandments.

Elder Bruce R. McConkie said, "To be valiant in the testimony of Jesus is to take the Lord's side on every issue."[5] As a step toward greater obedience, I invite us each to take inventory of where we stand on every issue about which the Lord or His servants have declared a position—everything from modesty to the precision with which we honor our temple covenants. A simple test applies to everything: Whose agenda does it support, the Lord's or the adversary's? Discipleship requires escalating submission to the Lord.

For me, the best part of the Good News is that the Lord works with imperfect people—meaning all of us. Nothing brings more joy more quickly than precise obedience.

Attribute number 4: Purity. Other than Jesus Christ, there may not be a finer mortal example of purity than His mother, who prophets foretold would be "beautiful and fair above all other virgins" (1 Nephi 11:15). That Mary lived up to her premortal assignment was clear when Gabriel declared, "Blessed art thou among women . . . for thou hast found favour with God" (Luke 1:28, 30). Said Elder Bruce R. McConkie: "As there is only one Christ, so there is only one Mary. . . . [W]e may confidently conclude that [the Father] selected the most worthy . . . of all his spirit daughters to be the mortal mother of his Eternal Son."[6] To be worthy to bear the Son of God, Mary had to be pure—not perfect, but pure, pure in thought, word, deed, and motive.

The object of this life is not to become perfect. Give that up! It is to become increasingly pure, which will eventually lead to perfection. We are the only ones who can show our young women that it is possible to live with purity in a polluted world. We are the only ones who can show them that purity is not piety and that vulgarity is not funny. We are the only ones who can show them that a woman who has the Spirit with her is radiant!

Obedience and repentance are the keys to purity, which will increasingly distinguish women of God from the women of the world.

Attribute number 5: Integrity. While Eve was fiercely obedient to the Lord's command to multiply and replenish the earth, she was also beguiled by Satan (see Moses 4:19). And yet, her response in the Garden was remarkable.

First, she immediately acknowledged her deed and accepted the consequences. She didn't lie. She didn't pout. She didn't get defensive or blame Adam. What humility and integrity from "our glorious Mother Eve" (D&C 138:39)!

Second, Satan mixed a lie, "Ye shall not surely die," with the truth, "Your eyes shall be opened, and ye shall . . . [know] good and evil" (Moses 4:10, 11). That is still Satan's game—to muddle error and truth until we are hard-pressed to tell the difference. While we don't know the exact nature of her beguilement, we do know that Eve then instantly recognized Satan. And here is the eye-popping part—there is no scriptural evidence to suggest that she ever fell for his deceit again.

We too must learn to identify Satan, for his tactics against covenant-making women are sinister in their subtlety. I do not care how valiant you are—no one is resilient enough to tango with Satan and survive. He is too experienced at spiritual ambush. One meaning of the name *Satan* is "the one who lies in wait."[7] And does he ever, which is why the only way to deal with him—and to teach our youth to deal with him—is to shun him like the snake that he is and leave him completely alone. Forsaking Satan may mean changing things. It may require changing wardrobes or changing channels, or changing attitudes, because it is not possible to "sort of" dress modestly, or "almost" tell the truth or be "kind of" morally clean. Nine percent tithing isn't tithing. It's a donation. Both Mary and Eve demonstrated that it is possible to have the integrity to entirely forsake Satan.

Attribute number 6: Identity. God named Eve the mother of all living before she was placed in the Garden (see Moses 4:26), and He elected Mary to bear His Son before she entered mortality. Their identities and callings were determined long before they were born and were surely a reflection of premortal spiritual valor. None of us comes to this earth to gain our worth; we bring it with us. Nothing was left to chance for them, and neither is it left to chance for us.

Said President Wilford Woodruff, "The Lord has chosen a small number of choice spirits . . . out of all the creations of God, . . . [who] have been kept in the spirit world for six thousand years to come forth in the last days . . . to build . . . up and to defend [the kingdom of God]."[8] There is not a woman in this Church who doesn't have a specific mission to perform in helping build up the kingdom of God. And the more we come to really believe that, the more immune we become to the world's distractions.

I offer as Exhibit A the recent rash of reality shows—*Survivor, The Weakest Link,* and don't even get me started on *The Bachelor*—each of which crowns one lucky winner. These awful programs perpetuate the big fat lie that only one can win. Satan, who is the quintessential exclusionist, loves to leave people out, probably because he knows he will never be included in the only group that matters.

In stunning contrast, our Father is staggeringly inclusive. Every one of us can be "joint-heirs with Christ" and receive all our Father has (Romans 8:16–17). Exaltation is for everyone who is wise in this agonizing, magnificent probation of ours (see Mormon 9:28).

My dear sisters, that includes you who have been reserved for this eleventh hour (see D&C 33:3). You are here now because you were divinely elected to be here now. The simple fact is that Mary and Eve and countless other glorious women were not assigned to this dispensation. We were. It is humbling and scary. But do you think God would have left the last days to chance by sending women He couldn't depend on? There is no chance He would have been that careless. The cumulative verdict of patriarchal blessings in our time is that we were sent now because some of the most trustworthy women would be needed in the final decisive battle for righteousness. That is who we are, and it is who we have always been.

Now, Mary and Eve exemplified many other attributes that are core to our divine nature that we could mention. But I come to the final, perhaps most compelling attribute, which is actually an outgrowth of all the others.

Attribute number 7: Courage. Eve's decision in the Garden was the most courageous any woman has ever made. But that was neither the beginning nor the end of her courage. Imagine the courage to be the first female mortal pioneer. Then imagine the courage to tame an unknown wilderness. Mary's assignment was no less daunting. Espoused to Joseph, she was suddenly, unexplainably with child. Yet her immediate response was both obedient and brave. And her challenges only began there. When others, choked with fear, abandoned Jesus, there stood by the cross His mother. Both Mary and Eve had unflinching moral courage.

We too need unflinching moral courage. A recent experience demonstrated this vividly for me. To my surprise, in March 2003 I found myself at the United Nations as a White House delegate to an international commission focused on issues relevant to women. From day one, I observed something that seemed incongruous. Women who impressed me as God-fearing souls in search of honest solutions to their problems often lobbied for the same things as women who had blatantly evil designs. I struggled to know how, apart from spiritual discernment, to detect the motives of these women. I listened carefully to everything they said, and at night I searched the scriptures for insight. But it was a puzzle.

Then one evening as our United States delegation held a briefing, a group of angry lobbyists began to attack the President's position on HIV-AIDS. These women were vicious. But it was as I prayed silently to know what to say when I took the podium that I had a clear impression: "Sheri, do you see? The mean ones are the evil ones." My fear vanished instantly. Now that I knew how to identify those on the other side, I wasn't afraid, because Satan never backs up his followers but the Master always does. The power of Jesus Christ is always stronger than any power emanating from the dark underbelly of the adversary.

Believing the Lord would fill my mouth if I'd just open it, I plunged in, uncertain how to both teach truth and support the administration. But as I began I heard these words come out of my mouth: "The first point of President Bush's plan to fight AIDS is abstinence," I said. "Surely anyone reasonable would agree that the only way to stop AIDS is for those who aren't infected to have no sexual relations with those who are." (I was tempted to say that they were looking at someone who'd had a whole lot of experience with abstinence and knew what she was talking about.) Several women looked ready to pounce, but I kept going.

"The next point is to be faithful to one partner in marriage. If sexual relations were restricted to husband and wife, AIDS would not spread." At that, two women attacked, but it didn't last long because their arguments were, frankly, dumb. Remember, Satan abandons his prey. And then, the women who agreed with me began to cheer, silencing the attackers for good.

What did I learn at the U.N.? That vigorous differences of opinion can be discussed respectfully, but when people become vicious, they are likely working for the adversary. That even in a spiritually hostile environment, there is power in truth. That when we have faith in the Lord, we, like Paul, "may boldly say, The Lord is my helper, and I will not fear" (Hebrews 13:6). And that the gospel is so practical. During two weeks I heard no issue debated that couldn't have been resolved by applying truth. The gospel of Jesus Christ has the answer to every conflict in our lives, families, and even nations. It also inspires courage— the courage to stand alone, the courage to open our mouths when prompted, the courage to prepare the greatest generation of missionaries, mentor the greatest generation of youth, and share the gospel in any setting. Unflinching moral courage.

Every time we exercise our faith in the face of fear or discover a doctrinal insight in the scriptures or the temple, we are better able to build the kingdom of God. Every time we discard a sin or an ulterior motive, every time we keep a trust or gain another glimpse of who we really are or speak truth, we are better able to build the kingdom of God. In short, every small step we take to develop our God-given attributes of faith, knowledge, obedience, purity, integrity, identity, and courage makes us better able to build up the kingdom of God.

From the beginning, women of God have shown that it can be done. Mary and Eve were elected for difficult assignments, and so were we. They came to earth precisely when they were needed and, in Mary's case, even in the right lineage. So have we. They endured heartache and opposition. So must we. Neither was perfect, but both lived up to their stewardships perfectly. And so must we. For being a latter-day woman of God is a sacred trust.

I believe Mary and Eve are the two greatest women who have ever lived. But I also believe we are the greatest generation of women to have ever lived, which means we have more responsibility than any group of women has ever had.

The Lord doesn't ask us to be more than who we are. But I'll bet each of us is further along the path than we think. And the reality of mortality is that our work never stops. Not if we are serious about immortality. So I ask you, Will you join me in identifying one thing you can do to increase your faith and knowledge? If you will, your obedience and purity, integrity and sense of identity, will also increase. Unflinching moral courage will be the result, the courage we as latter-day women of God must have if we are to be a light and a standard, if we are to open our mouths, if we are to build up the kingdom of God. We can do it. I know we can!

Jesus is the Christ. He redeemed us from the Fall. There is no "other way nor name given . . . whereby [we] can be saved in the kingdom of God" (2 Nephi 31:21). And there is no greater joy and no greater work than helping the Lord with His work, because His work is our work.

May we have the courage to do what we were elected to do and what we agreed to do, so that every day, when we wake up, the Lord will say, "Terrific! They are awake again, ready to help me build my kingdom."

Notes

1. Joseph Fielding Smith, *Doctrines of Salvation*, compiled by Bruce R. McConkie, 3 vols. (Salt Lake City: Bookcraft, 1954–56), 1:114–15.

2. Joseph Fielding Smith, Conference Report, October 1967, 121; also Joseph Fielding Smith, *Seek Ye Earnestly* (Salt Lake City: Deseret Book, 1970), 4.

3. John A. Widtsoe, *Evidences and Reconciliations* (Salt Lake City: Bookcraft, 1987), 194.

4. Joseph Smith, *Teachings of the Prophet Joseph Smith*, selected by Joseph Fielding Smith (Salt Lake City: Deseret Book, 1976), 305.

5. Bruce R. McConkie, *Sermons and Writings of Bruce R. McConkie*, compiled by Mark L. McConkie (Salt Lake City: Bookcraft, 1998), 363.

6. Bruce R. McConkie, *Doctrinal New Testament Commentary*, 3 vols. (Salt Lake City: Bookcraft, 1965–73), 1:85.

7. Hugh Nibley, *Approaching Zion* (Salt Lake City: Deseret Book; Provo, Utah: Foundation for Ancient Research and Mormon Studies, 1989), 92.

8. Quoted in Ezra Taft Benson, *The Teachings of Ezra Taft Benson* (Salt Lake City: Bookcraft, 1988), 555.

"WILLING TO OBSERVE THEIR COVENANTS BY SACRIFICE"

Elaine S. Marshall

Like thousands of faithful members of the Church celebrating the completion of a new temple, my husband and I traveled to Nauvoo last year. Unlike most who made the pilgrimage, however, we did not go in the summer when the sky was big and blue, the grass green, the flowers in bloom, and new friends were discovered in the long prededication lines to see the temple. We had declined an invitation to go with friends near the time of the temple dedication. Later, I regretted giving up such an opportunity.

At the time, my life seemed too full and busy. That spring, I had been called to be a ward Relief Society president. I was heavily involved in professional assignments. My father had surgery. My children were launched, but as any mother knows, life only becomes more complicated as children grow older and maternal worries stretch across a larger geography.

I grew up believing that work and worry were the two ultimate virtues. Anything resembling pleasure or peace was somehow unrighteous. My mother used to tease that it didn't matter to me if my work was efficient, effective, or productive—just as long as I sweat. My husband announces happily that since he married me, he doesn't have to

---

Elaine Sorensen Marshall is professor and dean of the College of Nursing at Brigham Young University. She served a mission in Colombia and has served on a general Church writing committee. Her book, Children's Stress and Coping: A Family Perspective, *won the New Professional's Book Award from the National Council on Family Relations. She serves as the Relief Society president in her ward. Married to Dr. John Marshall, she is the mother of four children.*

worry about anything because I am so good at worrying about every-thing. Paraphrasing a quip from George Bernard Shaw, he says of my British ancestors and me, "We think we are being virtuous when we are only uncomfortable."[1]

Last summer, my "fretting time" was overscheduled—I was reach-ing the point where I had to make an appointment with myself to con-sider a new worry. I was overwhelmed and personal time was crowded out. Have you been so busy you feel like you need a snorkel to keep your head above water? In his zeal to protect me, my husband John had even challenged the bishop about the wisdom of my new calling. So a summer vacation, even to Nauvoo, seemed out of the question.

But a blessing emerged as we were able to take a side trip to Nauvoo during a business trip in the Midwest. We drove into Nauvoo late on the night before Halloween. It was dark and cold and rainy. Though the wind howled and the pouring rain challenged the best speed of our rental car's windshield wipers, I will never forget that moment.

You know the moment. You have felt it on the I-5 freeway at La Jolla on the way to San Diego, on the Capitol Beltway at Silver Spring, Maryland, on Highway 89 between Ephraim and Manti, or perhaps even on that crowded street in Tokyo. I remember the first time I felt that divine pause that leaves one slightly breathless. I was very young, but the vision is forever in my memory of the moment when I saw the Salt Lake Temple spires for the first time. My father, mother, and Aunt Mildred exclaimed the obvious to me in unison: "See! There is the temple!" What is it that touches the divine in us when we catch the first glimpse of a temple? Is it the elegant architecture? The well-designed landscape and lighting? Is it the memory of milestone expe-riences of mission or marriage? The thought of a divine residence—the house of God?

That dreary night in Nauvoo, as we drove up the highway to Wells Street, the temple was larger than life, bathed in light that seemed brighter than day, and the rain seemed only to enhance its glisten. I knew at that moment that my "tourist side-trip to Church historical sites" had changed to a journey of holiness.

My husband left me in the parked car as he checked into our lodgings. I sat in silent awe and then whispered a prayer of thanks: thanks for those Saints who showed such commitment, such understanding of their covenants, such sacrifice, and such consecration that they left a legacy of holiness to all the world. That temple that night for me became a powerful symbol of covenant and sacrifice—a place of consecration.

Over the next three days, we walked the ground made holy by those early Saints. We peered into their homes and stores and barns like voyeurs into their private past. We went to the Land and Records Office and searched out my great-great-great-grandparents and found the place where they had lived. We went to the cemetery where my grandfather's first wife was buried. (That was nothing new—I love to wander old cemeteries and wonder about the lives of their residents. My husband says I go to a cemetery in every city I visit). Throughout our time in Nauvoo, I was consumed by a continual wonder at the daily lives of the sisters whose influence seemed to linger in the quilts and the butter churns and the porcelain dishes on the rough wooden tables. My heart was drawn to them in gratitude that they so willingly observed "their covenants by sacrifice" (D&C 97:8).

My great-great-great-grandmother Elizabeth Ann Garnett Reid was just twenty years old when she married Newman Greenleaf Blodgett in Nauvoo. Each one of her first three children died in the first year of life. She was among the faithful women who loaded her wagon and crossed the icy Mississippi River in February 1846. Her fifth child, my great-great-grandfather, was born at the crossing of the Sweetwater River in Wyoming on the way west.

On our last day in Nauvoo, a bitter-cold November morning, we walked down Parley Street. We paused at each signpost now placed as remembrances of the valor of those Saints. The harsh wind was so cold that it froze the tears on my face. Well aware that the Saints began their exodus down Parley Street, crossing the frozen Mississippi River or wallowing knee-deep in bone-chilling mud, we knew that we could not turn around. So, though freezing, we walked the entire length of the road. When we reached the river, we turned around and raced each other back up the hill, hoping to stir the blood to warmth again. As we climbed into the car and turned on our modern heater, my shivering husband turned to me and said with a promise so earnest that it surprised me: "I will never complain again. I will do anything the Lord asks of me—I will even support you as Relief Society president!" We were both overcome with gratitude and a desire to affirm the sacrifices of our ancestors with a commitment to our own covenants.

I think about Grandma Elizabeth Blodgett. What did she know? What was it in her soul that gave her the strength to leave the beautiful "City of Joseph"? How did she seem to heed so easily the call to "come unto him, and offer your whole souls as an offering"? (Omni 1:26). What did she take and what did she leave? What would she expect of me as her granddaughter? I learned much about consecration from my impressions of Grandma Blodgett that I would like to share.

First, *consecration is born of making and keeping covenants*. Grandma Blodgett and her Nauvoo sisters made precious covenants. The very purpose of their devotion to the building of the temple was to create a sacred setting for making divine covenants. The familiar stories of temple sessions continuing on into the night before they left Nauvoo illustrates their knowledge of the importance of official priesthood ordinances and covenants. Their faithful obedience in leaving their beautiful city and struggling into the unknown was an expression of their keeping their covenants.

Sister Bonnie D. Parkin reminded us: "Covenants—or binding promises between us and Heavenly Father—are essential for our eternal progression. Step-by-step, He tutors us to become like Him by enlisting us in His work. At baptism we covenant to love Him with all our hearts and love our sisters and brothers as ourselves. In the temple we further covenant to be obedient, selfless, faithful, honorable, charitable. We covenant to make sacrifices and consecrate all that we have. Forged through priesthood authority, our kept covenants bring blessings to fill our cups to overflowing. . . . Making covenants is the expression of a willing heart; keeping covenants, the expression of a faithful heart."[2]

Last night I went to a nearby temple with our ward, where my husband and I participated in sealing ordinances. I sat in a heavenly environment, with people I loved and other good people. As I knelt in behalf of sisters who had gone before, listening to their beautiful Scandinavian names and pondering the marvelous blessings promised for faithfulness, I thought of how little our sacrifice is compared to how great our blessings are when we commit to these covenants. I have learned that it is not enough simply to go to the temple and make sacred covenants. I must also practice keeping my covenants each day, living them with willingness, obedience, and faith.

The second principle I learned is that *consecration is the act of making our gifts holy*. It is not simply giving up everything. It certainly includes the sacrifice of worldly goods and time, but it is more than that. Grandma Elizabeth Blodgett surely lived the law of consecration as we understand it: She gave all her worldly goods, her time, and her talents to the Lord for the building of Zion. After being set apart as Relief Society president, I remember taking very seriously my own temple covenant of consecration. I was willing for this time to give all my energy and resources to what I perceived as my calling to serve others at home, at church, and even at work. I announced to my family and in my prayers that I would live the law of consecration—or my version of it.

What is my version of consecration? I work and worry to the fullest extent. I am good at working hard and fast, at sacrificing energy and rest. I can wake up at four o'clock in the morning, whether I want to or not, and sweat and think and worry and attend to any and all details. I am an expert at "multitasking." I can make being busy an art form. I am especially good at critiquing the work of others who don't seem busy enough!

But I have learned from our sisters in Nauvoo that consecration is not simply being busy, or the willing sacrifice of everything you have, or even the martyrdom of having goods taken away. It is not working and fretting as much and as fast as you can. Consecration is not weariness. Consecration is love and peace and taking the time to make our gifts holy.

Other valiant groups of the nineteenth century suffered and sacrificed to come west. The forty-niners, or perhaps the Donner party, suffered no less than did our mothers of Nauvoo. They left homes, packed wagons, walked long miles, and suffered harsh weather and sickness and loss. What was the difference? I believe that the trek of our mothers and sisters, as well as our brothers and fathers, was one of consecration because they made their journey holy. The Saints of Nauvoo were dedicated to a sacred purpose. Their steps were sanctified by faith and obedience to their covenants.

I have learned that my busyness is not enough. It is not enough to believe in the "work" of sacrifice alone. We must find a place for the Spirit. My journey must be made holy by prayer, by testimony, by love—and by accepting the Lord's gift of the Atonement to make up the difference when my efforts seem not enough. I must stop and listen to the quiet voice of the Spirit. I must find peace and holiness in my giving.

My third lesson is that *consecration requires testimony and faith*: a testimony of the truth of the gospel and faith in the gift of the Atonement. When my son Chad was about six years old, his Primary teacher helped him make a full figure of himself as "a child of God" with brass cotter-pin hinges at the joints of the arms and legs. Before we even left the church building, he began to take apart the limbs by removing the cotter pins. I warned in the usual motherly tone, "Don't take it apart until you get home, or you'll lose something." He didn't listen, and I didn't pay any more attention. When we arrived home, you know what happened. He had lost part of an arm and a leg. He cried over the lost parts, and I responded in my most patiently maternal "I told you so" voice, "Chad, didn't I warn you that if you took it apart, you would lose some pieces?" His response still rings in my mind. He wailed, "But, I didn't know you were true!"

How often have I just as suddenly learned a principle that I challenged? How often have I been reminded of my weaknesses and the Lord's willingness to guide by the Spirit and answer my flailing prayers? How often after dark nights of doubt did the answer come as a sweet light in the morning? And how often in my heart have I half-whispered, "But I didn't know you were true!" To live consecration, we must have the faith and courage to listen, believe, and live what we know is true.

To consecrate our work, to keep covenants, to dedicate our performance to a sacred purpose, to make our gifts holy—all are very personal and private acts. Nevertheless, they are not solitary in their purpose or effect. *Consecration brings us closer to each other as a Zion community.* When we dedicate our service to a holy purpose, we become more sensitive to others, more generous, more patient, and more willing and able to see others' needs and perspectives. We become more useful in our service and more like our Savior.

Our sisters of Nauvoo eagerly engaged in helping one another. They attended each other at illness, childbirth, and death. I like to imagine my Grandma Blodgett sharing provisions of her wagon as she left Nauvoo. Stories abound of our pioneer sisters' commitment to Zion. I have been blessed to watch the sisters of the Provo Pleasant View Fifth Ward serving each other. Within the last month, I reported to my bishop that the number of meals delivered in our ward seemed actually to exceed the number of ward members. Just twenty-one days ago, I witnessed sisters and brothers prepare special treatments, launder clothing, take watch at night, clean house, prepare food, bring flowers, fast and pray, and ultimately mourn with one another at the passing of one of our own. This process repeats itself daily across thousands of Zion wards of the Church throughout the world. Elder Neal A. Maxwell explained, "Consecration is . . . both a principle and a process, and it is not tied to a single moment. Instead, it is freely given, drop by drop, until the cup of consecration brims and finally runs over."[3]

When we set apart our lives for the holy purpose of service, we engage in the divine work of the Savior. Our influence for good is felt by friends (and, I hope and trust, even strangers within our own families and neighborhoods) and might even be felt, like that of my Grandmother Blodgett, across generations. "This is our Father's work," President Gordon B. Hinckley admonished, "and He has laid upon us a divine injunction to seek out and strengthen those in need and those who are weak. As we do so, the homes of our people will be filled with an increased measure of love; the nation, whatever nation it be, will be strengthened by reason of the virtue of such people; and the Church and the kingdom of God will roll forward in majesty and power on its divinely appointed mission."[4]

By keeping a covenant of consecration to build His kingdom, we are building our personal relationship with the Savior. Sacrifice is a gift that brings us closer to the Divine, but *consecration* uniquely *brings us closer to the Savior,* for we are engaged in His work. It was the Savior, after all, who gave the greatest gift of consecration: His Atonement, wherein He sacrificed all—the divine sacrifice—for us. When we become "swallowed up in the will of the Father," we become more like Him (Mosiah 15:7). Elder Maxwell reminded us: "The submission of one's will is really the only uniquely personal thing we have to place on God's altar. The many other things we 'give' . . . are actually the things He has already given or loaned to us. However, when you and I finally submit ourselves, by letting our individual wills be swallowed up in God's will, then we are really giving something to Him! It is the only possession which is truly ours to give!

"Consecration thus constitutes the only unconditional surrender which is also a total victory!"[5]

To live a life of consecration requires uncommon commitment and abandon. It is an act of giving freely without expectation of return. As Grandma Blodgett packed her wagon, I wonder what she painfully left behind. Was there a beloved chair or table or dress or book that her wagon simply would not hold? Did she stroke the object and then turn with resolve to follow the Lord and His prophets? What am I willing to let go in order to consecrate my life?

"I always weep on Parley Street," Sister Sheri Dew admitted, "because I can't help but wonder, Would I have loaded that wagon? Would my testimony of a modern-day prophet and Jesus Christ have been strong enough that I would have given up everything and gone anywhere? . . .

"Each day we stand at the end of our own Parley Street. The Lord needed the strength of the women of this Church as the seeds of the Restoration were planted and nourished. And He needs us today. . . . He needs us to develop the spiritual maturity to hear the voice of the Lord. . . . He delights in women who keep their covenants with precision, women who reverence the power of the priesthood, women who are willing to 'lay aside the things of this world, and seek for the things of a better' (D&C 25:10)."[6]

To consecrate is to set aside for a holy purpose. I pray that I will consecrate my life, that my time on earth will be set apart for some divine purpose, that I will meet Grandma Elizabeth Blodgett and report that I learned from her sacrifice and I continued her acts of consecration, that I may receive the promise given to her and her sisters: "Verily I say unto you, all among them who know their hearts are honest, and are broken, and their spirits contrite, and are willing to observe their covenants by sacrifice—yea, every sacrifice which I, the Lord, shall command—they are accepted of me" (D&C 97:8).

Notes

1. George Bernard Shaw, available at http:www.madwed.com/Quotations, s.v., "England/English." Retrieved 14 April 2003.
2. Bonnie D. Parkin, "With Holiness of Heart," *Ensign*, November 2002, 103.
3. Neal A. Maxwell, "Swallowed Up in the Will of the Father," *Ensign*, November 1995, 24.
4. Gordon B. Hinckley, "What This Work Is All About," *Ensign*, August 2002, 7.
5. Maxwell, "Swallowed Up," 24.
6. Sheri L. Dew, "Are You the Woman I Think You Are?" *Ensign*, November 1997, 92–93.

UNITED HEART AND HAND

🙟❦🙝

Cecil O. Samuelson

For almost two years, I have worked closely with all of the general auxiliary presidencies. I don't know when I have enjoyed an assignment or association more. Consistently, these exceptional women are wonderfully competent, faithful, strong, and effective, all the while being pleasant, always cooperative, and fully supportive of their priesthood leaders. If I could "bottle" what it is they do and what they are, I would do so and distribute it throughout the Church and the world.

In my years of traveling about the Church, I have also consistently met women leaders of capacity and devotion who contribute significantly to the work and success of the Church, while being positive and important influences on the families of the kingdom, particularly their own. The stellar qualities of the faithful sisters of this Church have been present from the beginning, and much of what I see in our emerging young women comforts me as well—even considering the challenges they face and the pressures today's world create for them.

In spite of my optimism about the present and future, I also candidly believe that things can and must be even better. I speak specifically of communication, work, and cooperation among sister and

Cecil O. Samuelson, a member of the First Quorum of the Seventy since 1994, was appointed the twelfth president of Brigham Young University in May 2003. He has worked as a physician and senior vice president of Intermountain Health Care. He is also the former vice president for health services and dean of the School of Medicine at the University of Utah, where he received his bachelor's, master's, and doctor of medicine degrees. Elder Samuelson and his wife, Sharon Giauque, are the parents of five children and the grandparents of three.

priesthood leaders in our families and the Church, as well as our community endeavors.

We must ask the question: Even though we want to be united in serving the Lord and building His kingdom, why do we continue to have occasional glitches or misunderstandings as we go about our work? That question has as many answers as there are people trying to work together. Let me focus on a few positive things we might consider doing to improve our communication and thus cooperation as we strive to fulfill our common goals.

First, we must always remember that we live in a world of individual differences. Men and women are different in very important ways. Most of us notice this fairly early in life. We must also recognize that women are different from women, and men from men. No stereotype accurately describes any particular person. Each one of us brings to every social encounter—be it marriage, a ward council, a profession, or a PTA committee—perceptions, past experiences, and expectations that color what we see and hear and how we attempt to communicate (or to avoid revealing) our feelings, attitudes, concerns, and suggestions. Because our individual differences are in large part God-given, Heavenly Father's plan must include our learning to deal with and accommodate quirks or traits—our own and others—as we live and work together.

The scriptures teach ways that we can communicate and cooperate with others, even those who differ from us—and that includes everyone at least part of the time. Let me review with you a few examples and then offer some suggestions that might be useful as you consider the circumstances, challenges, and opportunities that you face in your family, Church, and community associations.

What has the Lord said that will help us improve our relationships and communication? Think of Jesus dealing with His specially chosen Apostles. While these disciples had much in common, they also had distinct personalities and characteristics. Consider, for example, impetuous Peter or doubting Thomas. While we don't know everything about them, we know that they were different in easily recognizable ways. Nevertheless, Jesus wanted them to be one in some very vital ways, as He clearly stated in His great intercessory prayer for them to Heavenly Father (see John 17). I don't believe that Jesus was praying that they would lose their individual identities, their charming personalities, or other unique characteristics. But I do believe that He was unmistakably concerned that they be united firmly and permanently in the great cause of advancing the Church and kingdom, as well as that they themselves progress toward eternal life. Jesus had His priorities straight, and He expected the Apostles to have theirs properly positioned as well (see John 21:15–17).

Think of Mary and Martha. The Savior didn't demand uniformity in their service or offerings, but He did teach them both important principles of priority (see Luke 10:40–42). You will readily think of other examples.

How did Jesus teach and how did He communicate? The resurrected Christ was absolutely faithful in delivering His Father's message, but He also was sensitive to the circumstances of His audience, as can be seen in these verses from 3 Nephi 17:1–3: "Behold, now it came to pass that when Jesus had spoken these words he looked round about again on the multitude, and he said unto them: Behold, my time is at hand.

"I perceive that ye are weak, that ye cannot understand all my words which I am commanded of the Father to speak unto you at this time.

"Therefore, go ye unto your homes, and ponder upon the things which I have said, and ask of the Father, in my name, that ye may understand, and prepare your minds for the morrow, and I come unto you again."

While the Redeemer loved these people more than we can imagine, He also measured their capacity to understand what He was teaching and was patient enough to realize that often real learning takes significant time and effort.

We know that Jesus was a master teacher. What do we know about His ability to listen? Think of His conversations with Nicodemus, who came to Him by night to ask vital questions (see John 3:1–5) or the Samaritan woman at Jacob's well who initially did not understand what "living water" really meant (see John 4:6–26). In both cases, He answered the questions they asked, but also the ones they should have asked. He not only listened carefully to them but He also waited until they were ready to really hear His important message.

Other questions might occur to us as we use Jesus as a model of communication. How did Jesus target His teachings to His audience? Did He teach His Apostles and disciples in different ways than He did the multitudes? Given His stature, did He save all His best lessons for the masses or did He also deliver carefully crafted messages to individuals? Did He respond to every criticism or unfair comment directed to Him? What was His capacity to forgive those who had wronged Him? I believe we can safely say that as we search the scriptures, we find that the living Christ is the perfect example of virtually every form of effective and proper communication.

I, too, am impressed with the special communication skills of women, both those whom I read about in the scriptures and also those I observe. Think, for example, of Abish, the wonderful Lamanite woman who had both a firm testimony of the gospel and a testimony that she could make a difference. Like so many faithful women, she not only said what she knew but also had the courage and wisdom to reach out her hand to her queen, lifting her from the ground and helping change the history of her people for the good (see Alma 19:16–31).

Or consider the faithful slave girl from Israel who served the Syrian wife of Captain Naaman, who suffered from leprosy (see 2 Kings 5:1–4). In a subservient but appropriately assertive way, she shared with her mistress important information, combined with unmistakable testimony, that eventually led to Naaman's cure.

Like many of you, I remember correction and counsel from my own mother that made a difference in my life and continues to make a difference today. Both of my grandmothers were also master communicators. I remember vividly almost fifty years later the lessons of faith and commitment their lives reflected. Clearly, my most important teacher, counselor, and confidant for over thirty-eight years has been my wife, Sharon. A master of nonverbal communication, she is also never shy about explaining to me exactly how things really are! She has her own customized techniques that work most of the time with her husband and has the special capacity to completely connect with each of our children, who are in no way "clones"—even the twins—in ways uniquely responsive to their individual needs and circumstances.

As important as pondering examples may be, baptized and confirmed members of the Church have access to the most magnificent of all resources of communication: the inspiration of the Holy Spirit. This valuable resource is the vehicle through which pure communication of all kinds is received (see Moroni 10:5). In addition, the Holy Ghost can monitor or modify the communication we have with others (see D&C 84:85; 121:43–46).

Let me now make some suggestions for you to consider and perhaps even implement. Remember that President Hinckley shared his famous "Six Bs" with the youth of the Church.[1] While my effort will be more modest, allow me to propose Ten Cs, or words that begin with C, that may assist all of us in becoming more "United Heart and Hand" and improving our communication in all venues of our lives.

The first word is *careful*. Disappointments and even tragedies occur when there is miscommunication. We need to be very careful to say what we mean and to mean what we say. Skilled translators know that it is essential to listen carefully not only to the specific words but also to what is meant so that what we say really reflects what we intend to communicate.

The second word is *considerate*. We can become so focused on what we are feeling, wishing, or needing to share that we don't recognize how our message is being received. Even when our content is absolutely accurate, real communication is also influenced by context—how and where it is shared. The wise advice that we should commend people publicly but correct them privately underscores the importance of being considerate.

The third word is *confidential*. While not everything we share with others is secret, much, particularly when we are entrusted with leader-ship responsibilities in the Church or when we are dealing with impor-tant matters of family sensitivity, is confidential and must remain so. One of the easiest ways to spoil an important relationship is to betray a confidence. Lost trust is not easily recovered. Likewise, when we hear things that might be hurtful, embarrassing, or sensitive to another, we should consider it both a responsibility and a privilege to hold what we have heard in confidence, even when the facts are true and might be reported by other people anyway.

The fourth word is *courageous*. At times it takes significant courage to communicate things that we properly should share. We live in a world of changing values and, increasingly, no values at all. While we must always be careful and considerate, we need to take a stand for things we know to be right and against things that we know to be wrong. Think of the young Prophet Joseph Smith being both surprised and saddened at negative responses from people he thought would wel-come his account of his experience with the Father and the Son. In spite of the criticism, hostility, and the physical peril that he faced, he was always consistently courageous in stating his testimony of what he knew was right and what he knew God expected of him.

The fifth word is *clear*. Most of us have to work to make certain our feelings, concerns, observations, and suggestions are absolutely clear. Some have made a living by being obscure, and some perhaps consider obfuscation to be a key to survival in politics and certain other endeav-ors. Nevertheless, for most of us, striving to speak with clarity is essen-tial if we expect to be understood, appreciated, and effective in our relationships.

The sixth word is *complete*. In the Sermon on the Mount, the Savior taught, "Be ye therefore perfect, even as your Father which is in heaven is perfect" (Matthew 5:48). I have been grateful for the foot-note found in our LDS edition of the scriptures that equates the per-fection meant by the Savior with being "complete, finished, fully developed." While we rarely have either the time or talent to craft carefully every communication, we should do all we can to make the messages we share complete, appropriately detailed, and whenever necessary, reflecting consideration, planning, and development. While we all know people who seem to have something to say about every topic, those who contribute most are often those who say little but offer complete ideas and suggestions when they have something to say.

The next word is *concise*. After all I have said about such things as clarity and completeness, being concise may not seem desirable or even possible. Not so. I would again refer to the examples of the Savior. Think of those first verses of the Sermon on the Mount.

"Blessed are the poor in spirit: for theirs is the kingdom of heaven.

"Blessed are they that mourn: for they shall be comforted.

"Blessed are the meek: for they shall inherit the earth.

"Blessed are they which do hunger and thirst after righteousness: for they shall be filled.

"Blessed are the merciful: for they shall obtain mercy.

"Blessed are the pure in heart: for they shall see God.

"Blessed are the peacemakers: for they shall be called the children of God.

"Blessed are they which are persecuted for righteousness' sake: for theirs is the kingdom of heaven.

"Blessed are ye, when men shall revile you, and persecute you, and shall say all manner of evil against you falsely, for my sake" (Matthew 5:3–11; see also 3 Nephi 12:1–11).

These wonderful words that we refer to as the Beatitudes model the great power of what can be conveyed through concise communication.

The eighth word is *capacity*. Just as Jesus was always able to measure the capacity of His audience, we need to measure the capacity of ours. Explanations we share with children differ from how we teach the same principles to adults. Similar concerns apply to timing, context, and other factors related to the learning capacity of those we are trying to teach. Too often, perfectly appropriate communication is spoiled because the timing or environment isn't right. We need to spend as much time on the proper setting and circumstances for our communication as on the message itself. Likewise, if we want to be optimally effective, we need to communicate as the Lord did when He gave us the Word of Wisdom: "Given for a principle with promise, adapted to the capacity of the weak and the weakest of all saints, who are or can be called saints" (D&C 89:3). We need to remember, first of all, that our capacity or desire to expound or communicate may exceed the capacity or capability or interest of those we would like to receive our message. Second, keep in mind that "Rome was not built in a day"; even the Lord when dealing with most urgent matters counseled clearly about the issue of capacity. We are told not to run faster or labor more than our strength or means allow us. This was His counsel to the Prophet Joseph during the translation of the Book of Mormon (see D&C 10:4), and the same principle was expounded upon by King Benjamin (see Mosiah 4:27). While we should always strive to increase our capacity and that of others, we need to be objective about the limitations everyone faces.

The ninth word is *counsel*. One of the most effective and necessary types of communication occurs in counsel. The Lord reminds us that when we give counsel, it should be as if we are speaking in His name, meaning that we would say, under the inspiration of the Holy Ghost, what He would say rather than advancing our own agenda (see D&C 1:19–20). To be truly effective communicators, we need to both give counsel and receive counsel that is consistent with the spirit and mind of the Lord. We should gather information, advice, and even counsel from every appropriate source. But we must also remember our priorities and that "To be learned is good if [we] hearken unto the counsels of God" (2 Nephi 9:29).

The last "C word" I would ask you to consider is *council*. Our councils are a significant part of the government of the Church.[2] I speak not only of our ward or branch and stake or district councils but also the councils within our presidencies or group leadership assignments and especially the councils that should exist in our homes. A coun*cil* is not only a place to share coun*sel* but a place for us to communicate using all of the ideas or considerations found in these ten C words.

You will notice that there are some C words that I didn't mention.

Words or ideas like *carping* or *criticism* or *condescension* have no place in our communication. These behaviors are destructive and have no role in building the kinds of relationships that truly unite us heart and hand.

All that we do and all that we are should be focused on the Savior, His work, and His glory. Communications that cause us to be "United Heart and Hand" lead us to Him. Let me conclude with the words of Amaleki: "And now, my beloved [sisters], I would that ye should come unto Christ, who is the Holy One of Israel, and partake of his salvation, and the power of his redemption. Yea, come unto him, and offer your whole souls as an offering unto him, and continue in fasting and praying, and endure to the end; and as the Lord liveth ye will be saved" (Omni 1:26).

Notes

1. Gordon B. Hinckley, "The Six Bs," *Friend*, February 2001, 24–25.
2. See, for example, M. Russell Ballard, "Strength in Counsel," *Ensign*, November 1993, 76–78, and "Counseling with Our Councils," *Ensign*, May 1994, 24–26.

IN COUNCIL WITH MEN

Kathleen H. Hughes

In the many opportunities I have had to work in council with men, I have learned much about how men and women think and communicate, but of more importance, I have seen how much strength and power comes from uniting our efforts to bless lives. In a letter to Relief Society branches dated April 1875, Eliza R. Snow wrote: "There is nothing that appertains to the welfare of Zion, in which the interests of man and woman are not equal, and in which their efforts should not be mutual."[1] Consider with me some ways in which men and women can more effectively unite to serve and support each other in our homes and in the Church family.

Doctrine and Covenants 121 sets out seven "principles of righteousness" that describe the sons and daughters of God. While these qualities are described in connection with the righteous exercise of the priesthood, we also learn that the "powers of heaven cannot be controlled nor handled only upon the principles of righteousness" (v. 36). Therefore, when we refer to the "principles of righteousness,"[2] let's not just assign these attributes to men. To be entitled to call upon the powers of heaven in our families and in our church service, women too

Kathleen H. Hughes, first counselor in the Relief Society general presidency, earned her bachelor's degree at Weber State College and her master's degree at Central Missouri State University. After teaching school for many years, she worked as an administrator in the Provo School District. She has served as a Young Women General Board member, multistake public affairs co-director, and ward Young Women president. She and her husband, Dean Hughes, have three children and eight grandchildren.

need to possess these same character attributes. Like men, we should not be guilty of unrighteous dominion in our stewardships in the home or the Church or in places of employment. We must all be striving to develop the personal qualities of the Father and the Son, who work in unity of purpose and thought.

Verses 41 and 42 of section 121 describe the principles of righteousness. First is *persuasion*. In terms of our work together, this means that though we usually come to a meeting prepared with an idea, we must not try to usurp another's agency to get our idea accepted. We do not "bulldoze" our proposal forward without regard to others' thoughts and feelings. Likewise, we listen to each other, making sure that while someone is speaking we are not formulating our next sentence. We listen to hear and to understand.

The second principle of righteousness listed is *long-suffering*. Simply stated, we learn to wait. Because I am not naturally patient, I have had to learn, sometimes the hard way, that if I can just be still and wait upon the Lord, I can often see the power of God manifest itself in my life. When dealing with my children, my husband has taught me to "trust more and talk less." It may sometimes take longer to conclude a discussion, but invariably the results are better and last longer. For parents whose children have chosen, for now, another path, long-suffering is especially important. The person with a chronic illness will learn in this refiner's fire what it means to be long-suffering.

Gentleness means being sensitive to the feelings and choices of others. In our homes and elsewhere, gentleness implies respect for one another and regard for the agency we each possess. As Relief Society women, we should be charitable toward one another in our words and actions, avoiding gossip or unkind words.

Meekness is a quality the world does not value because it seems to imply weakness. But Christ tells us, in the Sermon on the Mount, that the "[meek] shall inherit the earth" (Matthew 5:5). Meekness, then, implies that when we choose to give ourselves to the Lord and to conform our lives to His teachings, we overcome the world; we become more like Him.

Love unfeigned is love that is real, authentic, true. In our interactions with others, we should love without regard to status, power, or what we can gain by association. The Lord gave us the example when He asked us to love Him and then to love one another as He loves us (see John 13:34–35).

The sixth principle is *kindness*. In our homes, the Church, and our community, we should use information given to us about others with care and sensitivity. For me, it means never sharing another's story without permission. Some stories and situations I will never share simply because they are too personal and/or too sacred.

Pure knowledge is the final attribute named. As covenant women and men, we should always be concerned that what we say reflects the truth. We need to become well informed about the issue before us. We need to explore as many options as possible and then present them as clearly and completely as possible. Our Relief Society general president, Bonnie Parkin, always tells us, "Good information makes for good inspiration." She is right. President Cecil O. Samuelson gave our Relief Society presidency and general board some great counsel about evaluating inspiration. He stated that we should ask ourselves four questions: First, is our inspiration consistent with the scriptures; second, is it consistent with the words of the living prophets; third, is it consistent with our callings; and fourth, does our inspiration infringe on someone else's agency? If we can answer the first three questions affirmatively and the last with "no," we can be assured that we have received "good inspiration."[3]

As we develop these personal qualities, we become more like the Father and Son—able to both minister and administer in ways that they do. In 2 Nephi 1:21 we read how father Lehi exhorts his sons (and daughters) regarding their need to be "determined in one mind and in one heart, united in all things." The same is true for us. Unless we are united, the work of our homes and the Church cannot go forth as the Savior desires.

Let me briefly discuss how men and women communicate with one another. If you haven't already noticed, men and women, more often than not, seem to think and express themselves quite differently. Let me illustrate with two humorous stories, one of them true. A young husband and wife were driving home from a party together. He was very quiet and unresponsive to her repeated attempts at conversation. Finally, she quit trying, but she began saying to herself, "Maybe our marriage is over. He must not be interested in me anymore because he certainly doesn't want to talk to me." When they got home, her husband said, "Did you hear that ping in the engine as we were driving home? I've really got to get the car in and get it serviced."

Another illustration: My daughter, not too many months into her marriage, celebrated her birthday. A day or two after this event, she called me and tearfully related that Brad hadn't given her a present. Her dad and I asked if he had asked her what she wanted. She responded that he had, but she had told him not to buy her anything. "Well," we said, "he did what you told him to." "But," she said, "he should have known that I didn't mean it."

Yes, men and women often do approach things differently—and that's good—or it can be if we remember that communication is never finished. No matter how long we've been together, there is always something new to discover about each other and the ways we think and work. Our differences also teach us that if we are to work unitedly, developing those principles of righteousness named in Doctrine and Covenants 121 is critical.

Home is obviously the first and most important setting in which men and women work together. Home is also the most challenging place to apply those attributes. Why is this so, when we are dealing with the people we love most and with whom we have the most to lose when things don't go well? Why is it so much easier for me to be patient with my neighbor's son who is doing weird things than with my own? I believe it is because we are so emotionally invested in our family members. We want so much for them and of them that we often forget to allow them the agency that is their birthright. Sometimes our own needs cause us to exercise unrighteous dominion over those whom we care most about.

In our homes, leadership is a cooperative partnership. Husbands and wives should counsel together regarding their needs and the needs of their families. While the father and husband presides in the home, women stand as equal partners in guiding the affairs of the home. Sisters, remember that you receive revelation in the same way that your husband does, and you are entitled, through your righteous leadership in the home, to receive revelation for your family as well. Many years ago, when our first son was just a baby, he cried most of the night; the next morning I took him to the doctor's office. I felt something was wrong, so when the doctor's examination revealed nothing, I was not satisfied and took him to see another physician. This doctor determined that both of Tom's ears were badly infected; this little baby was in much pain. I have always felt that the Lord inspired me, as his mother, to know something was wrong. I suspect you can identify instances in your life where you have felt similar promptings—revelation from the Lord regarding your family. As we ask the Lord to bless our families, each of us individually, or as couples, will receive the inspiration to know what is best for those in our care.

What about women who don't have a husband or father in the home? Remember what I said before: You have the right to inspiration for your family. Recall the example of Rebekah, who inquired of the Lord regarding her family.[4] She was given a very specific and direct answer from heaven: "Two nations are in thy womb, and two manner of people shall be separated from thy bowels; and the one people shall be stronger than the other people" (Genesis 25:23).

As we work unitedly within our families, we must remember that each family member is a work in progress. The weightier issues of home and family are often difficult, and solutions are neither swift nor simple. If communication is difficult, learn all you can about how to communicate more effectively with one another and practice what you learn. Pray often, with full purpose of heart, to know how to lead in your home. Exercise self-control and keep a sense of humor. I have discovered that often the most stressful situations our family encounters have become, over time, the best family stories. Keep in mind that words are not the most important thing; the feelings of family members are. *The conclusion of a discussion should never be a matter of who can out-think or out-reason the other.*

Please remember that we have been counseled by the brethren to hold regular family home evenings and family councils. These specific occasions allow us to unite as families to counsel together and learn the gospel together. These meetings offer opportunities to function in unity and love. Is it always easy? No. We are naïve to think it should be. There have been times in our home when family councils or family home evenings have had to be adjourned to let family members cool off. Yet we have had wonderfully fun and spiritual times as well. Do I get frustrated? Yes. Do we sometimes think that everyone else's families must be doing better than our own? I'm sure we do. But should we persist? Absolutely. Our persistence will help us and our children learn, through increasingly good examples, the way to work together effectively in a family.

Do effective family councils and family home evenings just happen? Usually not. They are created by carefully assessing family needs and purposefully planning to meet those needs. The *Family Home Evening Resource Book* states, "No one knows your family better than you do. You live with them every day—work, play, struggle, laugh, grow, and learn with them. You are in the best position to know their needs and abilities, their weaknesses and strengths."[5] If we will hold sacred this night set aside in the Church for family home evening and carefully plan what we desire to have happen, we can with patience and persistence make those things happen.

Ideally, fathers and mothers plan together meaningful family councils and family home evenings. We recognize, however, that in some homes, women often carry this responsibility alone. If this is your situation, listen to the words of a prophet and don't become angry or discouraged. If your spouse is uninvolved, encourage him to become more involved, but don't override his agency. If you are a single parent, persist in holding these important meetings.

Since most LDS women at some time or another will probably

serve in a leadership position in our wards and stakes, we also need to learn how to be an effective part of a church council. To a large degree, I believe we learn how to do so through our family council experiences in our homes. As we serve in our wards and stakes, we need to be certain that we understand our united goal. It is the same goal we should have within our families: to bring families and children to Christ. But how do we do this effectively and efficiently? Let me offer some suggestions.

In ward councils we do more than just schedule ward activities. We should, in confidential, prayerful discussions with the priesthood and with sister auxiliaries, plan how to strengthen families and individuals within the ward. Though we may represent a particular auxiliary, we also need to keep a "big picture" mentality and as a council member look to and represent the needs of the entire ward. Bishops sometimes become concerned and frustrated when auxiliary leaders complain that "everyone else gets the best people." Rather than think only of our own auxiliary's needs, in ward councils we must think of the people who will be aided by our auxiliary. Ward councils create a safety net for members, and each member of the council needs to think about what they can offer that will assist those with needs.

In priesthood interviews we have an opportunity to represent to the bishop or stake president specific needs of an organization. President Cecil O. Samuelson has been our priesthood adviser this year. As a presidency, we have met with him monthly. Since priesthood interviews at the general level are very much like those at a ward or stake level, let me share with you a few things that can be done to make these meetings effective and efficient: (1) Schedule a regular time to meet monthly with the priesthood representative over the organization. Set a time limit for the meeting. Sisters, bishops are particularly busy men, and the last thing they need is to have more of their time used than is necessary. Limiting the time in an appointment will also help you to be more exact in your requests and observations.

(2) As a presidency, carefully and prayerfully plan discussion topics. Sometimes women like to process things—talk about all the

possibilities. Men, on the other hand, often want to make a decision and move on. Presidency members should do the processing together, ahead of time. Then take an agenda to your council meeting and stick to it. A former stake president related that he could not believe the difference in the effectiveness of his meetings with the stake Relief Society president when she brought an agenda to their monthly meetings. There may not be time to cover all the items listed, but end when scheduled anyway. Unfinished items can be completed at the next regularly scheduled meeting.

(3) Communicate openly and freely with one another. Questions should be as direct and clear as possible. If you don't understand something, ask for clarification—this is not a time to guess what another person is saying. Open, direct communication patterns develop over time; therefore, it is important to begin each meeting with this goal in mind.

(4) When meeting with priesthood leaders assigned to your auxiliary, represent those you have been called to serve. Sometimes, priesthood leaders will help us in ways we don't expect. Let me share a delightful story about this. When Belle Spafford was Relief Society general president, she and her counselors and board raised the funds to begin construction on the long-promised Relief Society building. LeGrand Richards, serving then as the Presiding Bishop of the Church, counseled her that when she met with the First Presidency, she ought to make the point that the funds raised were depreciating in value faster than the cost of building was going up. He further said, "[I]f he asks you where you want to build, tell him that corner [where the building now stands], and if he asks for your second choice, tell him that corner, and if he asks you for a third choice, tell him that same corner. It won't be any harder for them to decide where you can build it today than it will ten years from now." Sister Spafford took his advice, and within ten days, the decision had been made and the Relief Society building now stands where she wanted it to be.[6]

(5) Speak with respect for both the person and the calling. This is when we need to remember the "principles of righteousness" I discussed

earlier. Persuasion, kindness, and gentleness will carry the day more quickly than anger or frustration.

(6) Finally, if a decision is made that day or a few days later, accept the decision when it comes and move forward. If you are unhappy, do not sabotage the decision or speak to others of your concerns. Be loyal to the priesthood. Remember, you don't have, nor can have, all the information the bishop has at his disposal.

Let me describe another council experience. As most of you probably know, the First Presidency has sent a letter to all wards and stakes describing suggestions for transitioning young women to womanhood.[7] In a ward I am familiar with, the auxiliary presidents—Primary, Young Women, and Relief Society—determined that successful transition was their combined concern, not just a concern for Young Women and Relief Society. With the approval of the bishopric, these women spent an afternoon together discussing and formulating a transition plan for the children, young women, and young adult women in their ward. Once it is finalized in their individual presidencies, they will take the plan to their priesthood leaders for approval. What a great example of women counseling together in council for the benefit of all.

Elder M. Russell Ballard has taught us: "God, the Master Organizer, has inspired a creation of a system of committees and councils. If understood and put to proper use, this system will decrease the burden on all individual leaders and will extend the reach and the impact of their ministry through the combined help of others."[8]

Why is all of this important? Let me answer by reminding you of the purpose of Relief Society and its sixth objective as set forth in the Church handbook: "The purpose of Relief Society is to assist priesthood leaders in carrying out the mission of the Church by helping sisters and families come unto Christ . . . [and] become full participants in the blessings of the Priesthood."[9] Temple blessings for all is the purpose of our work. President Gordon B. Hinckley has taught us: "Until you have received the sacred . . . ordinances of the [temple], you have not received all of the wonderful blessings which this Church has to offer. The great and crowning blessings of membership in The Church of Jesus Christ of Latter-day Saints are those blessings which come to us in the house of the Lord."[10]

Our purpose in our wards, and especially in our homes, is to give each family member an opportunity to receive temple blessings. It is not easy work, but it is holy work. It is the ultimate purpose of our strivings. It is the reason that we must be "united heart and hand," as are our Heavenly Father and His Son.

Notes

1. Eliza R. Snow, letter, *Women's Exponent* 4 (1 April 1875): 164–65.
2. For a more in-depth discussion and description of "principles of righteousness," see Harold Glenn Clark, "Priesthood Leadership," in *The Art of Governing Zion* (Provo: Brigham Young University Extension Publications, Division of Continuing Education, 1966), 547–54.
3. Relief Society General Board meeting, 16 April 2003; notes in possession of author.
4. See Robert L. Millet, "Restoring the Patriarchal Order," Family Expo Conference, Brigham Young University, 6 April 1998, 5; available at http://ce.byu.edu/cw/cwfamily/archives.
5. "Creating Your Own Lessons," *Family Home Evening Resource Book* (Salt Lake City: The Church of Jesus Christ of Latter-day Saints, 1997), 169.
6. Jill Mulvay Derr, Janath Russell Cannon, and Maureen Ursenbach Beecher, *Women of Covenant: The Story of Relief Society* (Salt Lake City: Deseret Book, 1992), 327.
7. First Presidency letter, 19 March 2003, available at www.lds.org/ywtransition/ywtransitionletter.pdf; see also James E. Faust, "The Virtues of Righteous Daughters of God," *Ensign*, May 2003, 108.
8. M. Russell Ballard, Conference Report, April 1994, 31; or "Counseling Our Councils," *Ensign*, May 1994, 24.
9. "Relief Society," section 3 of the *Church Handbook of Instructions, Book 2: Priesthood and Auxiliary Leaders* (2001).
10. "Recurring Themes of President Hinckley," *Ensign*, June 2000, 19.

I NOW TURN THE KEY IN THE NAME OF THE LORD

❧

Camille Fronk

Prophets have often lauded the greatness of women and their defining influence in righteous societies. For example, President Spencer W. Kimball said: "Much of the major growth that is coming to the Church in the last days . . . will happen to the degree that the women of the Church reflect righteousness and articulateness in their lives and to the degree that women of the Church are seen as distinct and different—in happy ways—from the women of the world."[1]

Women love quoting statements such as this one, hoping that in so doing we already are what prophets have envisioned. But just as often we hear ourselves simply described as *special, lovely,* and *beautiful,* all the while silently knowing that we aren't quite as special, lovely, or beautiful as we are being given credit for. We long to contribute our spiritual gifts in leadership councils, church callings, and community service. We want to make a difference, to have our spiritual sensitivities desired and used to build the kingdom, rather than simply acknowledged in an oft-repeated quote.

ORIGIN OF THE SOCIETY

In 1842, a small group of women in the Church felt the same way. They sensed the need for an organization to combine their means and

---

Camille Fronk, an author and popular speaker, is an associate professor of ancient scripture at Brigham Young University. Formerly a counselor in her stake Relief Society presidency, she now serves as a Primary teacher. She has served as a member of the Young Women General Board, as dean of students at LDS Business College, and as a seminary and institute instructor. Sister Fronk recently married Dr. Paul Olson.

efforts in meaningful charitable work. Certainly, this desire was not born of boredom or lives of ease. At that time in Nauvoo, many of the men were away from home serving missions. Others were heavily involved in temple building or other public works projects in the city. In their benchmark history of the Relief Society, Sisters Jill Mulvay Derr, Janath Russell Cannon, and Maureen Ursenbach Beecher observed, "The economic success, if not survival, of most Nauvoo households depended upon the resourcefulness and hard work of women."[2] Nauvoo women often needed to augment family income with school-teaching, sewing, quilting, spinning, millinery work, and fine laundering. They were also the ones called upon to nurse the sick, including the many sufferers from a malaria-like illness that plagued the area, prolonged by the mosquito-breeding swampland bordering the city.

This was a time in America when women were organizing in all sorts of prayer, missionary, and benevolent societies. But this group of about twenty women in Nauvoo—women Joseph Smith described as "some of our most intelligent, humane, philanthropic and respectable ladies"[3]—felt their organization should be different from all others. Eliza R. Snow petitioned "that the popular Institutions of the day should not be our guide—that as daughters of Zion, we should set an example for all the world, rather than confine ourselves to the course which had been heretofore pursued."[4] So they sought out the Prophet Joseph Smith for guidance. He did not disappoint them. While the Prophet Joseph praised their constitution and bylaws, drafted by Eliza R. Snow, as "the best he had ever seen," the women's plans were myopic compared to what God had in store for them. The Prophet promised "something better for them. . . . I will organize the women . . . under the priesthood after the pattern of the priesthood."[5]

During the first year of the Society's formal meetings, Joseph Smith provided the vision for the Society's essential mission: specifically, to unite for "the relief of the poor, the destitute, the widow and the orphan, and for the exercise of all benevolent purposes."[6] He foresaw "that with the resources they will have at command, they will fly to the relief of the stranger; they will pour in oil and wine to the wounded heart of the distressed; they will dry up the tears of the orphan and make the widow's heart to rejoice."[7]

Eleven weeks later, the Prophet expanded their mission of service when he commissioned the Society "not only to relieve the poor, but to save souls."[8] For women who wanted to make a difference in the world, this was the Society to join. It would provide opportunities unlike any other. The Prophet, speaking at one of their first meetings, observed: "You are now placed in a situation where you can act according to those sympathies which God has planted in your bosoms." He then promised them divine assistance, noting that "if you live up to your privilege the angels cannot be restrained from being your associates."[9]

To receive this final blessing, however, the Society required something more. The temple endowment was first revealed by the Prophet in May 1842. Several days before, on 28 April 1842, Joseph Smith taught the women: "This Society is to get instruction through the order which God has established—thro' the medium of those appointed to lead—and I now turn the key to you in the name of God and this Society shall rejoice and knowledge and intelligence shall flow down from this time—this is the beginning of better days to this Society."[10] Many of these women were among the first to receive the temple endowment in September 1843, having been "prepared by the instructions Joseph Smith gave to the . . . Society."[11]

What do we learn from these crucial elements of the Society? We can learn that the Society's success depends on its members' reliance on Christ and being true to sacred covenants made in the holy temple. Only in Christ do we know how to succor others. Only through the enabling power of Christ's atonement can we receive sufficient intelligence and capacity to truly help those in need.

CARE FOR THE POOR AND SAVING SOULS

What does all this mean to women today? How does this inspired beginning affect contemporary women's contributions in the home,

Church, and community? To answer these questions, we must understand what it means to care for the poor and save souls.

In my mind, "the poor" refers to those who have a depleted supply: those who have lost something precious and essential, such as a loved one, the connection with the Spirit, or the ability to care for themselves. The Lord has always been mindful of the vulnerable in our midst—the weak, the innocent, the unprotected (see Isaiah 1:17, 23; 10:1–2; Jeremiah 7:5–7). Through the prophet Malachi, He declared "I will be a swift witness against . . . those that oppress the hireling in his wages, the widow, and the fatherless, and that turn aside the stranger" (Malachi 3:5; 3 Nephi 24:5). On the other hand, visiting "the fatherless and the widows in their affliction" is defined as pure and undefiled religion (James 1:27).

Since Joseph Smith included saving souls as part of caring for the poor, surely more is asked of us than striving for statistics to wow a stake president or making the finest casseroles, designer ducks, and doilies. Joseph Smith taught that "the object [of this charitable society of women] is to make those not so good, equal with the good."[12]

With that perspective in mind, the question may not be "How can I meet this person's needs?" or "How can I fix this person's problem?" but "How can I assist this person to develop the skills, resources, knowledge, and, above all, spiritual strength to discover and implement her own solutions?" Or as Brigham Young University professor Chauncey Riddle put it: "The test of true help is this: does it leave the person helped better able to meet his problems . . . ?"[13] When saving souls is part of the mission of caring for the poor and destitute, assistance in basic physical needs—health, security, and shelter—is only the beginning. From the Prophet Joseph's perspective in setting up the Society, saving souls included educating the mind, increasing gospel knowledge, even imparting the same "doctrine of the priesthood" that priesthood quorums are taught.[14]

Even before the Nauvoo sisters had dreamed of their Society, Emma Hale Smith had been "ordained [or set apart] . . . to expound scriptures, and to exhort the church, according as it shall be given [her by the Lord's] Spirit" (D&C 25:7). At an early organizing meeting, the Prophet Joseph declared "that the revelation was then fulfilled by Sister Emma's election to the Presidency of the Society."[15] Clearly, expounding scripture and exhorting the Church are central to the mission of the Society when women are serious about saving souls.[16]

Other women in the Society were not exempt from the responsibility to expound scripture. The revelation addressed to Emma concludes, "this is my voice unto all" (D&C 25:16). Gospel education is not about posing mind-boggling gospel questions or about always having a crisp, impressively succinct answer. It isn't striving to become the designated ward scriptorian, nor feeling relief when that role is filled by another woman in the ward.

On the contrary, even gospel instruction should be founded on charity, namely, caring for the poor and saving souls. President Spencer W. Kimball challenged women: "Become scholars of the scriptures—not to put others down, but to lift them up!"[17] "A Christlike teacher," noted Brother Riddle, "will rejoice in the opportunity he has to make his . . . students, rich like unto himself in knowledge and ability"[18]—thus heeding the Prophet's admonition to "make those not so good, equal with the good."

Saving souls also suggests that some souls need rescuing. Not everyone who came to the Nauvoo Society was spiritually and morally whole. In one meeting, the Prophet Joseph discussed welcoming outcasts into their circle and tenderly supporting them along the road of repentance. He explained, "Christ was condemn'd by the righteous Jews because he took sinners into his society—He took them upon the principle that they repented of their sins. It is the object of this Society to reform persons. . . .

"Nothing is so much calculated to lead people to forsake sin as to take them by the hand and watch over them with tenderness. When persons manifest the least kindness and love to me, O what pow'r it has over my mind, while the opposite course has a tendency to harrow up all the harsh feelings and depress the human mind.

" . . . The nearer we get to our heavenly Father the more are we disposed to look with compassion on perishing souls to take them upon our shoulders and cast their sins behind our back."[19]

CAUTIONS

While we modern sisters are often praised for our unique abilities and worthy efforts, warnings about stumbling blocks that often prove devastating to women are rare. That is not true of the Society's early meetings, according to their minutes. Personally, I would welcome inspired words of chastisement or correction intended to stretch and refocus me in my quest to actually become one of those articulate, capable, God-fearing women that Joseph Smith and other prophets describe.

The Prophet Joseph certainly supplied plenty of cautions in his instruction to the women of the Society. He warned of women's tendency toward "self-righteousness," zeal without knowledge, creating divisions among themselves through "strife" and judging, an "aspiring" disposition, and ostracizing many by their sharp tongues.[20]

Let's consider more of Joseph Smith's concerns. "Don't be limited in your views with regard to your neighbors' virtues," he admonished the women of the Society, "but be limited towards your own virtues, and not think yourselves more righteous than others; you must enlarge your souls toward others if you would do like Jesus. . . .

"As you increase in innocence and virtue, as you increase in goodness, let your hearts expand—let them be enlarged towards others—you must be longsuffering and bear with the faults and errors of mankind. How precious are the souls of man! The female part of community are apt to be contracted, in their views. You must not be contracted but you must be liberal in your feelings."[21]

How often do we feel fear or distrust when a woman who is different from us joins our community? We take a quick inventory of her figure, clothing, hairstyle, approximate age, marital status, and socioeconomic status. From this shallow investigation, we compare ourselves and then choose to feel either intimidated or superior to the newcomer. Either response validates our instinct to withhold friendship and genuine communication. While we publicly announce that visitors are welcome, we privately establish a fence around our comfort zone to keep strangers out.

By contrast, the Prophet Joseph invited us to respond like the Savior would. The woman captured in adultery, Martha cumbered about with much serving, Mary who was always found at Jesus' feet, and the Samaritan woman previously married to five husbands and now living with a man not her husband: each discovered that Christ's invitation to "Come" included her. Would those same women find similar hospitality and succor among us? The Prophet admonished us to let our hearts expand to tolerate the weaknesses of others who desire fellowship with the Lord, knowing that Christ's sacrifice is infinite, even as "broad as eternity" (Moses 7:53). Certainly that is large enough to cover all of us.

In addition to warning us about withholding companionship and love, Joseph Smith cautioned women to tame their tongues and curb their propensity towards religious rigidity. He explained, "As females possess refined feelings and sensitiveness; they are also subject to an over much zeal which must ever prove dangerous, and cause them to be rigid in a religious capacity." He cautioned them to "put a double watch over the tongue" and "don't do more hurt than good with your tongues—be pure in heart—Said Jesus ye shall do the work which ye see me do."[22]

Here the Prophet identified religious fanaticism as the weakness that often undermines a woman's true spiritual sensitivity, replacing it with vanity and pride. In 1913, the First Presidency of the Church cautioned members who "pride themselves on their strict observance of the rules and ordinances and ceremonies of the Church." Such persons, they warned, lose discernment, "think they are 'the very elect'" and "are led astray by false spirits, who exercise an influence so imitative of that which proceeds from a Divine source."[23] If we ever hope to "be different—in happy ways—from the women of the world," we can't afford to let our own egos get in the way of discerning the still small voice.

Since the Prophet organized this Society of women "under the priesthood and after the order of the priesthood," the revelation, recorded in Doctrine and Covenants 121, about the righteous exercise of those priesthood powers can also remind women of the tremendous power that accompanies their Society while also warning them against religious fanaticism. Consider verse 37 with adjustments to reflect its meaning for the Society for women. "That they [the powers of heaven] may be conferred upon us [through the watch-care of priesthood leaders], it is true; but when we [women] undertake to cover our sins, or to gratify our pride, our vain ambition, or to exercise control or dominion or compulsion upon [our sisters], in any degree of unrighteousness, behold, the heavens withdraw themselves; the Spirit of the Lord is grieved; and when it is withdrawn, Amen to the priesthood or the authority [that had been available to bless that woman in her calling]."

Sisters, this Society was *not* like other women's benevolent societies of that day, or of this day. It was organized under the power and direction of the priesthood of God. We are held under the same strict guidelines as our priesthood brothers to keep the channels of inspiration and power open. We cannot succeed in caring for the poor in a way that souls are saved without the blessing of the priesthood. With it, we cannot fail.

CONCLUSION

The Society of which I have spoken is available to all of us today. From its beginning, it was properly called the "Relief Society." I purposely avoided referring to it as such because of the narrowing meaning the name has assumed over the years. The Relief Society as Joseph Smith envisioned it is more than a class we attend on Sunday, more than a single auxiliary organization in the Church, and more than a convenient label to distinguish women from priesthood-holding men. Wherever we are called to serve in the name of Jesus Christ, women are organized and guided under priesthood power. When our diverse God-given talents are magnified by the enabling power of Jesus Christ, the potential for positive influence by the Society is endless. We can change the world.

In 1945, President George Albert Smith recognized the same magnificent potential. He told the Relief Society sisters of that day: "You possess all that the world has that is really essential to eternal happiness, plus the gospel of Jesus Christ our Lord. . . . You were the first women to have the franchise; the first women to have a voice in the work of a church. It was God who gave it to you and it came as a result of revelation to a prophet of the Lord. Since that time, think of the benefits the women of this world have enjoyed. It was not just for us who belong to the Church to enjoy the blessings of equality. When the Prophet Joseph Smith turned the key for the emancipation of womankind, it was turned for all the world, and from generation to generation the number of women who can enjoy the blessings of religious liberty and civil liberty has been increasing."[24]

The potential for women's contribution to the Church and to the world exceeds our present imagination. It certainly exceeds getting instant credit for merely looking lovely and being special. Are we ready to be counted as a member of this visionary Society? Committed to care for the poor so that souls are saved? Prepared to relinquish all self-righteousness and a judgmental tongue? Ready to qualify for direction through the priesthood of God? More than being special, lovely, and beautiful, we can be those distinctly different and happy women who will influence the growth of the Church and thereby impact the world through righteousness and articulateness. Emma Smith caught the vision at the Society's inception when she declared, "We are going to do something *extraordinary*."[25] May we have the faith and conviction to follow their lead.

Notes

1. Spencer W. Kimball, "The Role of Righteous Women," *Ensign*, November 1979, 103–4.

2. Jill Mulvay Derr, Janath Russell Cannon, Maureen Ursenbach Beecher, *Women of Covenant: The Story of Relief Society* (Salt Lake City: Deseret Book, 1992), 24.

3. Joseph Smith, *History of The Church of Jesus Christ of Latter-day Saints*, edited by B. H. Roberts, 2d ed. rev., 7 vols. (Salt Lake City: The Church of Jesus Christ of Latter-day Saints, 1932–51), 4:567.

4. Derr et al., *Women of Covenant*, 27.

5. Derr et al., *Women of Covenant*, 26–27.

6. Smith, *History of the Church*, 4:567.

7. Smith, *History of the Church*, 4:567.

8. Smith, *History of the Church*, 5:25; see also Relief Society Minutes, 9 June 1842, in *The Words of Joseph Smith: The Contemporary Accounts of the Nauvoo Discourses of The Prophet Joseph*, compiled and edited by Andrew F. Ehat and Lyndon W. Cook (Orem, Utah: Grandin Book, 1991), 124.

9. Relief Society Minutes, 28 April 1842, in *Words of Joseph Smith*, 117.

10. Relief Society Minutes, 28 April 1842, in *Words of Joseph Smith*, 118.

11. Derr et al., *Women of Covenant*, 45.

12. Relief Society Minutes, 26 May 1842, in *Words of Joseph Smith*, 120–21.

13. Chauncey Riddle, "A BYU for Zion," *BYU Studies* 16 (Summer 1976), no. 4, 491–92.

14. Derr et al., *Women of Covenant*, 42.

15. Smith, *History of the Church*, 4:552–53.

16. "I could not ordain these sisters [of the first Relief Society Presidency] to anything more or to greater powers than had been conferred upon Sister Emma who had previously been ordained to expound the Scriptures" (Eliza R. Snow, *Woman's Exponent* 9 [1 September 1880]: 53).

17. Spencer W. Kimball, *Teachings of Spencer W. Kimball*, ed. Edward L. Kimball (Salt Lake City: Bookcraft, 1982), 321.

18. Riddle, "BYU for Zion," 493.

19. Relief Society Minutes, 9 June 1842, in *Words of Joseph Smith*, 123; see also Smith, *History of the Church*, 5:23–24.

20. Relief Society Minutes, 30 March, 28 April, 26 May, 9 June, 31 August 1842, in *Words of Joseph Smith*, 110, 114–19, 120–21, 122–24, 129–31.

21. Relief Society Minutes, 28 April 1842, in *Words of Joseph Smith*, 118.

22. Relief Society Minutes, 26 May 1842, in *Words of Joseph Smith*, 120–21.

23. Joseph F. Smith, Anthon H. Lund, and Charles W. Penrose, "Editors' Table: A Warning Voice," *Improvement Era*, September 1913, 1148.

24. George Albert Smith, "Address to the Members of the Relief Society," Relief Society General Conference, 4 October 1945; in *Relief Society Magazine*, 32 (December 1945): 717.

25. Derr et al., *Women of Covenant*, 31; emphasis in original.

HUNGRY FIRES OF COURAGE: THE RECIPROCITY OF PRIESTHOOD COVENANTS

Marie K. Hafen

I want to offer both my testimony about the priesthood and my theme for this article in one sentence—sustain the priesthood, and the priesthood will sustain you. "Sustaining" and "being sustained by" the priesthood imply two different types of reciprocal relationships. The first is between priesthood holders and those who receive priesthood help. The second is between those who make priesthood covenants and the Lord, whose power the priesthood is.[1]

We see both types of reciprocity in the story of Elijah and the widow. Because of Israel's wickedness, the Lord commands Elijah to seal up the heavens. In the drought that follows, even the prophet Elijah sits by a parched brook hoping for water. Instead he receives instruction from the Lord: "Arise, get thee to Zarephath. . . . I have commanded a widow woman there to sustain thee" (1 Kings 17:9). As Elijah enters the city, the widow is gathering sticks. He calls to her, asking for a little water and a morsel of bread. She has been "commanded" by the Lord to "sustain" Elijah. She replies, I have only "an handful of meal . . . and a little oil. . . . I am gathering two sticks, that I may go in and dress it for me and my son, that we may eat it, and die."

Marie Kartchner Hafen, an author and former teacher at the University of Utah, Ricks College, and Brigham Young University, holds a master's degree in English from Brigham Young University. She has served on the Young Women General Board and also on the board of directors of the Deseret News. She served with her husband, Bruce C. Hafen, in his calling as a member of the First Quorum of the Seventy. They are the parents of seven children and grandparents of a quiverful of energetic grandchildren.

"Fear not," says Elijah. "Go and do as thou hast said." But Elijah then asks a hard thing, "Make *me* thereof a little cake *first*, . . . and *after* make for thee and thy son." Of course, this is hard for her to hear and equally hard for him to ask. But the Lord has promised that "the barrel of meal shall not waste, neither shall the cruse of oil fail, until the day that the Lord sendeth rain upon the earth" (v. 14). Faithfully, the widow heeds the Lord's command and does what Elijah has asked. "And she, and he, and her house, did eat many days" (1 Kings 17:12–15; emphasis added).

But this is not the end of the story—nor of the reciprocity. In the midst of the drought, the widow's son falls so sick that "there [is] no breath left in him." In great grief, and even bitterness, she cries out to Elijah and to the Lord asking why. In compassionate response, Elijah says only, "Give me thy son." Again, in faith, she gives him her son "out of her bosom." Elijah lays the boy on a bed and cries to the Lord with his own wrenching question; in essence, Is this *Thy* doing, Lord? Then Elijah pleads three times, "O Lord my God, I pray thee, let this child's soul come into him again." And the Lord answers, Yes. The child's soul *does* come into him again, "and he revive[s]." Elijah delivers the boy to his mother's arms with this grateful elation: "See, thy son liveth" (1 Kings 17:17–23)!

In his oratorio *Elijah*, Felix Mendelsohn adds his gift of music to this intense exchange between Elijah and the widow. "What shall I render to the Lord for all His benefits to me?" is the widow's humble question. For them and for me the answer is: "Thou shalt love the Lord thy God, love him with all thine heart, and with all thy soul, and with all thy might. O blessed are they who fear Him!" The widow sustains Elijah; and Elijah sustains the widow; both act on commandments from, and faith in, the Lord. The power of the priesthood surges into their lives because they love God with all their souls.

In a much later time, the life of Lydia Knight offers another witness of the same reciprocity between people who honor the priesthood and between those people and God. Lydia lived through the infant years of the Church—from Kirtland to Missouri to Nauvoo, across the plains, through the early years of Salt Lake City, and finally to St. George. Her life displays a pattern of events strikingly similar to what we see with Elijah and the widow.

Lydia's "sustaining" of the priesthood began almost as soon as her foot touched the ground in Kirtland as a twenty-two-year-old convert desiring to gather with the Saints. Vincent Knight approached her, "Sister, the Prophet is in bondage, . . . and if you have any means to give, it will be a benefit to him." That Lydia had first heard the gospel from Joseph Smith himself made it even easier to reply, "Oh yes, sir. Here is all I have. I only wish it was more." She emptied "her purse, containing perhaps fifty dollars, [into] his hand as she spoke."[2] Handing over *all* the money her parents had given her to travel and to begin her life respectably in Kirtland left Lydia without means to buy even "a handful of meal and a little oil." Brother Knight used the money to free the Prophet, then later that night invited Lydia to stay with his family.

A few months later, Lydia met Newel Knight (not related to Vincent)—who had been called back from Missouri to help build the Kirtland Temple—while they were both boarding with Hyrum and Jerusha Smith. Quickly attracted to each other, their friendship grew into love and marriage later that year. Lydia and Newel's lives together demonstrate reciprocal relationships between them, as husband and wife, and between each of them and the Lord.

In April 1836, after the temple's dedication, Newel prepared to take his new bride to rejoin the extended Knight clan in the thick of turmoil in Missouri. "Are you not in rather straightened circumstances?" Joseph Smith asked, while talking with them about their pending thousand-mile journey to Clay County. Newel, having received no pay for his work on the temple for more than a year, replied with understatement, "We are rather cramped."

"Sister Lydia," Joseph continued, "I have not forgotten how generously you helped me when I was in trouble." The Prophet left and returned, handing the couple almost twice as much money as Lydia had given him.[3] Lydia's earlier gift to Joseph and Joseph's increased gift back to her is a temporal example of Lydia's sustaining the priesthood and the priesthood sustaining her and her family. Both Lydia's gift and Joseph's gift came not from a contract but as an act of generous grace. That is how blessings to and from the priesthood always work.

Surviving the abysmal conditions of Missouri, Lydia and Newel retreated with the Saints to Nauvoo, where again Newel was called to help build a temple. Once, when Newel fell ill for two weeks, Lydia sent a message to their priesthood leaders, first to apologize for his absence and second to request "on behalf of my husband . . . whom I love and reverence, even as Sarah did Abraham" that they pray for him and consecrate a bottle of oil for him (which she sent with the letter).[4] Her love for him, her support for his calling, and her faith in the priesthood sustained Newel.

And Newel sustained Lydia. Three months after their marriage was sealed in the unfinished though partially dedicated Nauvoo Temple, Lydia and Newel, with their seven children, fled Illinois. After they crossed Iowa to Council Bluffs, Brigham Young sent the Knights with two companies of Saints up the Missouri River in search of an alternate route west. The Saints accepted the kind invitation of the Ponca Indians to camp with them for the winter, hoping to continue west in the spring. One cold January night, Newel felt an acute pain in his side. No tried remedy brought relief. Through seven days and nights of excruciating anxiety, Lydia watched "the breath of the being she loved better than life itself slowly cease."[5]

"'Lydia,' his dying voice faintly whispered, 'it is necessary for me to go. Joseph wants me [on the other side]. . . . Don't grieve too much, for you will be protected.'"[6]

"'Oh, Newel, . . . don't give up; oh I could not bear it. Think of me, Newel, here . . . with seven little children. . . . I cannot let you go.'"[7]

In agony he tried to hang on, and Lydia writhed in pain with him. But, unable to bear his pain any longer, Lydia knelt by his bedside, praying for forgiveness if she had asked amiss that Newel might remain, and released her husband to God's will. Within moments his pain ceased, and his spirit went in peace.[8]

A month later, after an organization meeting for the trek west, Lydia wondered how she could possibly prepare her fatherless family for the journey—especially since she was expecting another baby. "Oh, Newel," she cried out, "why have you left me?!"

"As she spoke, he [came to] her, a lovely smile on his face, saying, 'Be calm, let not sorrow overcome you. I was needed behind the veil to represent the true condition of this camp. You cannot fully comprehend it now; but the time will come when you shall know why I left you and our little ones. Therefore, dry up your tears. Be patient, I will go before you and protect you in your journeyings . . . although the ravens of the valley should feed you and your little ones you shall not perish for the want of bread.'"[9] *Ravens will feed you*—note the echo of Elijah.

Newel's visit was a direct fulfillment of Lydia's patriarchal blessing, given to her by Joseph Smith Sr. soon after she and Newel had married in Kirtland. That blessing affirmed to her that "the Lord has given thee a kind and loving companion for thy comfort . . . your souls shall be knit together and nothing shall be able to dissolve them: neither distresses nor death shall separate you." The blessing continued, "Angels shall visit thee, and thy heart shall be comforted."[10]

A week after their baby was born, Lydia cried out to Newel again as rain poured through her cabin roof, soaking the bedclothes. He came to her once more, repeating his promise of protection. Even in the drenched linens, "a pleasant warmth crept over her."[11]

The reciprocity that lifted Lydia and Newel's burdens and afflictions grew out of a relationship between two covenant-making and covenant-keeping people and their God. Their covenants were made with God through the power of His priesthood, and kept by them and Him through the demands of everyday life. Relationships based in the true order of the priesthood are relationships that lift, and comfort, and strengthen, and sustain. The goodness of this reciprocity grows until burdens become light, the kind of light that shines through the darkness and casts out all fear.

This kind of reciprocity can exist among *all* of God's people, married or single, with or without children, who keep their covenants in honest faithfulness. While Newel brought Lydia strength from beyond the veil, priesthood brethren also gave her physical and spiritual support through the ensuing years of single motherhood.

In an incident reminiscent of Elijah's intervention with the widow's son and the Lord's response to *their* faith, Lydia's youngest son, Hyrum, was once snatched lifeless from a creek. Lydia called for the elders to act upon their "commission" in the Lord's name. But it appeared to be too late; "there was no breath left in him" (1 Kings 17:17). She clutched little Hyrum to her chest and recalled the promise in her patriarchal blessing that her "heart [would] not be pained because of the loss of [her] children." The priesthood brethren felt the child was too far gone; a blessing would be useless. But, Lydia wrote, "I could not be denied. They finally laid their hands on the lifeless child and prayed for him. Life returned and he began to breathe."[12]

Why did the Lord continually sustain Lydia? Because, I believe, she continually sustained Him by doing all she could to build His kingdom. His kingdom is built to sustain her, and us. When she felt it was time in 1848 to begin her trek to Zion, she counseled with Brigham Young, who had returned to Winter Quarters for his family. He was tender and thoughtful of her circumstances as well as the harsh conditions that awaited them in the valley. He reminded her that she needed not only enough provisions to get her family across the plains but also another year's worth of supplies to establish crops once she got to Utah. Brigham Young counseled her to remain in Winter Quarters "until she could find something to come to."

Then he gave her a faith-provoking suggestion: "If you feel so disposed, you can let your three yoke of oxen and two wagons go towards helping to fit out some one who can go and take care of themselves when there."[13] Recalling the covenant Newel had made in Nauvoo to give all they possessed to assist the Saints who went west, she unflinchingly responded as she had earlier when Joseph needed help, "Certainly, President Young. They are at your disposal."

She regarded Newel's covenant as her covenant. She lived a year with her seven children in "a half-cave, half-hut on the bank of the creek."[14] The hut "flooded when it rained," was cold in the winter and stiflingly hot in the summer, and "impossible to make or keep, clean."[15] When her own time came in 1850 to leave Winter Quarters for Zion, Lydia had to borrow money to rent the oxen she needed to complete her "fit out" for the journey, a debt she later repaid in Utah.

Lydia was sustained by priesthood power, reflecting her reciprocal relationship with both priesthood holders and with the Savior, whose power the priesthood is. All Church members are entitled to these same two forms of reciprocity. Elder Bruce R. McConkie once said that the blessings of the priesthood include becoming a member of the Church; becoming sanctified by the Spirit; and becoming a servant of God; being sealed for eternity; gaining eternal life; and, if pure in heart, seeing the face of God while yet in mortality.[16] These blessings made possible by the priesthood are accessible to women as well as to men. As Section 84 of the Doctrine and Covenants states, "In the ordinances [of the Melchizedek Priesthood], the power of godliness is manifest. And without the ordinances thereof, and the authority of the priesthood, the power of godliness is not manifest unto men in the flesh" (vv. 20–21).

Most of these blessings come as we receive the priesthood ordinances—baptism, the gift of the Holy Ghost, the temple ordinances—and as we are called and set apart in Church callings. The gifts flowing from these ordinances and blessings include faith, revelation, testimony, wisdom, tongues, healing, and prophecy. As Elder Dallin H. Oaks said, "These gifts come from the Holy Ghost and . . . are available to every member, male and female."[17]

The life of Lydia's son Jesse Knight shows how the priesthood's power reverberates not just between those who are in one another's presence, but also across time and space—to both our posterity *and* our ancestors. Even though Jesse had come west with the wagon-train Saints as a child and had grown up with a mother of extraordinary faith, he was not an active Church member for many years. During Lydia's last visit to Jesse's home in Payson from her home in St.

George—where she was doing temple work for more than 700 of her deceased family and friends—Jesse asked her, "Mother, how is it you are not preaching to me as you usually do?"

She answered, "Jesse, I have prayed in the Temple for my children many times and on one occasion the Lord made known to me that I was not to worry about you any more, that you would one day understand . . . [and] see the Gospel for yourself. . . . I never intend to argue again with you about religion."[18]

Jesse did come to "understand" and "see" the gospel for himself, though it took three more years and his oldest daughter's death to awaken his senses. Millie died from poisoned well-water exactly when she knew she would—thirty days after she had offered the Lord her life in exchange for the life of her youngest sister, who was, in their words, "the idol of the whole family." The same tainted water had drawn the younger child into the clutches of death, but she was miraculously called back through the faith of her mother, who, Lydia-like, called for the elders despite Jesse's protest. At that time, Millie offered the Lord her own life as a sacrifice so that her two-year-old sister might live. Millie's "breath" left her as she prayed, "Oh God, bless our household." The combination of his baby's life and Millie's death softened Jesse's heart and drew him toward God. When Jesse allowed himself to reverberate with the pattern of the priesthood, the blessings extended far beyond the life of his own family. His later wealth from mining allowed him to help pay some sizeable debts for the Church and to donate much of the land Brigham Young University sits on today. The BYU humanities building now carries his name.[19]

Indeed, the blessings the Lord extended to Lydia *do* flow by the power of the priesthood—across time and space—to and through each of hundreds of ancestors, and to and through the thousands of her posterity *if* each one will choose for him or herself to live by the same faith and be sustained by the same priesthood. Somehow Lydia's faithful, covenant-keeping life draws her lineage that much closer to the purifying fire of the gospel where they can be sanctified by God's glory—*if* they will. And—*if* they will—they can "behold" that Christ "[has en]graven [us] upon the palms of [His] hands" (1 Nephi 21:16).

A poem by Vilate Raile describes the kind of energy Lydia Knight allowed the Lord to set in motion through her, and on through Jesse and Millie, and on and on. It's entitled, simply, "Pioneers."

> *They cut desire into short lengths*
> *And fed it to the hungry fires of courage.*
> *Long after—when the flames died—*
> *Molten Gold gleamed in the ashes.*
> *They gathered it into bruised palms*
> *And handed it to their children*
> *And their children's children.*[20]

What is "it" they gathered? Molten gold. Why molten gold? It is a symbol of having the dross removed, of having been through covenant-keeping, backbreaking, mind-bending, yet spirit-refining fire. "Grace shall be as [our] day,"[21] and as one soul-stretched friend recently put it, "Grace is really hard work." As I understand the words of the poem "Pioneers," God's desires for them became their desires and fueled their courage. As the darkness of dross was removed from their desires, they had within them ever more gleaming light. "Your whole bodies shall be filled with light . . . and the days will come that you shall see him; for he will unveil his face unto you" (D&C 88:67–68). The gleam of this gold is the doctrine that if we sustain the priesthood, the priesthood will sustain us.

Ray Kartchner is a great-great grandson of Newel and Lydia Knight. He is my father. I tell you this not to claim undeserved fame from pioneer ancestors, but to testify that no matter when a family joins this Church, the blessings of the priesthood flow to God's temples and through the covenants we make there to lift, comfort, strengthen, and sustain our children and our children's children. I know this because I am one of Lydia's daughters. I have also been sustained by my husband, whom I "love and reverence" *and* sustain. My father was raised by a mother whose hands were bruised somewhat as Lydia's were—minus the relentless trek west. With those hands, my grandmother led her family after her husband died when my father was just two years old. She continued to teach the pattern and proper order of the priesthood to her children and her children's children. Her son learned that pattern well, and he handed it to me with a gentle reverence that has made it easy for me to envision God as both the source of law and the source of love. I testify that the priesthood's pattern is a "hungry fire of courage" that consumes my desire and transforms it into ashes *and* molten gold. I pray that my children, and their children, will stay close enough to that fire to see the gleaming in the dust.

Notes

1. For an earlier treatment of this subject, see Marie K. Hafen, "Sustaining—and being Sustained by—the Priesthood," *Ensign*, March 1987, 6–8.
2. Susa Young Gates, *Lydia Knight's History* (Salt Lake City: Juvenile Instructor Office, 1883), 25; reprint, [vol. 1] in *Noble Women's Lives* series (West Jordan, Utah: Early Church Reprints, 1983).
3. William G. Hartley, *They Are My Friends: A History of the Joseph Knight Family, 1825–1850* (Provo: Grandin Book, 1986), 115; see also Hartley, *Stand by My Servant Joseph: The Story of the Joseph Knight Family and the Restoration* (Salt Lake City: Deseret Book, 2003).
4. Hartley, *My Friends*, 156.
5. Gates, *Lydia Knight's History*, 69.
6. Gates, *Lydia Knight's History*, 69.
7. Gates, *Lydia Knight's History*, 70.
8. Gates, *Lydia Knight's History*, 70.
9. Gates, *Lydia Knight's History*, 72.
10. Patriarchal Blessing, 3 April 1836, Kirtland, Ohio; in Archives of The Church of Jesus Christ of Latter-day Saints, Salt Lake City.
11. Gates, *Lydia Knight's History*, 74–75.
12. *Letters and Papers of Lydia Knight and Newel Knight* (Provo: Brigham Young University Library, 1960), 28–29.
13. Gates, *Lydia Knight's History*, 76.
14. Gates, *Lydia Knight's History*, 77.
15. Gates, *Lydia Knight's History*, 79.
16. Bruce R. McConkie, "Ten Blessings of the Priesthood," *Ensign*, November 1977, 33–35; see Alma 13; D&C 84, 107.
17. Dallin H. Oaks, "Spiritual Gifts," *Ensign*, September 1986, 72.

18. Jesse William Knight, *The Jesse Knight Family: Jesse Knight, His Forebears and Family* (Salt Lake City: Deseret News Press, 1940), 33; see also LeGrand Richards, Conference Report, October 1941, 126.

19. For a more complete story of Jesse's life, see Jeffrey D. Keith's excellent BYU Devotional talk, "Feeling the Atonement," *Brigham Young University Speeches, 2001–2002* (Provo: Brigham Young University Press, 2002); also available at http//www.speeches.byu.edu/ devo/2001–02/KeithF01.html.

20. Vilate Raile, in Asahel D. Woodruff, *Parent and Youth* (Salt Lake City: Deseret Sunday School Union Board, 1952), 124; also in *Selected Writings of Gerald N. Lund*, Gospel Scholars Series (Salt Lake City: Deseret Book, 1999), 402–3.

21. "Come, Come, Ye Saints," *Hymns of The Church of Jesus Christ of Latter-day Saints* (Salt Lake City: The Church of Jesus Christ of Latter-day Saints, 1985), no. 30.

FAMILY PEACEMAKERS

✦

Henry B. Eyring

Nothing fills us with longing quite so much as thoughts of living in loving, peaceful families. The purpose of the plan of salvation is to allow us to live forever in such happiness. The Lord holds out that hope to us in these beautiful words from the Doctrine and Covenants: "When the Savior shall appear we shall see him as he is. We shall see that he is a man like ourselves.

"And that same sociality which exists among us here will exist among us there, only it will be coupled with eternal glory, which glory we do not now enjoy" (D&C 130:1–2).

There is comfort in the words, *that same sociality*. Heaven would be no heaven without our association with our families. And in the words *same* and *now*, there is a challenge to find family peace in this life.

Finding that peace will not be simple or easy for any of us. Consider your extended family. With a little reflection, you'll remember divorces, children estranged from parents, perhaps brothers and sisters at odds, flashes of anger and intemperate words, and in some cases, grudges that have lasted for days, months, years, or even through generations. You may remember patterns of harshness followed by reconciliation, and then repetitions of the hurt and conflict. It is not

Henry B. Eyring, a member of the Quorum of the Twelve Apostles, received a bachelor's degree from the University of Utah and a master's degree and doctorate from Harvard. Elder Eyring is Church commissioner of eduation and has served as a counselor in the Presiding Bishopric. He was deputy commissioner of education as well as president of Ricks College. Elder Eyring and his wife, Kathleen Johnson, are the parents of six children and the grandparents of nineteen.

surprising that the Lord chose the story of Lehi and his family as the thread to run through the Book of Mormon. It both humbles us and helps us to know that a good and great prophet of God from long ago dealt with the same cycles of family conflict that are familiar to us today. It has never been easy.

My earnest hope is that you are reading this with a smile. If you are, it is because there is little contention in your family and much peace. You know to whom you owe thanks for that miracle. The Lord sent Elijah as He promised the Prophet Joseph Smith He would. He had you and me and our families in mind and the challenging times in which we live. Because of His promise, we can expect help softening hearts in our families: "Behold, I will reveal unto you the Priesthood, by the hand of Elijah the prophet, before the coming of the great and dreadful day of the Lord.

"And he shall plant in the hearts of the children the promises made to the fathers, and the hearts of the children shall turn to their fathers.

"If it were not so, the whole earth would be utterly wasted at his coming" (D&C 2:1–3).

Elijah came, and the Lord's promise is being fulfilled. The hearts of many children are being drawn to their parents, toward each other, and toward their ancestors. That was the Lord's promise for the last days, and many of us are enjoying it.

But just as God promised to pour out blessings on families as part of the last restoration of the gospel of Jesus Christ, He also warned us that Satan would accelerate his schemes to replace peace in families with strife, anger, hatred, and great wickedness. The Prophet Joseph Smith prophesied: "The time is soon coming, when no man will have any peace but in Zion and her stakes.

"I saw men hunting the lives of their own sons, and brother murdering brother, women killing their own daughters, and daughters seeking the lives of their mothers. . . . I saw blood, desolation, fires. The Son of Man has said that the mother shall be against the daughter, and the daughter against the mother. These things are at our doors. They will follow the saints of God from city to city. Satan will rage, and the spirit of the devil is now enraged." The Prophet Joseph went on, "I know not how soon these things will take place; but with a view of them, shall I cry peace?"[1]

So, my message here must be of both gratitude and of encouragement. We give thanks for what God has done for our families. Through His prophets, He has poured out light and understanding upon us. We have discovered the power of regular family prayer, of reading the scriptures as a family, of family home evening, of putting the temple at the center of our family aspirations, and of excluding every influence from our homes that would offend the Holy Ghost.

But there is still danger. It is in being complacent. Just as there is risk in saying to ourselves, "All is well in Zion," it is not safe to assume that "All will always be well in my family." Satan tries relentlessly to create anger and contention in our homes. I once served as a counselor to a wise president. I was young; he was older. At the time I thought he was terribly pessimistic. He used to say something like this, "Hal, if you think you know a family that doesn't have to deal with contention, you either don't know them very well or you haven't known them long enough." I have lived long enough to know that he was not a pessimist; he was an inspired realist.

Let me give you two kinds of counsel. First, I will tell you how to close the gaps in your family defenses where Satan will try to enter and create strife. Second, I will tell you what I know about how to be peacemakers in a family when, as it must have been for Lehi and Sariah, contention reigns and peace seems beyond your reach. As I do this, I think of Sariah and of our mother Eve. They could tell us much about dealing with the heartbreak of families torn asunder by the wiles of Satan. Oh, what they could tell us about the value of patience and hope when tragedy threatens to overwhelm us!

I realize that if you are reading this article, you probably are the peacemakers in your families. You have experienced the joy of being with family members you love, who love each other, and who show it. You have known times of peace in your families and hoped they would never end. Those times form the sweetest memories of your life. You have also been quick to sense the first signs of conflict and contention. You have learned to move swiftly to calm the troubled waters. What I say here will be for most of you, therefore, a reminder of what you already know.

Satan's most destructive tool is, and always has been, selfishness. That is his own nature. Listen how selfishness rings in his defiant words: "Behold, here am I, send me, I will be thy son, and I will redeem all mankind, that one soul shall not be lost, and surely I will do it; wherefore give me thine honor" (Moses 4:1). Now, feel the sorrow of the Father for His spirit children in these words: "Behold, the devil was before Adam, for he rebelled against me, saying, Give me thine honor, which is my power; and also a third part of the hosts of heaven turned he away from me because of their agency" (D&C 29:36).

Because of that precious agency, Satan was able to tempt Adam and Eve and to tempt all their descendants. The tragedy of Cain and Abel illustrates the pattern by which conflict has been sown in families from the beginning. It always begins with selfishness. With that selfishness, Satan can foster pride and greed and deceit and finally the desire to destroy.

Cain was tempted by pride to believe that God honored Abel's gifts more than his and by greed to take Abel's property by murder. As he always does, Satan used deception: He taught Cain to cover his terrible deed with a lie. "And the Lord said unto Cain, Where is Abel thy brother? And he said, I know not: Am I my brother's keeper?" (Genesis 4:9).

Similar patterns of selfishness leading to pride and greed and finally to conflict remain our challenge today. Family peacemakers know what to do to stop that escalation toward contention and hatred: Stop the terrible sequence at its root. The Lord's defenses always begin with a great and miraculous change of heart from selfishness to selflessness. That change is an antidote to the diseases of pride, greed, and dishonesty. The Lord was speaking of peace in our hearts and in our families when He said: "Peace I leave with you, my peace I give unto you: not as the world giveth, give I unto you. Let not your heart be troubled, neither let it be afraid" (John 14:27).

The peace we seek in our families is a gift from God, not our own creation. It comes only from selfless hearts. We are dependent on the effects of the Atonement of the Savior. Knowing that, there is still much we can do to be peacemakers in our families. We can and must plead in faith for those we love to choose to hear and obey the voice of the Holy Spirit leading them toward righteousness. When they do, we can and must give thanks to God and watch for the fruits of the gospel to appear in their hearts. You will see those fruits when they love others as themselves. Pleasure in the success of another will replace envy. Mark it when it comes; nurture it as the seedling of a plant that will produce the sweetest fruit.

A few weeks ago, our third son was called to be the second counselor in a stake presidency. His younger brother is his neighbor. They have gone to the same schools, worked in the same company, married women who were friends, and had the same successful experiences in the mission field. Do you get the idea they just might compare and perhaps even compete with each other? I heard about the calling from the younger of the two who phoned to tell me that his brother had been called as counselor in their stake presidency. He started to chuckle and said, "I thought I'd call you because I knew *he* wouldn't ever do it. He's not very good at self-promotion."

I hope that younger brother heard in my voice gratitude to God and admiration for him. It is a gift of God to find joy in someone else's happiness. It is a mark of the Atonement working in a life. Because you may feel that charity yourself so often that you do not recognize its rarity, you may neither appreciate nor encourage it when you see it in the heart of a family member. Please never fail to notice it. Never fail to appreciate it. If you can, find ways to make it happen more often. Begin when children are young. Watch for the delight in a child's eyes for the good fortune of a brother, sister, cousin, or friend. What you see will be a glimpse into heaven.

That generosity of spirit, that selflessness, makes possible the keeping of the second great commandment: "Thou shalt love the Lord thy God with all thy heart, and with all thy soul, and with all thy mind.

"This is the first and great commandment.

"And the second is like unto it, Thou shalt love thy neighbour as thyself.

"On these two commandments hang all the law and the prophets" (Matthew 22:37–40).

And on these two commandments hangs peace in your home.

The key words are "thy neighbour as thyself." When the Atonement has done its work on our hearts, the good that comes to another has come to us. That is far more than generosity as the world might see it. A sister might give something to her sister out of her abundance. But the Savior's gospel holds out the possibility, for instance, that a woman denied the blessing of childbearing would feel her sister's joy in a full quiver of children. I've seen that pure charity and so have you. That gift of God in the hearts of our family members is a sure defense against Satan's attempts to disrupt and divide us. We can pray for it. We can teach that it is possible. We can give thanks for it when it happens. And we can encourage it.

You can teach your children that the feelings of charity they have for each other come naturally to those who feel the charity of a loving Father and His Son, Jesus Christ. That is why those who feel forgiven are more forgiving of others, and those who feel the kindness of God want to be kind to His children. That is also why knowing how to reprove and yet add love under the direction of the Holy Ghost is at the heart of being a peacemaker in your family. Only such inspired correction can lead to repentance. Without those promptings from the Spirit, we may fail to correct, or we may correct in a way that actually creates contention. But, if we are guided to reprove when the Lord would have us reprove and with the love He would have us show, repentance and a change of heart are more likely.

King Benjamin described what our family members can become. Just as a pattern of selfishness tempts our families towards contention, a process of yielding to God leads us where our hearts truly want to go, to the peace of a little child. We can teach it as King Benjamin did: "For the natural man is an enemy to God, and has been from the fall

of Adam, and will be, forever and ever, unless he yields to the enticings of the Holy Spirit, and putteth off the natural man and becometh
a saint through the atonement of Christ the Lord, and becometh as a
child, submissive, meek, humble, patient, full of love, willing to submit to all things which the Lord seeth fit to inflict upon him, even as a
child doth submit to his father" (Mosiah 3:19).

You will find ways to teach that path to peace in your families and
to help them move along it. I pray with all my heart that you will think
of other ways to build defenses against selfishness. All of them will
have one feature in common: They will invoke the power of the
Atonement to soften hearts.

But what should you do when conflict has become a pattern in your
family? Contention can take many forms. It may be constant bickering.
It may have moved past words to actions. In time, contention can grow
and you may someday say, as I heard not long ago from an anguished
mother of such a troubled family, "Can I ever find peace again?"

The answer is always, "Yes," but you will need to understand some
things. First, the peace the Lord promises is in an individual heart. The
peace comes when the heart is purified. Second, only through faith in
the Lord Jesus Christ and keeping His commandments can the Atonement cleanse us. That anguished mother can find the Lord's peace for
herself. Being a mother, however, her cry for peace is for her children as
much, or more, as for herself. Their hearts locked in the prison of conflict can break hers. And so her cry will be: "What can I do to get peace
for them?"

The answer is this: They can find peace the same way you will,
through the effects of the gospel of Jesus Christ. Contention and conflict are products of sin. They always produce spiritual darkness. The
only way to peace is for them to choose to let in the light of the gospel.
That is a hard truth for any mother: Her children must choose peace
for themselves. She can persuade, direct, and set an example of finding peace in righteous living. But they must choose the path to peace
through obedience to the commandments. That is the Lord's way. He
will never compel the human soul.

With the Lord's help, though, the mother is not powerless. She can pray, teach, and correct for Him. And He has other faithful servants upon whom she can call. Think of that great mother, Sariah, who saw her sons try to kill their brother. Those rebellious sons resisted even angels the Lord sent to call them to repentance. Their hatred only grew. But the Lord made Sariah a promise through her prophetic husband. Though Lehi saw that their rebellion would go on for generations, he promised that their seed would be preserved.

After generations of terrible conflict, the Lord in His mercy and surely through the prayers of Sariah, sent missionaries to them. Her descendants, her family, heard and believed. They repented so fully that their hearts were changed. They were willing to give up their lives rather than take the risk that the sins of hatred and killing would return to them. When you read of their marvelous journey back into the light, think of Sariah looking down on her family. Think of her joy. Think of her peace.

Now, it may take patience. It will surely take faith, hope, and charity. But any mother can know that her desire to be a peacemaker will be honored by the Lord. He is the Prince of Peace. "And blessed are all the peacemakers; for they shall be called the children of God" (JST Matthew 5:11).

You will have the righteous desires of your heart. God will reach out across time and space to touch hearts in your family. You and they will have the chance to choose the peace that the gospel always brings.

As His witness, I testify that Jesus is the Christ. I bear you my testimony that we are the children of a loving, living Heavenly Father. We can in this life taste the sweetness of that sociality we once knew in His family. I know that He works with us, using His matchless power, to bless us and our families with peace. I pray that for you, for your family, and for mine.

Notes

1. Joseph Smith, *Teachings of the Prophet Joseph Smith*, sel. Joseph Fielding Smith (Salt Lake City: Deseret Book, 1938), 161.

"FORSAKE ME NOT
WHEN MY STRENGTH FAILETH"

꒰⊙꒱

Kate L. Kirkham

A photograph of the sun at the water's horizon on an island in the Bahamas sits on my bookcase. Visitors often ask, "Is it sunrise or sunset?" I always reply, "Well, what do you think?" I've been amazed at the different responses and what sunrises and sunsets mean to people in terms of life's beginnings or endings. This photo has become a conversation piece about the dawn and dusk of our lives.

In January 1996, my mother fell and broke her hip walking to the front door of her Salt Lake City home. That began a series of health challenges. In May of that same year, my dad, who had been Mom's primary caregiver, had a stroke. Mom and Dad had always been active, independent, and private, as well as loving parents and grandparents; my brother, sister, and I were not ready for the sunset of their independence. By August 1996, they were living with me and sleeping in my bedroom, as I planned an addition to my home that would be an apartment for them. The apartment didn't get started until spring of the following year. It was a long winter on the futon—for me; my parents were fine. Finally, by October 1997, we were able to invite their Salt Lake City friends to see their new home in Springville.

Kate L. Kirkham holds a Ph.D. from the Union Graduate School, Union of Experimenting Colleges and Universities. An associate professor in the Department of Leadership and Strategy at Brigham Young University, she is the organizational behavior and human resource group leader. Former director of the EMBA program at BYU and a popular teacher and mentor, she has received numerous awards recognizing her excellence. She has served as a member of the Relief Society General Board and as stake Relief Society president.

On the last day of September 2001, with my sister and me at his bedside, my father left this mortal life. Mother, who'd been in a nursing home, had left us first in May. Diabetes and expressive aphasia, an element of dementia, had magnified her needs to the point we couldn't take care of her. The doctor said she probably could think but couldn't connect her thinking with her speech. There was no way to tell how much she really understood, nor was she able to respond to our demands or requests.

Somewhere in the middle of those almost six years, I became aware that while this was the sunset of their mortal lives, it was in fact the sunrise of their eternity. And I named us—the aides and the relatives involved with their care—the Transition Home Team. We were committed to celebrating the lifetime that they had shared, making sure the generations of our family and friends, and especially the new little grandbabies, knew of our love for Mom and Dad. We hoped that our compassion as elder-care providers would be evidence of charity, what Moroni 7:47 calls "the pure love of Christ," whose gospel our parents had steadfastly taught us.

Why do the circumstances of this transition to eternity vary so much? Why are our needs as we age, our circumstances and our resources as caregivers so varied? Why is my mother's dear friend of ninety-five-plus years still struggling to live alone in Salt Lake City after all of her family, and many of her friends as well, have gone? And why do some transitions happen so early in life without any notice? I don't know the answers to any of these questions. Borrowing a passage from Alma, I might say: "Now these mysteries are not yet fully made known unto me; therefore I shall forebear. And it may suffice if I only say they are preserved for a wise purpose, which purpose is known unto God; for he doth counsel in wisdom over all his works, and his paths are straight, and his course is one eternal round" (Alma 37:11–12). Alma, of course, is not talking about the elderly, but the point is the same: "Whose purpose is known unto God . . . whose course is one eternal round."

My experience as a fulltime care provider taught me many things and strengthened my belief that we are all on this earth to be caregivers across the entire range of our mortal life. It's part of our eternal round of progression. As we work out our own salvation, we seek to express charity and caring for others. The time we have and the timing will vary according to His purposes.

Isn't it curious that in the beginning, in the sunrise of mortal life, we celebrate caring for the newly born and are intensely interested in a baby's body functions? Just the other night, we were enjoying my sister's brand new grandbaby of five weeks, amused by her burping noises and laughing at her facial expressions as she passed gas.

But as caregivers in the twilight, we took a bit longer to gain both a respect for and ability to see the humor in an eighty-six-year-old's body functions and noises. I once sat across from Dad, midway in our care, when he pounded his fist on the rocking chair and said in disappointment and frustration, "I'm wet as a hen." I looked at him and said, "I can make you dry as a bone." He said, "You can?" I said, "Yes," and we finally had a discussion about adult Depends™, a conversation that we didn't know how to engage in before. I was able to reassure him that it wasn't his fault that his bathroom needs and his ability to get there were no longer evenly matched.

I would like to address the blessings and hardships of being a care provider for my parents by concentrating on two dimensions of Psalm 71:9: "Forsake me not when my strength faileth." This psalm can be read as a plea of the elderly. It can also be read as the plea of the families that support them. It is our plea to Heavenly Father and our Savior to be with us as we seek to do what we can, remembering that we still have to care for our young, our spouses, and ourselves. These equally important needs do not suddenly diminish when we step into the role of caregivers.

My sister, her family members, and I spent many hours looking at assisted living and care facilities before I decided to build an addition to my house. We found one facility that we thought was going to be wonderful and arrived at the same time a group came out on the porch to smoke. My mother said, "I'm not getting out of the car." Care decision is a long discussion that should start early and involve as many family members as possible. My brother's family lived in Layton so distance was a factor in their involvement in our care discussions.

Care giving should be a collaboration, not an isolation. Every family member has resources, and I learned to appreciate and integrate every opportunity to have others be involved in care giving. We were all blessed that my sister and her network of friends were able to find young women who had been trained in home health care but no longer wanted to work for an agency. Early in my parents' care we had multiple aides (which I realize is not feasible for all families), and Mother and Dad were able to spend some of their time alone. Eventually we settled into a pattern where an aide came at 7:30 A.M., so I could make an 8:00 class, and left at 5:00 P.M. Sometimes we had an evening aide for one or two hours. At night, I slept with a baby monitor on, which fortunately didn't bother me. The loving attitude and spirit of the young women who were our aides and others who came to work with Mom and Dad was itself a blessing. I believe we were guided to these resources.

Let me highlight the top ten principles of care that I learned in our efforts to give loving and effective care to my parents.

1. *Find out what the elderly value.* How did they structure their lives? What little things mattered to them? How could we replicate that in our care for them? For Mom and Dad, we found several important things. They wanted their own phone line. It bothered them to think that their calls would come through me or somebody else. Remember, these are the private, autonomous, independent parents I mentioned earlier. Mother wanted her own cable, which was fine with me because they never learned to love CNN 24-hour news, and I never learned to love country videos. Also the room temperature—the elderly need rooms to be either warm or even warmer. So I had a separate heating system put in their part of the house. As to their refreshment needs, Mother wanted a cold Tab any hour of the day; Dad wanted a toothpick. So we put a small refrigerator in their sitting room, and next to

Dad we placed a table with a toothpick holder and a letter opener for the mail.

It was harder to manage their sense of privacy. We tried to help aides and guests understand that Mom and Dad were very private people, whether dressing or moving through their day.

Mom liked having her nails done and her hair done. To the last weeks of Mom's life, Heather, one of our aides, would go to the nursing home to check on Mom and see how her nails were.

Dad liked to organize his shaving supplies a certain way, and we did it that way. I kept his car, which didn't run, parked in the driveway near the window where he sat so that he could see it as he walked slowly by with his walker. He would often comment, "You know, I may drive that car again." And I'd say, "Any time you want to, Dad." Both of us knew he probably would never drive again, but it gave him a sense of stability in a time of many changes.

It was easier to manage some of the core values—praying, home teachers—those things we all shared and understood. We kept the scriptures nearby, and for Dad, who had sung with the Tabernacle Choir for eighteen years, we kept tapes of the choir nearby. So the first challenge is finding out what the elderly value and respect, even the little things.

2. *Maintain an interest in their social lives as they age.* Looking back, I would be even more involved in some of the things that Mom and Dad were doing. Mom and Dad lived in the same neighborhood that we grew up in, so we knew who to call, who to ask about how their friends were doing, who their neighbors were. I had watched my sister check out her children's friends and talk to them. I did the same thing with my parents' friends who called, and it worked just as well. It can be hard to manage a phone conversation as you age. Either hearing, in Dad's case, or organizing thoughts, in Mother's case, made it hard for them to be on the phone with their friends. So I became their translator. I would talk with the friend, then stop to ask my parents one or two questions that they could respond to, and relay that message. Of course, this took up more of my time, but the blessing for me was the

notes from their friends thanking me for helping them stay in touch
with Mom and Dad and sharing the reasons why they loved them so
much. I got to learn more about my mother and father through the eyes
of their friends.

3. *Find ways to remind them that they are helping.* It's hard to go from
independence to dependence. We had projects for Mom and Dad to
work on. When they were both more able, Heather and Amie helped
them keep journals. They taped comments, wrote down things my parents said, listened to stories, and noted them for us. They compiled
photograph albums. They organized sock drawers. All the projects
helped Mom and Dad feel like they had things to work on during the
day. We also told them over and over again that we were glad they
were so near to us. We made productions of birthdays and anniversaries
and always took photos. When I was outside working in the yard, Dad
would say, "I just wish I could do more to help." And I would say, "Dad,
you are our spiritual supervisor, and we need all your prayers."
Sometimes Dad would stop talking to me right then and start praying.
He got the message.

4. *Understand what time means to the person you are giving care to.* I
think of time as one long, flexible continuum of ongoing, sometimes
overlapping activities. I get it done, I don't get it done, I'm on time,
I'm not on time. I'm not saying this is a good trait, just that my parents
were very different. If a doctor's appointment was at 2 o'clock, we
should be leaving at 1:37. I would come home and find Dad waiting
with his hat on or mother with her coat in her hand. Waiting is stressful for the elderly. They would say, "You're late," when I thought I was
pretty much on time. When I would say I would be gone a few minutes,
say to the store or the cleaners, when I got back I'd hear, "You've been
gone a long time." Being alone must stretch time. So we began to set a
specific time when I would be back. I'd say, "Dad, I'll be back when the
clock hands are at 5:30." He could watch that and see the numbers
progress rather than trying to judge how much is "a few minutes." I
learned to think of their experience regardless of my intent. What a

blessing it is to learn to understand what someone needs as they report it, rather than as we see it.

5. *Comprehend the physical changes for the ancient ones.* After a time we began to call Mom and Dad the ancient ones as a term of affection (and they knew we did). The physical changes for the aged can be astounding. In January 1996 I hadn't a clue what medications my mom and dad were taking. By August, we had created 3-by-5-inch laminated cards with all their medications and doses, insurance information, names of family members to be contacted, and the aides' phones numbers. We handed these out because no one knew when or with whom Mom and Dad might be going to the emergency room. We learned to give shots for diabetes. I learned to shave Dad, which I am sure he is still commenting on in heaven. We learned to treat a diabetic foot ulcer. We learned to do things we never thought we'd be able to do.

Any contact with medical professionals requires discretionary time to manage—lab appointments, doctor appointments, pharmacy needs, physical therapy, follow-ups, consults. I ended up juggling my available time with my parents' physical abilities and the doctors' openings. It's hard for the elderly to be mobile and have sufficient energy. "Just come by the lab on Tuesday. We'll take a blood sample" is a half-day investment of time. I ended up making and paying for appointments for me to meet with the physician or nursing home staff simply to talk about my parents, because it was easier and less costly in the long run than getting them there.

I became very concerned about age bias. I didn't worry so much about abuse, though I'm sure that goes on and it pains me. Rather, I detected a bias that the older you get, the less important the quality of your life is. I don't believe that. We became very assertive in offering information to medical personnel, who didn't always want to hear from us, about the condition or experience or the needs of Mom and Dad. We learned that it helps to collaborate with medical professionals.

Two medical issues took us by surprise. One was dehydration. The elderly sometimes don't consume enough fluids to keep their bodies hydrated. Dad had a mucous problem, and the discs in his neck were deteriorating, so he did not want to drink because it was uncomfortable. We had to insist that he drink liquids! We didn't recognize the signs of dehydration soon enough once, and he ended up in the emergency room. We now know what dehydration looks like in the elderly. Skin texture and body tone as well as lack of thirst can signal dehydration.

A second surprise was that some elderly are immobile during the day but mobile at night. One nurse called them "sundowners." As soon as the sun goes down, they get more energy. My mother was a sundowner. During the day we couldn't get her to move. Two or three times a week in the years when she was still somewhat mobile, she would show up late at night at my bedroom door. She would scare me to death. I'd look up and there she'd be saying, "Hi." *How did she get there?* My first thought was to be suspicious: *If Mother's not moving in the day, how is she moving at night?* Eventually I had to put a side guardrail on her bed because it was too dangerous for her to wander around at night. (Guardrails can also cause problems; so be careful.)

6. *Recognize the need to share information and help others.* Providing information helped others know how to help Mom and Dad. I struggled with this because sometimes the time it took to help others help Mom and Dad was additional time for me. Yet if I didn't spend that time, others couldn't really help. I also had to learn how to be exact about what help we needed. Relatives would come by and say, "We came by to see ElMoine and LaPreal." I was glad. Having company gave me time to do a few things. But they would sit down, talk to me, and never say one sentence to Mother and Dad. I finally learned to say, "Come in and sit down and talk with Mother and Dad. Shake their hands and give them a hug. They may not respond, but they know you are here." I had to help them know how to interact so they could stay in touch with Mom and Dad.

It's important to consider what you say in front of the elderly or about them. It frustrated Dad to hear us talking about him at a pace that he couldn't keep up with. We learned to say some very slow, thoughtful sentences to Dad about his condition, then we'd go out and talk more intensely with relatives so that Dad didn't feel like we were leaving him out.

7. *Decide what's fair about financial support and legal matters.* We barely made the eleventh hour deadline in getting Mother's signature notarized so that we could be on her bank account. In a few more weeks, she wouldn't have been able to sign her name, and we wouldn't have had access to the account without going through a lot of legal challenges. Know what the accounts are. Know where the trusts are. Know where the safety deposit box is.

We separated duties. My sister became the bookkeeper and had power of attorney. My brother, sister, and I were all co-executors of the estate. One of the craziest "you can't get there from here" things is trying to get information from an agency or a retirement plan on behalf of someone else. One day I realized I should find out about Dad's retirement plan as a long-time Utah state employee. *I'll just call them and ask,* I thought. Twice during the conversation I had to put the phone down and walk around the room. It is extremely hard to get information for someone else. Organizations evidently have reasons to suspect your motives in getting information and there are privacy issues. My advice is to find out as far in advance as you can from the elderly themselves about their resources, wills, insurance, and retirement programs. One thing we've learned from the challenges we've had is: don't put off financial conversations. My sister and I have written down what our coverage is. We have told her children where our papers are. We've organized safe deposit boxes. We're trying to make up for the failure to do that early with Mom and Dad.

8. *Expect personality changes.* I had to rethink my assumptions about what Mom and Dad were able or were willing to do, which were not the same thing. Dad would enjoy a meal one night, and the next time I fixed it he would say I was trying to poison him. I'd wonder, *Is Dad doing this just because he's frustrated?* Later I learned that taste buds and saliva change a lot as we age. What tastes good one week might taste awful another week, so Dad wasn't intentionally being difficult.

The inhibitions change too. Mother wasn't able to communicate as well, but her body movements showed that she was frustrated. Dad cried a lot. We didn't always know what Dad's tears meant—they weren't always from sadness. It's just hard to maintain emotional inhibition as you age. In the past, my father never swore. Then once, he told my niece and nephew they were dismissed and then swore at them. The room emptied instantly. They'd never heard Grandpa be that upset. We had to explain that it wasn't personal; Grandpa is frustrated, and he no longer has the capacity to omit words he would ordinarily screen from his vocabulary.

One of the most important things I had to learn was repetition, repetition, repetition. Even though my mother couldn't understand everything I was saying, she understood emotional pitch change in my voice. If I expressed feelings through repetition—"Mother, *Mother*, MOTHER"—she'd pick up only on my emotions. When I wanted her to pick up information, not emotion, I repeated commands to her in exactly the same pitch. "Mother, we are going to do this. Mother, we are going to do this." I spoke as flatly as I could because then she would start paying attention to the words, and finally she would hear me. When I changed pitch, she would tune in the emotion without understanding the words, and she'd feel like she had done something wrong or she'd disappointed me. It is important to keep the tension out of our voices so we can be better heard by those whom we are trying to help.

I developed compassion for those who could not come and see Mother and Dad as they aged because it was too difficult to see the way my parents had changed. Mother was the oldest of ten. I believe it was hard for her sisters to come and see their future. At first I wondered, "Why haven't *they* come?" That doesn't help. In time I understood. Eventually I began phoning mother's sisters. I would talk about what she was able to do or not do, sharing something fun that she was able to enjoy. I tried to find ways for them to join in and care about her. When they were able to come to Springville, I didn't insist that they spend a lot of time with her; it was enough that they could be in the home and be nearby but not have to spend a lot of time realizing they couldn't talk to her.

I really enjoyed discovering what made Mom and Dad happy as they aged. By accident we found out that Sesame Street's laughing Elmo toy was a big hit with Mom. She loved to laugh with Elmo. Children's toys and teddy bears became simple ways to give Mom the kind of laughs we hadn't heard from her for a long time.

9. *Understand that you won't always be able to control the quality of their experiences.* The first time I moved Mom into a nursing home I was traumatized because I couldn't maintain as much personal care of Mother there. I must have been the nursing home's all-time most obnoxious relative. I realized this one night when I found myself sorting through the nursing home's laundry looking for Mother's misplaced nightgown. Mom was comfortable. She wasn't sleeping in the nightgown I wanted her to sleep in, but she was okay. I learned we should help the nursing home staff, not complain about what they are trying to do. I really had to change my attitude about "quality of life" and look at how much they were trying to help Mom.

10. *Learn to see what is, not what was or what should have been or what we hoped had been done.* One night I stood in the nursing home cafeteria, looked around, and said, "This is Mother's community now. These are people that Mother sees every day. I'm going to learn more about them. I'm going to learn their names. I'm going to appreciate who they are right now at this point in their lives. I'm not going to be afraid of the people I don't understand." This attitude helped me be more patient and tolerant and helped me provide more care for Mom while she was there.

Why is it so important not to forsake the elderly? Each family builds a legacy of caregiving that lasts across generations and represents our best resources, abilities, and circumstances. As I cared for Mom and Dad, I remembered seeing my grandfather's face light up when as a little girl I visited him in his big grandpa chair in his old house on First Avenue. I talked to my aunts and got treats while my dad helped his father. I went with my dad to help move his sister and saw him visit her in the nursing home. I heard Mom and Dad pray over her welfare. I sat with my mom when we cared for her mom in her Salt Lake home and heard stories about Bear Lake. I hope the young people in my family, who also helped us, remember that we loved as much as we could. Expressing love is as important a part of the legacy of care as any financial or physical resource.

How do we know when we are doing enough? This passage from *Believing Christ* by Stephen Robinson is reassuring: "If we are doing what can reasonably be expected of a loyal disciple in our present circumstances, then we can have faith that our offering is accepted through the grace of God. . . .

"Do you feel the influence of the Holy Spirit in your life? Do you enjoy the gifts of the Spirit? Then you *know* that God accepts your faith, repentance, and baptism and has agreed that '[you] may always have his Spirit to be with [you]' (D&C 20:77). This is perhaps one reason why the Holy Ghost is called the Comforter, because if we enjoy that gift, we can know that our efforts are acceptable—for now—and that we are justified before God by our faith in Christ. And that is comfort indeed."[1] I learned that no matter what circumstance we are in, we can give comfort to others, and that comfort can be acceptable. We can know it is acceptable because the fruits of the Spirit will attend us.

The second dimension of my title concerns the pleas of the caregiver not to be forsaken. How did I know I was not forsaken? I experienced the evidence of His care in the voice of those who talked to me with an understanding heart, whose charity came across in spite of their own discomfort in not knowing what to do or say. As a caregiver, I felt love and support when instead of quickly asking, "What can I do?" people talked to me and then discerned what they could do.

Acknowledging the sacrifice caregivers make is extremely important. I appreciated all of those who sincerely inquired, "How are your mom and dad?" I was further touched by those who said, "And how are you?" Many days I knew that I was in trouble. When others helped me manage the little things I needed, I felt that I was not forsaken. People asked, "Are you aware that the Sunday meeting schedule has changed?" "Did you realize that this announcement was made in a meeting you missed?" Those things mattered a lot to me.

I also know I was not forsaken because my capacity for faith greatly increased. Sometimes on a Sunday evening I would think about the week ahead and not be able to see how I could manage it. I now have a different definition of faith, one that includes moving ahead, trusting I will be guided and prompted beyond my capacity to "manage." It took less control on my part and more humility, but I learned. *Go Forward with Faith* discusses challenges President Gordon B. Hinckley faced both in workload and policy as President Kimball became more feeble: "The prospects of what lay ahead might have been paralyzing had it not been for President Hinckley's innate optimism and his unwavering faith that the Lord knew the circumstances and would provide direction."[2] I had to learn that. The Lord does know our circumstances and He will provide direction.

Third, I knew I was not forsaken because I felt the power of a sustaining spirit. My mood would change, my priorities would shift, my spirit would be encouraged, my task would seem simpler beyond my capacity to explain, and clearly beyond my individual, emotional, and physical strength. We all have access to this sustaining spirit.[3]

What can we do to help with care giving? We can all pay attention to the caregivers and people who need care giving in our wards and stakes, and find out about that population. We can visit nursing homes without having someone we know in them. We can talk about the facilities in our wards and stakes. We can make it a normal part of our life to include the caregivers.[4]

Last, in our lessons, in our foyer conversations, and in our day-to-day activities we can take a sincere interest in the joys and the complexity of aging. A gentleman in my neighborhood who walks around the block with an oxygen tank stopped by when I was out pulling weeds and said, "I don't get to do much yard work anymore. I'm not of much use to anyone." I said, "Oh, I don't think that's true." And I paused to have a conversation with him. Before, I probably would have just nodded my head, smiled, and let him walk on. Take an interest in the lives of people around you. You are on somebody's "Transition Home Team." We all are. Though our focus in mortality may of necessity be on sunsetting, we are part of one eternal round, and someday there will be a glorious sunrise.

Notes

1. Stephen E. Robinson, *Believing Christ: The Parable of the Bicycle and Other Good News* (Salt Lake City: Deseret Book, 1992), 93–94; emphasis in original.

2. Sheri L. Dew, *Go Forward with Faith: The Biography of Gordon B. Hinckley* (Salt Lake City: Deseret Book, 1996), 396.

3. Ironically, the year after Mom and Dad died was the most challenging for me. I'd just spent six years giving intense care, and here I was, wondering, "Where should I be going? What should I be doing? What matters most?" People would ask, "Aren't you relieved?" And I'd say, "Relieved? I'm struggling to relearn how to manage my day." The post-caregiving experience brought readjustment challenges of its own.

4. We need to appreciate the individuality of caregivers. They don't fit one box, one size, one need. We need to pay attention to their interests and how best to support them. Some very practical suggestions for finding out how to be good individual caregivers is found in Marguerite Mauss Eliason and Susan Chieko Eliason, *Caregiving: An Errand of the Heart* (American Fork, Utah: Covenant Communications, 1995).

LAUGHTER: THE
ANTI-PRIDE INGREDIENT

⚡

Emily Watts

We don't fly much as a family—we have too many children and too little money. But last summer we took our children on a trip to Washington, D.C., and the airline seated my husband and me behind the galley on the airplane. We were congratulating ourselves and feeling pretty good about the fact that there was no one in front of us to recline the seat backs and crowd our already-crowded legs. The only drawback was that there were no tray tables. Many veteran flyers have since pointed out to me that the tray tables are in the arm between the seats in such a case, but we didn't know that, and the steward did not bother to enlighten us. I think he enjoyed seeing the rubes who hadn't ever flown before.

So, when they passed out the snacks, we didn't have anyplace to put them. Larry, my husband, was reading a magazine, and he was holding his little bag of pretzels and a cup of tomato juice. You know how you get sort of lulled in, turning pages, relaxing, when you're reading on a plane. At one point I caught sight of him in my peripheral vision just in time to realize that he had put the tomato juice in the same hand with the snacks and was in the process of shaking some pretzels

Emily Bennett Watts holds a bachelor's degree in English from the University of Utah. She works as senior editor for development and communications at Deseret Book Company. She has served as a Gospel Doctrine teacher, a counselor in ward Primary and Young Women presidencies and ward Relief Society president. Emily, who loves words and music, has written two books and sung in the Utah Symphony Chorus. She and her husband, Larry, are the parents of five children.

from the bag into his mouth, which of course resulted in his dumping the whole glass of tomato juice down his shirt.

I really, really tried not to laugh. I just sort of held my breath and shook silently. He got up and went to the restroom cubicle to try to clean himself up, and *then* I laughed just as hard as I could, as quickly as I could, knowing that he would be back soon and I would have to try to be sympathetic. I was fairly composed by the time he came back out, but his white polo shirt was still just such a mess, I couldn't contain myself. I laughed and laughed, and between laughs I said, "Honey, I am so sorry, but this really is going to be funny someday."

"It's funny now," he said. "I just don't feel like laughing."

Well, you know what? There is a time to laugh. I think we can all recognize that what kept my husband from laughing in that instance was that little bit of injured pride that said, "Oh, great, I get to land in Washington, D.C., the nation's capital, with a tomato-stained polo shirt." The truth is, pride keeps us from laughing, and laughing keeps us from pride. When we recognize how many bad things pride leads us into, I think we can recognize that we need more laughter. We need to have laughter as the anti-pride ingredient in our lives.

Let me tell you what kinds of stupid things pride will make you do. My extended family all went to France together one year. In one hotel the space was limited, and my twenty-something brother was appointed to stay in the room with me and my husband. The next morning, after we slept, my husband and brother went to breakfast, and I thought, *This will be a great time for me to have a bath.* I went in the little bathroom and was having a bath, and they came back before I came out. I don't know why I had not a stitch of clothing in the bathroom with me so that I could get out of the bathroom. I don't know why I didn't just call out through the bathroom door, "Guys, go away, I don't have a bathrobe." I have decided, after having thought about this in sort of excruciating detail for a long time, that what happened was, I was having some big-sister pride that was telling me, "My little brother is not going to prevent me from getting out of this bathroom."

I thought, *I will just drape a towel around myself and go out and grab the blanket off the bed so that I can wrap up better*. So I got the towel.

Now, in France, towels seem to be made for the petite Frenchwoman rather than the more statuesque American Amazon type, and when I draped this towel horizontally, there was not sufficient vertical coverage. But I was determined to solve this problem by now, and my creative ingenuity was at work, and I thought, *I will hold the towel vertically in front of me and inch out along the wall*. This was a clever, good, big-sister solution. I held the towel in front of me vertically, and I started inching out. The whole time my brother's face was this study in "how stupid are you?"—a look that I'm sure you have seen if you have a little brother. I was feeling quite proud of myself, though, as if I were really accomplishing something. I got to the bed, and I couldn't resist the big-sister gloat: "There, didn't I do that well?"

And he said, "Except for the mirror behind you, yes."

I had somehow failed to notice the full-length mirror on the closet door. That kid didn't get married for ten years after that! I think it was a formative experience in his young life.

Here's the point: Pride makes you do stupid things. If you succumb to pride, it makes you unable to admit your inadequacies, wanting to hide something that you don't do well, wanting people not to see. Laughter allows you to cross those barriers, to acknowledge inadequacies and to build bridges to people who can help you with things that you are inadequate with.

I remember when I was a young mother, I went to a Homemaking night where we were going to crochet a little chick to go around a plastic Easter egg. I had never successfully crocheted anything in my life. We had learned crocheting in Merrihands in Primary, but while my friends were crocheting darling little vests and shells, I was crocheting along one edge of a tea towel. I folded it discreetly so that the mothers couldn't see the unfinished edge on the day that we had to display our handwork.

But these women in Relief Society assured me that a six-year-old could crochet this little chick. (These are the same kind of people who tell you, "I can get anyone up on water skis." This is just a lie. I have disabused many proud boaters of that notion.) So I had the crochet hook, and the yarn, and all my hopes, and I went with my little plastic egg to do this chick-around, only to learn that apparently I have a problem with "tension." As I crocheted, instead of the cute little shape that it was supposed to be, my creation got sort of elliptical, to the effect that it clearly would not fit on the egg in the traditional fashion. However, if we laid the egg on its side, it fit nicely over it. I didn't particularly want a dead Easter chick, but someone suggested that it could be a mouse, and my sisters helped me crochet some little round ears to attach at one end and chain-stitch a little tail, and I ended up with an Easter mouse.

I'm not a six-year-old, that's the problem. If someone had taught me to do this when I was six, I might have been able to accomplish it. But the important thing was that twenty years later, those women in my ward are still laughing with me about the year that I made the Easter mouse. And they are laughing about it because it was a good memory for them, and it was a good memory for me because we laughed the whole time it was happening. I did kind of learn how to crochet, and I even crocheted a baby blanket for my first child, and if the edges kind of fanned out unevenly as we were going along, she didn't care. In fact, she used to turn it around to try to find the gimpy corner that stuck out. That was her favorite corner.

But pride keeps us away from doing things. Pride makes us stay home from Enrichment Night because we don't know how to do the thing they're doing, and we don't want to look stupid. Pride makes us afraid to make a mistake and, because we all *do* make mistakes since that is part of what happens in mortality, pride makes us try to hide the mistakes that we make. Laughter takes the sting out of the mistakes and puts us in a position to learn from them, which is what we are supposed to be doing with our mistakes.

We live right across the street from our chapel, and I'm not sure that I've gotten to church on time more than ten times in my entire life. I think if we lived half an hour away I could be on time, because we'd all have to drive together. But when you live just across the street, you get the kids ready, and you get the husband ready, and you push everybody out the door, and then finally you get the bathroom and you get the chance to get yourself ready. So I'm often not on time.

However, one day I was determined: We were going to all be on time to church! I had laid out the clothes the night before, and all the children had both matching shoes and stockings with no holes. It was a great moment. We were walking out the door, and our neighbors were out in their yard, and I was just glowing, feeling like a good example, all precious and prompt. We were doing so well. As I turned to wave, I thought I saw a kind of funny look on my neighbor's face. Turning back around, I caught a quick glimpse of my shadow on the driveway—just enough of a look to confirm that I had a head full of instant curlers. Yup, I'm going to church with curlers in my hair, but I'm going to be on time. . . . Well, I wasn't on time for church that day. I went back in the house and shook the stupid curlers out of my hair. But you know what? Everyone got to church that day, and church is three hours long, and I say, if you are a couple of minutes late, oh well! (I don't *really* say that. Don't tell my bishop. I'll try again next week to be on time.)

I think pride makes us embarrassed and laughter makes us human. One time when I was a young adult, before I was married, I had to leave a stake conference meeting a little early. I had sat on the front row of the overflow area, so there were maybe three hundred people behind me, but I thought, *Well, I'll just hurry out.* The door on my side of the chapel wasn't open, so I was going to go out the other door. The time came that I was just going to slip quickly and quietly out of the meeting, and I stood up and took a step on my left foot, and it felt kind of funny. I stepped right, stepped left again, and realized that it felt funny because my entire left leg was asleep. If you have ever stepped on an entirely asleep leg, you know that it doesn't support your weight. I went right down in front of several hundred people, hearing their collective gasp.

There is a moment when something like this happens to you when you think, *Okay, should I act really injured, and bid for the sympathy vote?*

Or should I just laugh this off and get up and go on? Well, I couldn't get up and go on because my leg was still asleep, but I couldn't bring myself to act really injured because I wasn't. So I did start to laugh, and then everybody just breathed again and settled back into their seats and relaxed. One of my friends told me afterward that he and the friend he was sitting next to drew straws to decide who was going to get up and come help me out. The happy thing is that I married the one who did—because he got it, that sometimes you make a mistake and you just get up and you go on. Pride makes you embarrassed about that, and laughter reminds you that everybody is human and everybody makes those mistakes.

I think that pride leads to anger. Pride takes us to a place where we are feeling self-justified, where we are trying to defend our position. And I think laughter dissolves anger quicker than almost anything else I can think of. I'm thinking of a time when I was pregnant and we were driving, by the grace of my mother-in-law, this big, old Ford station wagon. There were ten kids in my husband's family, and they had all fit in that car, which was roughly the size of an aircraft carrier, with fold-up seats in the back.

It was not a particularly aesthetically pleasing car, but the young people in my husband's family had used it for their dates, so it had sentimental value if no particular blue book value. It was our only car, and on the day in question I was going to pick him up at work, but I had to go to the bank first. Well, you know how the bank has those incredibly stupid pillars at a really inconvenient angle that you have to get your car around so that you can reach the drive-through? Sure enough, as I pulled into the bank, I heard, "Scraaaape." And I thought, *Oh great, I've scraped the car. But it's an old car, you probably wouldn't even be able to tell*, I thought. *Not that big a deal.* I was pregnant, I had two small children with me, and I was really tired. So I just kept going, and this horrible scraping sound went on all the way down the whole interminable length of that car. I couldn't believe how loud it was. I thought, *This is just so awful*, but I still didn't stop and get out to look. I just got the money and headed over to pick Larry up.

When we came out from his office, he walked over to the car, looked at it for a long minute, and finally said, "Honey, how do you propose that we get *in* the car?" I had shorn the door handles—front and back—right off. We drove back to the bank, and they were lying there in the drive-through. I wonder what the other people thought who came through: "Oh, someone's lost their door handles. Let's turn them in." And you know, my sweet husband just threw back his head and laughed and laughed. He escorted me in a gentlemanly fashion around to the other side of the car so that I could climb in and scoot over, which was how we had to get into the car the whole rest of the time we had it. And he never got angry. He never made it so that I had to bite back at him, "Well it's that I'm pregnant and I had to drive and I couldn't get in . . ." We never had a fight about that because he knew that no amount of angry yelling was going to get those door handles back on that car. I don't care how good you are with a glue gun, you're not fixing that. The point of this is that sometimes you get to choose your response. And sometimes, when you find yourself with anger being foremost in your mind, if you can stop and turn that response into something that can make you laugh, you can avert a lot of problems.

Especially when they were smaller, I used to bawl out my kids in French. I would say in loving tones: "Oh, tu me fais mal à la tête" ("You make me sick in the head"). They didn't know what I was saying, so they'd laugh and I'd laugh and then we'd be okay. My favorite phrase when they were little was *ça suffit*, which means "that's enough," and now they say to each other, "sauce your feet." That's close enough and accomplishes the same thing.

I want to close by suggesting that pride keeps us away from God because it makes us feel like we have to do everything ourselves, that we want to do it ourselves, that we should do it ourselves. I have one son who was so stubborn in this regard. In the era when he was wearing the one-piece, footed pajamas—he was about two—he always wanted to put them on by himself. It's hard for a mom to put those sleepers on a wiggly two-year-old; the child himself really can't do it. Every night we would lay the pajamas out and he would fight and struggle to don them. Finally at some point he would come to me with the pajamas in his hands and hold them up. I would put them on him and zip them up and get him to bed.

I sometimes wonder how often in our pride we insist on trying to do for ourselves things that we are entirely incapable of doing. This turns us away from our Father in Heaven. Laughter, on the other hand, lightens our hearts, clears our minds, shifts our perspective, and helps us remember that most of the clutter of mortality isn't worth spending even one ounce of emotional energy on.

If I could leave you one testimony in conjunction with what I've written here, it is that I believe the Lord loves a cheerful heart. If we will cultivate that quality of cheer in our hearts and in our lives, we will draw closer to him, closer to our families, and closer to each other.

ONLY THE HOME

✺❦✺

Janet S. Scharman

The LDS Bible Dictionary tells us that "only the home can compare with the temple in sacredness."[1] That's a powerful declaration, especially when combined with statements from our prophets. President Harold B. Lee told us, "Remember always that the most important of the Lord's work you and I will ever do will be within the walls of our own homes."[2] President Gordon B. Hinckley added: "I am satisfied that no other experiences of life draw us nearer to heaven than those that exist between happy parents and happy children."[3] In September 1995, "The Family: A Proclamation to the World" un-ambiguously set forth the paramount importance of family and our responsibility as parents.[4]

No one questions the high priority given to family or the prophets' counsel about the sanctity of the home, but we probably all wonder if our own homes could honestly be compared to a temple in sacredness. Why do we so often fall short of our aspirations? One reason is that family upsets and even minor disruptions in plans tend to distract from a feeling of serenity. Our lives simply don't always run on schedule or according to plan, not to mention that perhaps some of our plans may include impractical fantasies of what the "ideal" is—fantasies that could never be realized in the world in which we live.

Men's and women's different approaches to life mean a potential

Janet S. Scharman is the vice president of Student Life at Brigham Young University. A Laurel advisor in her ward, she served as chair of the BYU Women's Conference in 2001 and 2002. She and her husband, S. Brent Scharman, have a blended family of one son and nine daughters.

for conflict always exists—even when partners' opinions agree on most issues. Add children, and the complexity compounds exponentially. We sometimes set ourselves up for disappointment by thinking that if we want something desperately and are willing to work hard enough, we can, through sheer willpower or righteous intent, create a world that is exactly to our liking.

The Apostle Paul wisely counseled, "Hold fast that which is good"—not hold fast to *everything* (1 Thessalonians 5:21). We are to cling only to those things in this imperfect world that motivate us to be better and to appreciate the beauty we find here and the gifts we have from God.

Many people have had to deal with tremendous pain and heartbreak, particularly in sacred family relationships. Some mothers struggle with being single because of a death or divorce. Some women are married to faithless men. Others grieve over abuse or neglect. Some families have to deal with financial calamities and with physical or emotional illness. Still, in spite of it all and under the worst of circumstances, our Heavenly Father is watching over each of us and has promised us every blessing we need to return to His presence. That promise is also for those spirits who have been entrusted to us to teach, guide, and nurture.

In his professional life, my father often worked with disabled people whom he would sometimes invite to our home. I recall one gentleman who had lost both arms in the war. Instead of hands, he had hooks that he could maneuver with incredible accuracy. He could tie his own shoelaces, button his shirt, skillfully handle a knife and fork, and work as a mechanic full time. To prepare us for visits with him and others with disabilities, my father taught: "Focus on what they have, not on what they haven't." That is a good message for all of us, especially during those times when we are not feeling whole in exactly the way we would like to be.

My first year teaching junior high school English, during a unit from our literature book about heroic triumphs over disabilities, I invited a friend of my father's to be a guest speaker in my classes.

Totally blind as a result of a childhood accident, this man had later married a woman blind from birth. Together they raised three healthy, sighted children. He was obviously a very capable man who had adapted quite impressively to the world around him. After his remarks, he invited questions, and one young student asked: "If you had a chance to get your eyesight back or get one million dollars, which would you choose?" I well remember his careful, measured response. "I don't want to sound worldly," he began, "but I would probably have to choose the money. I'm well aware that my blindness is just a temporary state. I know that my eyesight will be restored to me fully at the time of the resurrection, that because of my Savior any inequity will be resolved. But my son is preparing to go on a mission which is very costly, and we are not wealthy people. The money would ensure that he could have the opportunity to serve the Lord—now, in this life, when he is privileged to receive such a calling."

I'm reminded again of the statement in the Bible dictionary: "Only the home can compare with the temple in sacredness." It gives no qualifiers to *the home*. It doesn't say: only the home where there is no disability or dysfunction can compare with the temple in sacredness, or only the home with two parents, or with a lot of money, or with no wayward children. This physically blind man clearly saw what was of most importance in this life, and that was exactly what he needed to be a good parent, a faithful son of God, and a promoter of sacred work within his home.

Let me tell you about three other men whose lives were in many ways less than perfect. The first, named Howard, contracted polio at age four and, although he recovered, endured back pain for the rest of his life. During his later years, he developed cancer that ultimately spread to his bones. Howard's mother was active in the Church, but his father was not a member, and he refused to let his son be baptized when Howard turned eight. Howard didn't go on a mission after graduating from high school, and rather than go to college, he decided to play in a band that toured the world. After returning home and going from one dead-end job to another, Howard began to attend night school. He married and had three children, one of whom died in early childhood.[5] Most of us would hardly characterize the course of Howard's life as ideal.

Vaughn is another man whose childhood was full of challenges. His father was an alcoholic who often drank away the family income, at times leaving them without adequate food. "We didn't have much clothing, either," Vaughn recalled. "I had a pair of shoes with soles that were worn clear through. I'd cut out pieces of cardboard and slide them inside the shoes to cover the holes. When I went to church, I would sit with both feet flat on the floor—I didn't want anyone to see 'Quaker Oats' through the bottoms of my shoes." Later his parents divorced. His mother joined the Church, but did not remarry. She worked nights so that she could be home with the children during the day.[6]

A third young man came from equally difficult financial circumstances. His family had to move from time to time because of ongoing financial problems. As a child, he was less interested in reading and study than his siblings.[7] As an adult, he spent much of his life dodging the law and in the end was killed while imprisoned.

In all three cases, I've focused on problems and difficulties in these men's lives, emphasizing what they lacked. Maybe some of their home circumstances sound similar to your own or to someone you know. It would be easy to assume that their lives were unhappy and, to put it mildly in the last case, turned out less than wonderful. But that would not be taking into account their life assets—things they did have: people who loved and supported them, their own strong work ethic, their acquisition at some point in life of a testimony of the gospel of Jesus Christ, and certain commitments they made a long time ago to our Heavenly Father. The first person I mentioned was our fourteenth president of the Church, Howard W. Hunter, the second is Elder Vaughn J. Featherstone of the First Quorum of the Seventy, and the last was our beloved Prophet, Joseph Smith.

Let me state this as clearly as I can. There is no question that the family headed by two healthy, stable, righteous parents who share the same vision and commitment is what each of us would hope for. That's what we should strive to achieve. We should behave in ways that would help us attract a worthy companion, that would allow us to be sealed in the temple and be true to the covenants we make there. We should do everything within our power to create an environment likely to promote successful experiences for our family and children. But, we must also remember that if, for whatever reason, we are diverted from that ideal path, all is not lost. "Every home," President Hinckley has said, "can provide an environment of love which will be an environment of salvation."[8] "What righteous families have in common," Sister Kathleen H. Hughes has added, "are the covenants that they hold sacred."[9]

Clear values, commitment to doing those things of eternal consequence, and loving, thoughtful parenting are what matter, whatever the configuration of the family in which we find ourselves. We have been counseled to bring up our children in light and truth (D&C 93:40). That means to teach and guide them. Children pay attention to our behavior and the spirit they feel when they are around us. Fortunately, we don't have to get it right every time to be a positive influence; but the more often we speak, act, and make choices consistent with gospel principles, the greater chance our children will do the same. Let me offer three final thoughts.

First, love the Lord. President Hinckley told us in a recent general conference: "God has made it clear that if we will not forsake Him, He will not forsake us."[10] Children need to see that we truly love the Lord with all our heart, soul, and mind (Matthew 22:37), and that we trust His redeeming love in return. Powerful teaching moments happen when our children catch us reading scriptures alone in our bedroom, saying personal prayers, or asking for divine help in dealing with difficult issues. Regular attendance at Church meetings, consistency in holding family home evenings, and willingness to accept Church callings, even when difficult or inconvenient, demonstrate our commitment to the Lord.

A letter from a missionary son brought tears to his mother's eyes when she read the following: "Mom, I read a scripture and I heard your voice because you had shared that scripture with me so many times before."[11] The lessons we teach in our homes, whether inadvertently or purposefully, stay with our children over time and across geographical distances.

Second, encourage the righteous exercise of agency. A great modern literary hero was told by his mentor, "It is our choices, Harry, that show what we truly are, far more than our abilities."[12]

"Have you ever thought about the wonder of the gift of agency," BYU devotional speaker Clayne Pope asked, "—this rare ability to make choices between good and evil that sets us apart from God's other creations? Volcanoes do not have the power to choose when to erupt in order to minimize death and destruction. Asteroids don't change their course in order to steer clear of the earth. Grizzly bears are not waking up from the winter hibernation telling themselves that this is the year that they are going to quit eating those tender young elk calves. Crabgrass doesn't repent and vow to stop growing in people's backyards. The rest of God's creations were created to be controlled by their nature and to be unaware of good and evil and the need for moral distinctions. But we as humans are different. We have been given this wonderful capacity to decide that something is right or wrong and change our actions. . . . Agency is essential to the plan of salvation and eternal life."[13]

That's easy to remember when all is going well. However, when those we love go astray, or we make our own mistakes, we have to work harder to remind ourselves that we chose this path. We chose agency with its sometimes-dreadful outcomes during the pre-existence when we first decided to follow Jesus. We fought in a terrible battle alongside our Savior for the opportunity to make many more choices in the future and to deal with the results of those decisions. We resisted Lucifer's enticements to relinquish our agency to him—though lured, no doubt, by promises that his plan guaranteed freedom from challenges and disappointments and heartache of our own making. Under his leadership, we would make no mistakes. We weren't fooled then, and we shouldn't allow ourselves to be confused now. We must encourage our children as they make righteous decisions and help them to right their wrongs when they don't. We came to life expecting learning, not perfection—either in our circumstances or choices.

Remember President James E. Faust's wise counsel: "Let us not be arrogant but rather humbly grateful if our children are obedient and respectful of our teachings of the ways of the Lord. To those broken-hearted parents who have been righteous, diligent, and prayerful in the teaching of their disobedient children, we say to you, the Good Shepherd is watching over them. God knows and understands your deep sorrow. There is hope."[14]

Finally, don't give up. Sometimes we focus our attention on raising successful children rather than on being a successful parent. There is a difference. Ultimately, we can't control our children. What we can determine is what *we* will personally do or not do, and we have been promised that our righteous efforts will not be in vain.

Henry Eyring, world-famous scientist, faithful member of the Church, and father of Apostle Henry B. Eyring, said: "I'm convinced that the prophets are inspired and that I'll be inspired in guiding my family if I listen to them. When I don't follow the counsel of those who are placed over me, then I'm in very deep water. I'm enough of a coward and a poor enough swimmer that that's not where I want to be."[15]

I'm a coward and a poor swimmer as well, and so I must rely on the gospel in my life and the wisdom of inspired leaders to help keep me afloat. The normal ups and downs of family life can cause us to feel uncertain, wondering if we will ever have the reassuring calm and peace we desire. We can dwell on what is missing in our lives and find ourselves being pulled down to the depths of despair. Or we can trust in the Lord's love for each of us, hanging on tightly to the truths, supports, and blessings of membership in this great Church, which can buoy our spirits and inspire us to greater efforts. As we do so, in time we will come to see that the work we do in our own homes—each one unique in both challenges and opportunities—can, in fact, compare with the temple in sacredness.

One last word of encouragement: The magnificence of your efforts may not be readily apparent. But I promise you that the Lord is aware of each one of you, He knows the end from the beginning, and, as you allow Him, He will be by your side, especially during those times when you worry that what you have to offer may not be enough. At those times, hold onto this truth from the Doctrine and Covenants: "Wherefore, be not weary in well-doing, for ye are laying the foundation of a great work. And out of small things proceedeth that which is great" (64:33).

Notes

1. LDS Bible Dictionary, s.v. "Temple," 781.
2. Harold B. Lee, *Stand Ye in Holy Places* (Salt Lake City: Deseret Book, 1974), 255.
3. Gordon B. Hinckley, Conference Report, October 1994, 74; or "Save the Children," *Ensign*, November 1994, 54.
4. "The Family: A Proclamation to the World," *Ensign*, November 1995, 102.
5. Available at http://personal.atl.bellsouth.net/w/o/w013/huntehw1.htm.
6. Vaughn J. Featherstone, "Acres of Diamonds," *Speeches of the Year, 1974* (Provo: Brigham Young University Press, 1975), 351–52.
7. Francis M. Gibbons, *Joseph Smith: Martyr, Prophet of God* (Salt Lake City: Deseret Book, 1977), 26.
8. Hinckley, "Save the Children," 54.
9. Kathleen H. Hughes, "Blessing Our Families through Our Covenants," *Ensign*, November 2002, 106.
10. Gordon B Hinckley, "'Til We Meet Again," *Ensign*, November 2001, 89.
11. Personal conversation with author.
12. J. K. Rowling, *Harry Potter and the Chamber of Secrets* (New York: Arthur A. Levine Books, 1999), 333.
13. Clayne L. Pope, "Remember That Ye Are Free to Act for Yourselves," *Brigham Young University 1996–97 Speeches* (Provo: Brigham Young University, 1997), 204.
14. James E. Faust, "Dear Are the Sheep That Have Wandered," *Ensign*, May 2003, 68.
15. Henry Eyring, *Reflections of a Scientist* (Salt Lake City: Deseret Book, 1983), 18.

"Be Taught More Perfectly": Principles and Practices

✺

Coleen K. Menlove

"It was nearing the end of October and I distinctly remember the crunch of leaves under our feet as we left the chapel, having attended three hours of Sunday meetings. After a seventeen-year absence from the Church, my husband and I were just not sure that this was a commitment we really wanted to make. As we took in the autumn sun and slowly made our course home, our five-year-old son began to tell us about Primary. His eyes were bright with the excitement of knowing something he was sure we did not. He began to stutter, 'Did you know that we got to vote about coming to earth?' He didn't wait for any responses but prattled off one question after the other.

"'The Primary president told us about this council in heaven where we all decided about how we wanted it to be on earth. And I didn't believe her and so you know what I said? I said "How do you know?" She told me that God talks to men on the earth—did you know that? And those men that He talks to are called prophets—and then they write down everything that God told them on this thin little paper and it has gold around the edges of the paper and the books are called scriptures. Do you think we could get some?'

Coleen K. Menlove is a wife, mother, grandmother, author, educator, avid gardener, and a leader who has special love and understanding for children. She was sustained as Primary general president in October 1999. She received a bachelor's degree from the University of Utah and a master's degree from Brigham Young University and has served on Church writing committees and the Young Women General Board. She and her husband, Dean W. Menlove, are the parents of seven children and grandparents of fifteen.

"I continued nodding my head yes and would squeeze in an 'Uh-huh' every moment he would let me. My husband and I exchanged glances and secretly were amused by his enthusiasm.

"He continued, 'And then any question—ANY QUESTION—you have in the whole world you can find the answer to in those books, Mom. Any question!'

"In my noncommittal tone, I answered him. 'Yes, that is nice, isn't it?'

"My small one's enthusiastic face changed. He stopped dead in his tracks and he turned to us in earnest. 'Did you know about this?' His face was sincere and serious.

"'Why of course, Jimmy, we—' He did not let me finish. His eyes welled with tears. 'But, Mom,' his lip curled and one single tear streaked his face, 'Why didn't you tell me?'

"I looked at my husband and we shared a moment of pain in our failure. I bent down on one knee and kissed his sweet face.

"'I don't know, Jimmy. I just don't know. But I promise you I will never keep the truth from you again.'"[1]

This story is from a letter I received as General Primary President. It emphasizes how deeply parents' choices matter in their children's lives. Elder L. Tom Perry has reminded us that our children are not yet ours. Our earthly work will determine if we keep them. To become eternal families, we must teach them the gospel in our homes.[2] Children must not be left to wander spiritually. Parental teaching and example have always been the most effective way to pass on a deep and enduring testimony of Jesus Christ from one generation to the next.

President Gordon B. Hinckley has said, "Eternal life will come only as men and women are taught with such effectiveness that they change and discipline their lives. They cannot be coerced into righteousness or into heaven. They must be led, and that means teaching."[3] In addition to family home evening, we know that unplanned moments can be defining moments for teaching gospel principles and bearing testimony. Elder Vaughn J. Featherstone has given an example of how this might happen: "A son may say to us, 'I sure think President Hinckley is a good man.' You could say, 'Indeed, he is wonderful.' What if instead we said, 'Son, I know he is a prophet of God, a seer, and a revelator. . . . ' Can you see the difference? Can you feel the difference?

"A daughter might say, 'We have a nice bishop.' We could respond, 'Yes, . . . he is.' What if we took this opportunity to say, 'Sweetheart, he was called of God by revelation. He has the mantle upon him, and he is guided by inspiration in his calling.'

"Children need to hear their parents testify."[4]

Children should not be left wondering about our faith and testimonies. They need to know what we know. President Boyd K. Packer counsels, "Keep the fire of your testimony of the restored gospel and your witness of our Redeemer burning so brightly that our children can warm their hands by the fire of your faith."[5]

All good teaching is based on certain fundamental principles and practices. I wish to identify four which are central to teaching the gospel "more perfectly" (D&C 105:10).

First, begin with the end in mind. The end purpose of the gospel is clearly stated in Moses: "Behold, this is my work and my glory—to bring to pass the immortality and eternal life of man" (1:39). A favorite painting of mine by Minerva Teichert reminds me of this scripture. It is a picture of Christ with children gathered around Him. Bringing souls unto Christ is the ultimate purpose of any gospel teaching.

I find another lesson in this painting: It has no artist's signature, yet its distinctive style makes the painting easily identifiable as Minerva Teichert's. An unsigned picture usually signals that the artist has not yet finished the work. Consider how that fact relates to a statement by Joseph F. Smith: "Jesus had not finished his work when his body was slain, neither did he finish it after his resurrection from the dead; although he had accomplished the purpose for which he then came to the earth, he had not fulfilled all his work. And when will he? Not until he has redeemed and saved every son and daughter of our father Adam that have been or ever will be born upon this earth to the end of time. . . . That is his mission."[6]

Joseph F. Smith continues: "We will not finish our work until we have saved ourselves, and then not until we shall have saved all depending upon us; for we are to become saviors upon Mount Zion, as well as Christ. We are called to this mission."[7]

Teachers assisting in the Lord's work are concerned with end results, namely, bringing eternal life to His children.

Second, show love. The preeminent reason to teach is to help others know and feel the love of God and His Son. Our desire to show our love will help us overcome many of the challenges we might face as teachers. Sister Beatrice Vilakazi, mother of eight grown children, is a popular seminary teacher in South Africa. But she is no ordinary seminary teacher. She is paralyzed from the neck down as a result of an illness that occurred eighteen years ago. Her students—more than fifty during the last eleven years—gather at her bedside for an hour after school. Sister Vilakazi's genuine love and vibrant testimony keep them coming back. She said: "Although I am physically disabled, the Lord has blessed me with eyes to read, a mind to think, and a mouth to proclaim the gospel. . . . These are the only things I can use to serve others."[8] Sister Vilakazi's love of the gospel and her love for her students enable her to overcome challenges and teach more perfectly. One meaning of the word *teach* is to show.[9] The Spirit can both inspire us with love for those we teach and teach us how to show it.

Third, be teachable. Study and internalize the scriptures. "Remember that it is upon the rock of our Redeemer, who is Christ, the Son of God, that ye must build your foundation" (Helaman 5:12). All the professional teaching methods we might study will not change ours or our students' hearts. Only doctrine and principles taught in the scriptures will do that. When we teach from the scriptures and from divinely inspired Church materials, we have the Spirit with us to bear witness. When the Spirit is present in gospel teaching, "the power of the Holy Ghost carrieth [the message] unto the hearts of the children of men" (2 Nephi 33:1).[10]

If you humble your heart, you may be surprised by what you learn. As I was pondering the topic of teachablity, I gazed out my kitchen window and became the beneficiary of a lesson from a nine-year-old neighbor, Rebekah. She was busily engaged in creating a playhouse at the foot of a large pine tree. In a short time, she had draped a blanket over a low branch, arranged twigs and rocks to mark the walls, and was energetically sweeping the hard-packed dirt. From my window, I could also see our own well-constructed family playhouse that had taken us five years to complete. Rebekah occasionally asks to play in our play-house. Curious to know why she had chosen to create her own that day rather than enjoy ours, I went outside to ask. In defense of her project, Rebekah said, "Well, it is not as professional as your playhouse, but it is mine and it's pretty good."

I immediately thought of the time I had tried to make a doll dress instead of playing with the ones my grandmother had so carefully stitched. As storms came over the next few days, I watched Rebekah fortify her playhouse with a sheet of plywood and other items to shore it up and make it more lasting. At times, those we teach must be in charge of their own learning, unrestricted by our limited understand-ing of the Lord's plan for them. Learning from life is, after all, the pur-pose for which we have come to this earth. Often the most effective lessons for us and for those we teach come from the Lord, not from our lesson plan book, and are a natural outgrowth of earth life.

Fourth, allow for the process of time. Just as children do not grow to full physical stature suddenly, spiritual growth takes place over the "process of time" (Moses 7:21). It begins with bedtime stories, prayer, doing chores, being kind to others, reading from the scriptures—and loving Heavenly Father and His Son, Jesus Christ.[11]

We often think of Jesus Christ as the master teacher, but He at one time was also taught. As John the Baptist stated, "He received not of the fullness at first, but continued from grace to grace" (D&C 93:13). In a similar vein, Luke stated, "Jesus increased in wisdom and stature, and in favour with God and man" (Luke 2:52). Who were His teach-ers? What was the process? *Knowledgeable and loving parents taught Him to pray and to be a student of the scriptures.*[12] He was raised in a family as we all are.

Remember five-year-old Jimmy and the promise his mother made to never keep the truth from him again? In the process of time, Jimmy is now twelve years old—and prefers to be called Jim. He and his parents were sealed as an eternal family in the Salt Lake Temple two years ago. His parents are not only continuing to share the truths of the gospel with Jim but they are also teaching others: Jim's father in a bishopric and his mother as a Sunday School teacher. Time will work for us when we continue with faith and patience. Elder Neal A. Maxwell teaches, "The work of eternity is not done in a moment, but, rather, in 'process of time.'"[13] The scripture that tells us to "wait upon the Lord" means a great deal to teachers who are also learners (Isaiah 40:31). We, and those we teach, are in the lifelong process of becoming Christlike.

We conclude where we started, with the end in mind. Think back to that beautiful, unfinished painting of the children gathered around the Savior. The Lord longs for all of His children to know and come unto Him. Our love for Him and for His children causes our joyful desire to be part of His work. As teachers and learners, we can be more perfectly taught by the Holy Spirit how to more perfectly teach the powerful message of our Savior's redeeming love.

Notes

1. Correspondence on file in General Primary office.
2. See L. Tom Perry, "The Importance of the Family," *Ensign*, May 2003, 42.
3. Gordon B. Hinckley, "How to Be a Teacher When Your Role as a Leader Requires You to Teach," address delivered at General Authority priesthood board meeting, 5 February 1969.
4. Vaughn J. Featherstone, "Things Too Wonderful for Me," *Brigham Young University 2000–2001 Speeches* (Provo: Brigham Young University Press, 2001), 172.
5. Boyd K. Packer, "The Golden Years," *Ensign*, May 2003, 84.
6. Joseph F. Smith, *Gospel Doctrine*, 5th ed. (Salt Lake City, Deseret Book, 1939), 442.
7. Smith, *Gospel Doctrine*, 442.
8. Craig and Kaye Baird, "Disabled Teacher Bears Testimony from Her Bed," *Church News*, 15 March 2003, Z11.
9. *Merriam-Webster Dictionary*, electronic version 2.6, s.v. "teach."
10. Within the Church we have opportunities to learn and renew basic teaching skills. We can ask to attend the *Teaching the Gospel* course. We

can also use *Teaching, No Greater Call;* "Gospel Teaching and Leadership," section 16 of *The Church Handbook of Instruction, Book 2: Priesthood and Auxiliary Leaders;* and the *Teaching Guidebook* as home study courses.

11. See M. Russell Ballard, "Teach the Children," *Ensign,* May 1991, 80.

12. Merrill J. Bateman and Marilyn S. Bateman, "How Knoweth This Man Letters," *Brigham Young University 2001–2002 Speeches,* (Provo: Brigham Young University Press, 2002), 166–67.

13. Neal A. Maxwell, "According to the Desire of [Our] Hearts," *Ensign,* November 1996, 23.

WELFARE PRINCIPLES IN THE HOME

✺⟨⟩✺

H. David Burton

One of the highlights of my assignment at Church headquarters is working with other Church leaders on a multitude of issues that affect people living on every continent in this wonderful but often troubled planet of ours. We see the delicious fruits of man's great humanity to man. Unfortunately on occasion we are exposed to man's inhumanity that brings much sadness and even despair. Too often, it seems, mother nature reminds us of her awesome destructive power. In each situation, we endeavor to apply welfare principles and assist in the Lord's own way.

We reach out to the community of Saints as well as to those not of our faith. For Saints we use the label "welfare." For others, we identify aid as "humanitarian service." Regardless of the brand or label, the result is the same—assisting our Father in Heaven's children who are in need.

Most of the responsibility for ministering to the welfare needs of Church members falls upon the broad shoulders of devoted bishops and Relief Society presidents. Sister Bonnie D. Parkin and I, along with our fellow committee members, see that Church storehouses are full and that other resources are available for bishops and Relief Society

H. David Burton, sustained as the Presiding Bishop of the Church in 1995, has served in the presiding bishopric office for many years, first as a secretary and then as counselor to Presiding Bishops Hale and Bateman. He received his bachelor's degree from the University of Utah in economics and a master's degree from the University of Michigan in business administration. He and his wife, Barbara Matheson, are the parents of five children and the grandparents of seventeen.

presidents to use in fulfilling their scriptural mandate of seeking out and providing for the poor.

The overwhelming generosity of Latter-day Saints around the world as well as our storehouse system uniquely position us to render humanitarian assistance around the world. We have learned that people want to help in times of crisis. Our phones literally ring off the hook when people hear about a disaster. "What can we do to help?" is always the question.

In October 1998, Hurricane Mitch hovered over Honduras for several days. More than forty inches of rain fell in some locations in a four-day period. Mud slides and flooding covered everything with a thick, rust-colored mud. More than 13,000 members of the Church were forced out of their homes, along with hundreds of thousands of their neighbors. Roads were impassable. Food and hygiene items were in critically short supply. Honduras urgently needed the Church's help. A sister from Ogden, Utah, phoned and said: "I have a son in the Honduras Tegucigalpa Mission. I want to help. What do you need the most? Let me get it for you." We responded, "Sister, thank you for your offer, but what we need worse than anything right now is an airplane." "Oh," she said immediately, "I can take care of that!"

And she did! Within a few hours she called back, having arranged for a giant U.S. military C-5 cargo airplane. Her husband, a recently retired Air Force colonel, was engaged in a new business with a retired two-star general who had been in charge of the Southern Command in Panama during the last part of his career. Those two good men were able to connect with the Joint Chiefs of Staff and secure the commitment to have the large plane made available to us at nearby Hill Air Force Base at no cost. The final hurdle to jump was to secure concurrence for the use of that aircraft for humanitarian purposes from the State Department in Washington, D.C. My phone call to Senator Orrin Hatch brought a quick, positive solution. We owe so much to so many.

There must be a lesson in this story. Could it be that if you need what seems to be impossible, just ask a woman? Or could it be that there is nothing impossible to a woman determined to succeed? Or perhaps the lesson to be learned is that great spiritual power comes from acting in behalf of those in need.

Contributions faithfully continue week after week. At this moment, the Church as an institution is assisting the needy in Iraq, Zimbabwe, and Ethiopia, to name just a few active projects.

I'm going to use the term *welfare* to include all that is done to reach out to bless lives, regardless of how it is administered in the Church. One of the founding fathers of our present welfare plan, President J. Reuben Clark Jr., remarked sixty-seven years ago that "the real long-term objective of the Welfare Plan is the building of character in the members of the Church, givers and receivers, rescuing all that is finest down deep inside of them, and bringing to flower and fruitage the latent richness of the spirit, which after all is the mission and purpose and reason for being of this Church."[1] His insightful statement remains one of the foundational elements of our mission to provide in the Lord's way.

President Marion G. Romney stated: "There is an interdependence between those who have and those who have not. The process of giving exalts the poor and humbles the rich. In the process, both are sanctified."[2] The idea that giving both exalts and humbles and thus brings us together is of great spiritual significance.

"The touchstone of compassion is a measure of our discipleship; it is a measure of our love for God and for one another," said President Howard W. Hunter.[3] From the lips of one of my heroes, President Spencer W. Kimball, comes this thought-provoking statement: "Isn't the plan beautiful? Don't you thrill to this part of the gospel that causes Zion to put on her beautiful garments? When viewed in this light, we can see that [welfare] is not a program, but the essence of the gospel. *It is the gospel in action.* It is the crowning principle of a Christian life."[4]

Let me summarize these powerful prophetic statements. Welfare is a means of rescuing all that is finest in givers and receivers. It is a means of exalting the poor and humbling the rich and a measure of our discipleship. It is the very essence of the gospel and the crowning principle of a Christian life. Though it may be simple, perhaps even obvious to most, may I suggest the following: *Faithfully living and practicing sacred welfare principles in the home brings great spiritual strength to families and individual family members.*

I have observed over the years that spiritually strong individuals and families share common characteristics. Among their virtues, they know and study the gospel; they follow the advice of the prophets; they are obedient to their covenants; they love and respect each other; they make prayer an integral part of life; and they display a great love of our Father in Heaven. In addition to all of that, they live and practice welfare principles in their homes.

Picture in your mind this scene described in the Church-produced pamphlet *Family First:* A father leaves the homestead on a tractor, his young son sitting behind him, with the early morning sun rising above the nearby mountains. The father begins to plow his field near a canal bank while his son plays there. Suddenly the father hears desperate calls for help and looks up from his plowing to see his son hanging onto a slippery, thin willow growing on the canal bank. "'Hang on, son,' the father reassures. 'Hang on till I plow just one more round.' Unbelievable? Absolutely. What parent would leave a child struggling against a swift-running stream of water, fighting for his very life? And yet as [our] children grow, many times they are struggling against a swift-running stream, currents in a world that threaten their sense of values and self-worth. How do [we] as parents give them the message, 'Hang on, I'll be right there.'?"[5]

I believe we can best deliver the message within the *home and family.* I also believe that *example* is by far the most effective delivery device. By living and teaching welfare principles in the home, we can both materially and spiritually strengthen our families, particularly our children, against the many challenges they face each day. Over a lifetime, welfare can truly become the crowning principle of an individual's Christian life, the living essence of the gospel, particularly if it is deeply rooted in the nourishing fiber of *home*, *family*, and *example*. Because of a special endowment of charity, love, and great sensitivity, women are uniquely qualified to lead out in practicing welfare principles in the home.[6]

Have you ever thought about welfare as it relates to the law of the fast? The law of the fast may be as old as the human family. In Old Testament times, prophets repeatedly expressed themselves about the commandment to observe the law of fasting and prayer. Most often prayer is mentioned in the scriptures as a companion to fasting. I know it is sometimes difficult to convince children, particularly teenagers, that there is value in obeying the law of the fast. On far more than one occasion, we have heard the moans and groans of children as they were reminded that it was fast day. Our youngest son, in particular, was always disgruntled to wake up on Sunday morning and be reminded—just as he was reaching for that cereal box in the cupboard—that it was fast day. Several years later, we received a letter from him in the mission field. "Mom and Dad, I have a testimony of fasting! One of our investigators was really wavering in his commitment to be baptized. . . . We fasted and prayed for him, and he is back on track! Fasting *really works!*"[7]

Our son had not yet experienced a strong personal desire to rely heavily on the Spirit for help, but his desire for the investigator to accept the gospel brought him a personal test of this principle. This is the same son who, at four years old, came home from sacrament meeting on the Sunday I was called to be bishop of our ward and asked his mother, "Is dad now the person that gets all the envelopes with money in them?" Barbara replied that, yes, the bishop receives the envelopes *for* our Father in Heaven. Our son then let out a loud squeal and exclaimed, "Oh, goody, we're gonna be rich!" We knew we had our work cut out for us way back then.

The Savior proclaimed that the greatest of all the commandments centered on loving our Father in Heaven and fellowmen (see Matthew 22:36–40). "Inasmuch as ye have done it unto one of the least of these," the Savior reminds us, "ye have done it unto me" (Matthew 25:40; see also D&C 42:38). One way we show our love to Him is through observance of the law of the fast. President David O. McKay explained, "We have in the church one of the best systems in the world of aiding one another—the fast offerings."[8] He further indicated that "if there were no other virtue in fasting but gaining strength of character, that alone would be sufficient justification for its universal acceptance."[9] Fifty-nine years later in a general priesthood meeting President Gordon B. Hinckley counseled: "Think, my brethren, of what would happen if the principles of fast day and the fast offering were observed throughout the world. The hungry would be fed, the naked clothed, the homeless sheltered. Our burden of taxes would be lightened. The giver would not suffer but would be blessed by his small abstinence. A new measure of concern and unselfishness would grow in the hearts of people everywhere."[10]

Our children need to see us respond to the deacons as they make their monthly rounds or see us include our fast offerings as we submit our tithing. They need to be a part of calculating what the family amount should be. Of course, when Mom and Dad feel they can be more generous than the value of two meals, they may wish their contribution to be a little more confidential. When discussing fast offerings, I always reflect on the well-chronicled statement of President Spencer W. Kimball: "Sometimes we have been a bit penurious and figured that we had for breakfast one egg and that cost so many cents and then we give that to the Lord. I think that when we are affluent, . . . that we ought to be very, very generous . . . and give, instead of the amount we saved by our two meals of fasting, perhaps much, much more—ten times more where we are in a position to do it."[11]

Living the law of the fast in the home brings not only increased spiritual strength to family members but also inner peace, and it helps hearts turn to the Lord and to other family members. A deep sense of gratitude is generated for the family's blessings as well as an increased sensitivity to the needs of others. As families prayerfully fast for specific purposes and see the promised blessings of the Lord come forth, they grow more united in purpose.

Is it easy to teach the law of the fast in the home? Of course not. Does it take patience, determination, and discipline? Sure. Is it worth it? Absolutely! As families live the law of the fast in their homes, they are blessed in many ways.

The law of the fast is one important arrow in the quiver of living welfare principles in the home. Another is reaching out to assist extended family members, neighbors, and friends. Children who take part can learn firsthand the meaning of kindness and compassion as they become aware of other people's circumstances. They can also learn to respect and appreciate the diversity of human lives. My wonderful mother practiced and taught the principles of welfare and charity as I was growing up. Losing her father during the Depression, when she was only fourteen, caused her to learn resourcefulness, charity, and sensitivity to the needs of others, particularly her four younger siblings. Over the ensuing years, she has continued to give to her family, her extended family, neighbors, and friends in a very quiet way, always concerned for the well-being of others before her own. Now, in her ninetieth year, she continues to reach out by regularly making and sending handmade blankets to the Primary Children's Medical Center in Salt Lake City. Over the last several years, she has sent along with her love more than 200 blankets. I'm certain I have violated her comfort zone by giving away this secret—I'm due for a scolding!—but I'm so grateful for her magnificent example to her children, grandchildren, and great-grandchildren.

Children can also learn marvelous lessons by helping to plan and execute a family preparedness plan. President Hinckley has repeated the family preparedness and self-reliance themes over and over again at recent general conferences. One important principle taught by participating and preparing is obedience—obedience to a prophet's voice.

When President Kimball suggested years ago that each family should have a vegetable garden and learn gardening techniques, our family decided to follow his direction. My grandfather invited us to use a small piece of land, and we launched our garden—or "farm," as the children referred to it. Initial interest and enthusiasm were high. We had fun preparing the soil and planting the seeds. Then the real work of raising a garden set in. Our children discovered that constant cultivating, watering, and weeding was backbreaking work. Their interest waned until the fruits of the harvest were apparent. All of us boasted about the quality and taste of our corn, peas, and potatoes. Though we probably didn't save any money, we did gain much as a family that cannot be quantified. In fact, we invested in our family. Participating in family preparedness and self-reliance not only teaches obedience and lifelong skills but also strengthens love and communication as families learn how to work together.

One challenge facing many families today is affluence. I can hear some of you say, "Please, dear Lord, give me that challenge." But be careful what you wish. Too often our affluence, if not carefully managed, gets in the way of our long-term spiritual welfare. Living a provident lifestyle can be a blessing for generations to come. Living within or beneath our means brings peace of mind and reduces financial stress. Children learn self-discipline and, perhaps more important, gain an understanding of the critical difference between needs and wants. If our children do not understand the difference, their decisions as adults may severely impact their families. Mothers in the workforce to provide wants rather than needs when there are children in the home, or fathers working second and third jobs to acquire wants mistakenly perceived as needs, represent decisions that may hurt the family unit and the children. If we live providentially, our children will be more likely to make correct decisions when it comes to needs versus wants.

President Gordon B. Hinckley has said: "I feel to invite women everywhere to rise to the great potential within you. I do not ask that you reach beyond your capacity. I hope you will not nag yourselves with thoughts of failure. I hope you will not try to set goals far beyond your capacity to achieve. I hope you will simply do what you can do in the best way you know how. If you do so, you will witness miracles come to pass."[12] May the Lord bless you as you play your vital and important role in helping to strengthen families and individuals by living sacred welfare principles in the home.

Notes

1. J. Reuben Clark, Jr., special meeting of stake presidents, 2 October 1936, quoted in *Providing in the Lord's Way: A Leader's Guide to Welfare* [welfare handbook] (Salt Lake City: The Church of Jesus Christ of Latter-day Saints, 1990), i; also quoted by Marion G. Romney, "Living Welfare Principles," *Ensign*, November 1981, 92.

2. Marion G. Romney, "The Celestial Nature of Self-Reliance," *Ensign*, November 1982, 93.

3. Howard W. Hunter, "The Lord's Touchstone," *Ensign*, November 1986, 35.

4. Spencer W. Kimball, "Welfare Services: The Gospel in Action," *Ensign*, November 1977, 77; emphasis in original.

5. *Family First* [booklet] (Salt Lake City: The Church of Jesus Christ of Latter-day Saints, 1992), 3.

6. I'm reminded of a story Elder Neal A. Maxwell tells about the persistent promptings he received from his wife. He tells of coming home after a long day's work to his wife's suggestion that he should go see Sister Pearl Lence. He acknowledged that he should go and said he would sometime soon, but that he was really very tired right now. Sister Maxwell persisted in gentle persuasion, and he finally went. When the door opened, Sister Lence greeted him, saying, "I have been praying all day you would come, Brother Maxwell, and the Spirit told me you would come." Elder Maxwell didn't elaborate on why he needed to be there but expressed gratitude for the sensitivity of a wife who was in tune with the Spirit at a time when perhaps he was not. (Neal A. Maxwell, "Women of Faith" [pamphlet] [Salt Lake City: Deseret Book, n.d.]; also in *As Women of Faith: Talks Selected from the BYU Women's Conferences*, ed. Carol Cornwall Madsen and Mary E. Stovall [Salt Lake City: Deseret Book, 1989], 13.)

7. Letter in possession of author.

8. David O. McKay, quoted in Francis M. Gibbons, *Harold B. Lee: Man of Vision, Prophet of God* (Salt Lake City: Deseret Book, 1993), 127.

9. David O. McKay, Conference Report, April 1932, 65.

10. Gordon B. Hinckley, "The State of the Church," *Ensign*, May 1991, 52–53.

11. Spencer W. Kimball, Conference Report, April 1974, 184.

12. Gordon B. Hinckley, *Teachings of Gordon B. Hinckley* (Salt Lake City: Deseret Book, 1997), 696.

WELFARE, "THE CROWNING PRINCIPLE OF CHRISTIAN LIFE"

Bonnie D. Parkin

Like Relief Society presidents across the Church, one of my responsibilities as the Relief Society general president is welfare. The first definition for *welfare* in my dictionary is: "Health, happiness, good fortune and well-being."[1] The second and third definitions refer to assisting those in need. Isn't it interesting that happiness *and* serving are wrapped up in one word? Let me share with you the story of a dear Relief Society sister named Kim Hak who lives in the Ta Khmau branch in Cambodia. Her rural branch has about 280 members who live in a community with dirt roads, no sewers, no running water, and *very* few homes with electricity. The missionaries there frequently teach at night by candlelight. Sister Kim has been a member of the Church for about two years and has served as a Relief Society president for a little over a year. Her branch president asked her to deliver rice and money to several families in the branch. Elder Lindmark, a senior missionary who, along with others from the branch, accompanied her, wrote of this experience:

"Sister Kim does not speak any English and I do not speak any Khmer but that's okay, as you will see, she knows what she is about. She pulled out this piece of paper with the names of the families we

Bonnie Dansie Parkin was called as Relief Society general president in 2002. A graduate of the Utah State University in elementary education, she has served on the Relief Society General Board and as a counselor in the Young Women general presidency. She served with her husband, James L. Parkin, as he presided over the England London South Mission. They are the parents of four sons and have sixteen grandchildren.

were to visit, and then using hand waving motions she signaled for me to back up the van. Also using hand waving, I checked to make sure she *wanted* me to back up. She assured me with the nod of her head. From then on there was no problem—she would point and I would drive.

"We went to fourteen homes that day. Each home had its own set of problems and we knew we could not solve all of them with a bag of rice and 10,000 riel. But Sister Kim did know that the rice would feed the family for seven, maybe even ten days. And the 10,000 riel, about $2.50 in U.S. dollars, could help buy some vegetables or maybe some fish.

"Sister Kim's directions, or finger pointing in this case, were flawless; she knew exactly how to get to each sister's home. Now the really good part—she knew each sister by name, she knew the names of the children, and while we were in the home her conversation with the family was pleasant and inviting. It was the conversation of a friend. You could see by her countenance that she cared for her sisters and these sisters—without exception—knew she cared for them."[2]

President Spencer W. Kimball taught, "[Welfare] is not a program, but the essence of the gospel. *It is the gospel in action.* It is the crowning principle of a Christian life."[3] Sister Kim exemplifies that spirit. She knows welfare isn't just a program. She understands that it encompasses both spiritual and temporal well-being. Sister Kim shared her love for the Lord as she loved others. My hope is to help us see welfare with new eyes and to understand that we each have something to contribute to the Lord's storehouse. Self-reliance is not just about having enough for ourselves, but about having enough to share with others.

When Joseph Smith organized the Relief Society, he called sisters to "relieve the poor" and "to save souls."[4] When we fulfill this mandate, we are living welfare. The bishop has responsibility to care for his flock, assisted by the Relief Society president. Together they access the bishops' storehouse and the Lord's storehouse to assist the needy in a dignified way. The bishops' storehouse is a physical place with goods and commodities lined up on shelves. But the Lord's storehouse—

where "there is enough and to spare"—is what the Lord has placed within each of us (D&C 104:17). It is one woman making a difference for another. It is one sister offering to listen or talk with a sister who may be lonely. It is a sister developing a close friendship with the sister she visit teaches. It is you and me, with our strengths, our skills, and our talents, blessing the life of another.

We choose what we give to the Lord's storehouse from what He has given us. Sisters, do you see the abundance we have to draw upon? What gifts can you bring to the Lord's storehouse? Each endowed Church member has covenanted to consecrate time, talents, and resources to the building up of the kingdom of God. Our consecration becomes part of the Lord's storehouse in our individual wards and branches.

Sister Sonia Duffles is the Relief Society president of the Anchorage Alaska Bush District, which encompasses thousands of miles of wilderness territory. Scattered across this land are small towns, many with only one or two Church members. Recently my counselors and I participated in an historic teleconference with sisters from the Bush district. Sister Duffles, who arranged our "meeting," sent each participating sister a phone card with a prearranged time and number to call. She asked Kay Root of the Bethel Branch, Tamara Furman from Cold Bay, and Jean Gabryszak from Yentna to share a message with the sisters over the phone. Some sixty-five sisters gathered in chapels or around kitchen tables. They held a roll call that stirred my heart. Each branch reported the number of sisters in attendance. It sounded something like this. "Cold Bay—one sister. Yentna—one. Nome—two. Bethel—ten." On the line were sisters from Dutch Harbor, Dillingham, Naknek, and Kotzebue. We will probably never see these sisters face to face. Many of them have not met each other, but when we sang "As Sisters in Zion," this much was clear: They knew each other's hearts. I will never forget the love that resonated over those phone lines.

In her talk, Sister Root shared how Sister Duffles travels several times a year to the outlying areas, bringing supplies and sisterhood. When Sister Root and her family first moved to Bethel, they had very little money and their meager belongings did not even include pillows. A few weeks later, Sister Duffles came to Bethel bearing a large box of pillows. How excited her children were! No longer would they have to sleep on their rolled-up coats. Sister Duffles' service exemplifies the mission of welfare and Relief Society: She is self-reliant, she knows her sisters and their needs, she follows the Spirit in serving them, and she encourages them to do the same.

Another sister shared how her e-mail address was given to a Dutch Harbor sister who was going through a very difficult time. "After visiting with her via e-mail for about a month, I came to find out that we had been through many of the same things. We were able to share, encourage, and lift one another. I looked forward to her e-mails; her contact with me was at times *my* lifeline." In giving to the Lord's storehouse, both souls were filled.

We stock the shelves in the Lord's storehouse with mercy and charity in the shape of thoughtful acts and silent service. The Spirit will prompt you, for only the Spirit can let you know where you are really needed. You can see if someone doesn't have shoes, but those needs that only the Lord knows must be discerned by the Spirit. Not everyone needs a food order or a bag of pillows. A young mother far from home tells of answering the door one day to find an older sister in the ward on her front step. She hadn't brought a meal with Jell-O™ or even cookies. She asked, "May I come in and rock your baby?" This new mother was so thrilled to have someone love and enjoy her baby. The seasoned sister was grateful to have a child in her arms. Both the giver and the receiver were blessed.

Welfare service depends on, and should in turn promote, temporal and spiritual self-reliance. President Marion G. Romney taught, "Without self-reliance one cannot exercise these innate desires to serve. How can we give if there is nothing there? Food for the hungry cannot come from empty shelves. Money to assist the needy cannot come from an empty purse. Support and understanding cannot come from the emotionally starved. Teaching cannot come from the unlearned. And most important of all, spiritual guidance cannot come from the spiritually weak. . . . Once a person has been made whole or self-reliant, he reaches out to aid others, and the cycle repeats itself."[5]

For the cycle of welfare to repeat itself in our families, we must actively teach it. President Romney once told a story that illustrates the danger of doing too much for our children. There was once a flock of seagulls in the seaside town of St. Augustine. Although fish were plentiful, these gulls were starving. Why? Generations of them had lived work-free on the fishermen's discards. The gulls no longer knew how to fish; parent birds had stopped teaching these once natural skills to their young. So when the fishermen eventually moved on, the gulls' lack of self-reliance threatened their very survival.[6] "We fear many parents in the Church are making 'gullible gulls' out of their children with their permissiveness and their doling out of family resources. . . . In fact, the actions of parents in this area can be more devastating than any government program."[7]

We received pointed counsel at the April 2003 general conference regarding parents' and grandparents' sacred responsibilities.[8] Such counsel extends to all who play meaningful roles in children's lives. Yes, parenting can be overwhelming. Some of us are still waiting for that promised peace of the golden years! But, by consistently and lovingly teaching the principles of welfare, we are teaching our children to fish; when we are gone, not only will our children eat but they will be able to feed others.

What must we do to cultivate an enduring legacy of self-reliance and service in our children?

We must teach our children to work. Elder Dallin H. Oaks said, "Relative poverty and hard work are not greater adversities than affluence and abundant free time."[9] Do we rob our children of their self-reliance by providing too much abundance and free time? Have we denied them the blessing of hard work? Have you ever heard someone stand in conference and thank their parents for giving them every temporal blessing they desired—for not making them work or earn anything?

My husband and I were blessed with parents who loved us enough to teach us to work, no matter how challenging we made it for them—which we often did! We had duties and little jobs. We didn't like a lot of those jobs, but we did them anyway. We worked hard in our home. I didn't think it was a blessing then, but I now know it is a legacy of priceless worth. We tried to give our children this same gift. Of course, by the time we finished, Jim and I were ready to write a book, *Free Agency and How to Enforce It.*

Yet surprisingly, after all those battles over mowing the lawn, cleaning the bathroom, or getting jobs working for others, our children regularly thank us for teaching them how to work. I know it is often easier to do the work ourselves, but remember the starving gulls, then consider the alternative. Work builds confidence and self-reliance and provides skills to serve others.

We must teach our children to live within their means and stay out of debt. For more years than we can count, our family has discussed the hazard of debt around the dinner table. Our sons learned that credit cards get paid off in full every month or they don't get used; that those who understand interest, earn it, those who don't, pay it. President Gordon B. Hinckley has counseled, "Be modest in your expenditures; discipline yourselves in your purchases to avoid debt to the extent possible."[10] Parents must teach the values of frugality and saving.

When my husband served as a stake president and spent time counseling couples with marital challenges, he would meet separately with the husband and the wife. In those cases where financial problems were a major concern, he would frequently hear this heartbreaking comment from the husband: "No matter how much money I earn, it is never enough." Sisters, does this describe us? I wonder if high-maintenance wives don't create high-maintenance children!

We must teach our children to value learning. I am grateful for parents who knew the importance of education and encouraged and sacrificed on my behalf. As our dear prophet teaches, education can bring self-reliance. Our children need the advantage that an education provides.

We must teach our children to serve others. My parents taught us to care for others. Annie, an older woman, lived across the road. When her husband died, she became very frightened of being alone. So my parents sent my sister Joyce and me to take turns sleeping at Annie's house. Each morning we helped Annie make the bed, then we returned home, got dressed, and went to school. This practice went on until she felt able to be alone. I was twelve; Annie was in her sixties. She helped me learn to make a mean bed; I helped her learn to be alone.

As the Prophet Joseph Smith expressed, "A man filled with the love of God is not content with blessing his family alone, but ranges through the whole world, anxious to bless the whole human race."[11] Remember, self-reliance is not just having enough for ourselves; it is having enough to share with others.

My family had very little growing up, but I never knew it. That is a tribute to my mother and father who were faithfully self-reliant. One Christmas Eve, my brothers and I decided to take Christmas to a family struggling to provide for their young children. Knowing full well that our finances were just as tight, my wise mother let us do this anyway. She must have known that what we would learn that night was worth far more than any gift we could receive.

As we went through the house looking for gifts, Mother said, "Sure, you can take this," and "Let them have some of that." We went to the freezer and took some meat. We gathered up oranges, bottled fruit, a loaf of bread, Mother's fruitcake. We went through our own drawers and closets and found one or two of our own special things to give. The effort was basic, but we cobbled together a little Christmas.

Even though I was only thirteen, I was chosen as the getaway driver because my brothers were faster runners. As we approached the family's house, I pulled the car up next to an irrigation ditch that ran alongside the road. My brothers sneaked from the car and ran to the porch with the box of gifts. When they placed it on the mat, the dog started barking.

The children swung the door open just as my brothers leaped into the ditch. Thankfully, the ditch was empty! I'll never forget those little children squealing and dancing with glee: "Santa came! Santa came!" With my brothers barely in the car, we sped off full of Christmas joy.

Years have passed, yet I still marvel that in the face of our own meager situation, my mother let us loot the house for another family. She
understood that our service did not have to be perfect. It only needed to
come from our hearts. My parents' examples created a powerful bond
between my siblings and me. To this day, we know that if one of us is
down to the wire, we can count on the others to rally 'round us.

On another Christmas when I was a sophomore in high school, we
were the family in need. On the way home from shopping in town, we
were involved in a car accident. My father was taken to the hospital,
leaving us with the sinking realization that Christmas would be slim-
mer than ever. There were things I had wished for, things that mattered
to a high school girl: a felt skirt, a Jantzen™ sweater.

On Christmas morning we awoke to what we were sure would be
just another day. But there on our front step was a box. Inside was a gift
for each of us, and it was something we really wanted. We never knew
who left those gifts. But after that day, we thought differently about the
people in our town. Sometimes we give and sometimes we receive.
That is the circle of welfare.

King Benjamin candidly asked, "*Are we not all beggars?* Do we not
all depend upon the same Being, even God, for all the substance which
we have? . . . *O then, how ye ought to impart of the substance that ye have
one to another*" (Mosiah 4:19, 21; emphasis added). Jesus taught,
"Inasmuch as ye have done it unto one of the least of these my
brethren, ye have done it unto me" (Matthew 25:40). Welfare, true
welfare, is simply how we take care of each other.

I am thankful to belong to a church that cares enough about me to
teach me these truths. I thank each of you for what you bring to the
Lord's storehouse. I promise that as you live and teach the eternal principles of welfare, your capacity for self-reliance will broaden, many will
be blessed by your contributions, and together we shall come unto
Christ and become like Him.

Notes

1. *American Heritage Dictionary*, 3d ed., s.v. "welfare."
2. Personal correspondence.

3. Spencer W. Kimball, Conference Report, October 1977, 123; or "Welfare Services: The Gospel in Action," *Ensign*, November 1977, 77; emphasis in original.

4. Joseph Smith, *History of The Church of Jesus Christ of Latter-day Saints*, edited by B. H. Roberts, 2d ed. rev., 7 vols. (Salt Lake City: The Church of Jesus Christ of Latter-day Saints, 1932–1951), 5:25.

5. Marion G. Romney, Conference Report, October 1982, 135–36; or "The Celestial Nature of Self-Reliance," *Ensign*, November 1982, 93.

6. "Fable of the Gullible Gull," *Reader's Digest*, October 1950, 32; as quoted in Romney, Conference Report, October 1982, 133; or "Celestial Nature of Self-Reliance," 91.

7. Romney, Conference Report, October 1982, 133; or "Celestial Nature of Self-Reliance," 91.

8. See, for example, James E. Faust, "Dear Are the Sheep That Have Wandered," *Ensign*, May 2003, 61–68; Susan W. Tanner, "Did I Tell You?" *Ensign*, May 2003, 73–75; Jeffrey R. Holland, "A Prayer for the Children," *Ensign*, May 2003, 85–87; Boyd K. Packer, "The Golden Years," *Ensign*, May 2003, 82–84.

9. Dallin H. Oaks, "Give Thanks in All Things," *Ensign*, May 2003, 97.

10. Gordon B. Hinckley, Conference Report, October 1998, 72; or "To the Boys and to the Men," *Ensign*, November 1998, 54.

11. Smith, *History of the Church*, 4:227.

MEEKNESS,
THE UNSUNG VIRTUE

꒰⌒꒱

Nora K. Nyland

Taken together, the Beatitudes as recorded in Matthew 5 describe attributes of spiritual perfection. To my mind, some of the statements make perfect sense and seem very natural, such as those who mourn will be comforted and the merciful will obtain mercy. Some connections, however, are harder to discern. Into that category falls the declaration, "Blessed are the meek, for they shall inherit the earth."

Though the immediate relationship of meekness and inheriting the earth may be a bit hard to see, study of the matter reveals a most glorious connection. In fact, this rather unsung virtue plays a key role in helping us achieve a Christlike life. The connection begins with an understanding of the nature of Heavenly Father and His desire to bless us. Joseph Smith said, "As God has designed our happiness—and the happiness of all His creatures, he never has—He never will institute an ordinance or give a commandment to His people that is not calculated in its nature to promote that happiness."[1]

That means that the commandments and conditions set forth by Heavenly Father are designed specifically to allow Him to bless us. He doesn't make laws to curtail our fun or burden our lives; He makes

---

Nora K. Nyland, a member of the BYU Women's Conference committee, is an associate professor of nutrition, dietetics, and food science at Brigham Young University. She has held leadership positions in professional organizations, including director for the dietetics program at BYU and president of the BYU Faculty Women's Association. She is a talented seamstress, cook, and teacher and has served as a welfare missionary in Taiwan, as a ward Relief Society and Primary president, and as a stake institute instructor.

them because He is blessing oriented. Heavenly Father wants to bless His children. He is, however, bound by eternal law and can bless only those who obey the laws that lead to the blessings, as explained in Doctrine and Covenants 130:20–21: "There is a law, irrevocably decreed in heaven before the foundations of this world, upon which all blessings are predicated—And when we obtain any blessing from God, it is by obedience to that law upon which it is predicated."

So, what does all of this have to do with being meek? Let's review: Heavenly Father wants to bless us, His commandments are calculated to guide us back to His presence, and being in His presence is His greatest gift and will bring us great happiness and joy. Among all the scriptural guidelines telling us what is required to return to the presence of our Father, we receive this gentle reminder in Moroni, "for none is acceptable before God, save the meek and lowly in heart" (Moroni 7:44). But meekness seems like such a nondescript virtue. How can it possibly determine our acceptability before God?

The human body is composed of trillions of cells, and in each cell are thousands of enzymes. Though small, each enzyme acts as a catalyst, or trigger, for a biochemical reaction. Enzymes are involved in digestion, in production of energy, and in many other vital physiological functions. Failure of an enzyme to function properly can result in disease or even death. Meekness, it seems to me, acts as a spiritual enzyme. All of the so-called greater virtues depend on meekness for their accomplishment. The meek will inherit the earth because only the meek will develop all of the other attributes required for entrance into the celestial kingdom.

One dictionary defines *meekness* as, "Deficient in spirit or courage: submissive."[2] This definition ascribes a negative connotation to the word, which probably reflects—and perpetuates—the world's view of this vital attribute. The common perception of a meek person is of someone afraid of her own shadow, cowering before the will of others, unable to defend herself or her position. I dare say that if you take a poll of friends and neighbors and ask what qualities they most want to develop, meekness will not be on many lists. We simply fail to grasp the importance of meekness because we so often misunderstand what it is.

Contrast that view of what it means to be meek with President Harold B. Lee's: "A meek man is defined as one who is not easily provoked or irritated and forbearing under injury or annoyance. Meekness is not synonymous with weakness. The meek man is the strong, the mighty, the man of complete self-mastery. He is the one who has the courage of his moral convictions, despite . . . pressure. . . . In controversy his judgment is the court of last-resort and his sobered counsel quells the rashness of the mob. He is humble-minded; he does not bluster. . . . He is a natural leader and is the chosen of army and navy, business and church, to lead where other men follow. He is the 'salt' of the earth and shall inherit it."[3]

This view of meekness is the antithesis of one lacking in confidence and courage. In fact, meekness before the Lord is the result of supreme confidence in Him. In Doctrine and Covenants 121, we learn that confidence and power are a result of righteousness. After the declaration that "No power or influence can or ought to be maintained by virtue of the priesthood, only by persuasion, by long-suffering, by . . . *meekness*, and by love unfeigned," we are told, "and let virtue garnish thy thoughts unceasingly; then shall thy confidence wax strong in the presence of God" (D&C 121:41, 45; emphasis added).

That confidence is a two-fold blessing. First, it occurs because our trust or faith in the Lord has been strengthened. Second, it reflects our increased faith or trust in ourselves to act appropriately and according to God's will. Confidence, both in the Lord and in ourselves, is a critical component of meekness. In Hebrews, Paul warns the Saints, "Cast not away therefore your confidence, which hath great recompence of reward. For ye have need of patience, that, after ye have done the will of God, ye might receive the promise" (Hebrews 10:35–36).

Elder Neal A. Maxwell said, "Meekness is neither alarmist nor shoulder-shrugging unconcern. It involves shoulder-squaring self-discipline, and what follows is the special composure that meekness brings."[4] *Special composure*—I think that's another way of describing confidence.

It is clear that the Lord considers meekness an essential attribute of sainthood. Meekness seldom shows up alone in scriptural context. Rather, it is generally found in a cluster of Christlike characteristics. For instance, King Benjamin teaches: "For the natural man is an enemy to God, and has been from the fall of Adam, and will be, forever and ever, unless he yields to the enticings of the Holy Spirit, and putteth off the natural man and becometh a saint through the atonement of Christ the Lord, and becometh as a child, submissive, meek, humble, patient, full of love, willing to submit to all things which the Lord seeth fit to inflict upon him, even as a child doth submit to his father" (Mosiah 3:19).

Meekness becomes the basis for many blessings. Here are some examples from the scriptures:

Psalm 25:9 "The meek will he guide in judgment: and the meek will he teach his way."

Psalm 37:11 "But the meek shall inherit the earth; and shall delight themselves in the abundance of peace."

Isaiah 29:19 "The meek also shall increase their joy in the Lord."

Zephaniah 2:3 "Seek righteousness, seek meekness: it may be ye shall be hid in the day of the Lord's anger."

Moroni 8:26 "And because of meekness and lowliness of heart cometh the visitation of the Holy Ghost, which Comforter filleth with hope and perfect love."

D&C 19:23 "Walk in the meekness of my Spirit, and you shall have peace in me."

Why will the meek be guided in judgment and learn the ways of the Lord? Why will they enjoy an abundance of peace and have joy in the Lord? Why will they be spared the Lord's anger and be visited by the Holy Ghost and thus filled with hope and perfect love? I think it is because the meek will *let* those things happen. The proud will fail to seek the Lord and fail to *let* Him into their lives. The verse in Mosiah suggests that it is not natural to be submissive to the Lord, nor to be humble, patient, and meek. These attributes come by putting off the natural man and becoming, or developing, the desired qualities.

The natural characteristic that most gets in the way of meekness is pride. When we allow ourselves to become puffed up with pride, we can be so easily deflated! Like a bird that fluffs up its feathers to look larger when in danger, our pride is just so much window dressing. It is not related to true confidence but to fear—fear that we will be shown up or found out. Pride is easily offended while meekness is gentle, understanding, and forgiving. Pride looks out for itself, meekness for its neighbor. Pride experiences success with attitude, while meekness succeeds with gratitude. Pride views disappointment or failure with anger and blame; meekness gets through it with patience and supplications for strength.

Wouldn't it be nice to have some sort of device to give us early warning signs of flagging meekness and impending pride? We could call it a "meekometer" and wear it near our hearts. The meekometer would beep (or better yet, drive us to our knees) when our responses to life situations showed decreasing meekness. The meekometer would help us find ways to deflate our own pride before it consumes us.

Let's look at situations where the meekometer might come in handy, and some examples of folks who have passed the test:

First, *being misjudged*. If anything can make us resentful and defensive, it's being misjudged; but consider Pahoran in the Book of Mormon. In the midst of battle, Moroni, who is unaware of an insurrection at home, sends a scathing letter to Pahoran, the governor. Instead of sputtering and holding a grudge, Pahoran responded to Moroni's letter this way: "And now, in your epistle you have censured me, but it mattereth not; I am not angry, but do rejoice in the greatness of your heart" (Alma 61:9).

Next, consider *receiving priesthood direction not of your choosing*. While I was serving in Taiwan, our mission was developing media presentations to expose people in that largely Buddhist area to Christianity as well as to the Church and principles of the gospel. One elder who was very skilled in electronics was heavily involved in work-ing with sound and lighting systems for the presentations. Another elder who absolutely loved teaching the gospel—nothing made him happier than knocking on doors and spreading the good word—was assigned to be the companion of the electronic wizard. That meant not tracting and teaching, but assisting with media productions. One day when I was talking to the mission president, this elder's name and cur-rent assignment came up. The president said, "You know why Elder Christensen is a great man? It's because he's not doing what *he* wants to do, he's doing what *I* want him to do."

What about a *perceived broken word?* One of my colleagues received a call to be a mission president, and a member of the Quorum of the Twelve assured him that, because of some health concerns, he would be assigned to an English-speaking mission where good healthcare would be available. A few weeks later, a letter came informing him he would be serving in Romania. After the initial shock, but with never a sign of anger or resentment, this humble man simply hired a Romanian tutor and began his preparations to serve. Several weeks later, a tele-phone call came asking him if he would consider presiding over a mis-sion in the United States instead.

Another situation for the meekometer is *receiving a Church calling that does not require all of your considerable skills.* After a shift in ward boundaries, a friend of mine attended her new ward for the first time. There, happily fulfilling her calling as the Relief Society pianist, was a former Relief Society general president. My own mission president, released from presiding over a mission, was called to be a Scoutmaster. A former bishop's first call after his release was to serve as the nursery leader for Home, Family, and Personal Enrichment night. And, of course, there was J. Reuben Clark Jr., who was released as first coun-selor to President George Albert Smith and then called to be the sec-ond counselor to President David O. McKay. Rather than take offence at what some considered a demotion, he taught, "In the service of the Lord, it is not where you serve but how."[5]

What happens when you *hold a responsible, visible position of author-*

ity in your profession or in the Church? Moses was a mighty man, but Numbers 12:3 informs us, "Now the man Moses was very meek, above all the men which were upon the face of the earth." I think it's hard for anyone who has seen Cecil B. DeMille's production of *The Ten Commandments* to picture Moses as meek, at least not by the world's definition. Moses was indeed a mighty prophet, liberator of the children of Israel, and the great lawgiver. However, Moses 1:6–10 describes the Lord's interaction with Moses and his vision of the world. When Moses's strength returned to him, he said, "Now, for this cause I know that man is nothing, which thing I never had supposed" (v. 10). Moses didn't mean that man had no worth, rather that man's ability is insignificant compared to that of God. Moses was meek because he submitted his will to the will of the Father.

Theodore Roosevelt was another great leader who knew how to take the measure of mankind. "Before retiring to bed, Roosevelt and his friend the naturalist William Beebe would go out and look at the skies, searching for a tiny patch of light near the constellation of Pegasus. 'That is the Spiral Galaxy in Andromeda,' they would chant. 'It is as large as our Milky Way. It is one of a hundred million galaxies. It consists of one billion suns, each larger than our sun.' Then Roosevelt would turn to his companion and say, 'Now I think we are small enough. Let's go to bed.'"[6] There's nothing like appreciating the immensity of space or the precision of a flower petal, the fury of a storm, or the calm of a summer breeze to keep our own abilities in perspective.

What about *being treated rudely?* Elder Wayne S. Peterson of the Seventy related a story in the October 2001 general conference. Waiting in his car while his wife ran into a store, he glanced into the car in front of him and saw several children looking at him. A small boy about six years old caught his eye and immediately stuck his tongue out at him. "My first reaction was to stick my tongue out at him. I thought, *What have I done to deserve this?* Fortunately, before I reacted, I remembered a principle taught in general conference the week before by Elder Marvin J. Ashton. He taught how important it was to act instead of react to the events around us. So I waved at the little boy. He stuck his tongue out at me again. I smiled and waved again. This time he waved back." Elder Peterson and the boy, soon joined by his siblings, exchanged waves until arms were tired. Finally the parents returned and drove off, with the children still waving and smiling. Elder Peterson then said, "I was grateful that I chose to act in a friendly way rather than react to my young friend's childish behavior. In doing so I avoided the negative feelings I would have felt had I followed my natural instinct."[7]

I like this small illustration precisely because it *is* small. Conquering our natural selves depends on our reactions to so many little occurrences. Every day we have opportunities to respond with meekness or with defensiveness and pride. When you know more about the gospel than your Sunday School teacher, or think you do, do you participate, pout, or pontificate? Only one of those responses escapes the meekometer's beep. How do we, as adults, respond to perhaps unsolicited (but probably insightful) counsel from a parent? How do we respond to a work supervisor's evaluation of our performance that points out areas for improvement? How do we respond when we feel unappreciated? How do we respond to counsel from our bishop, stake president, or from General Authorities in conference? How do we deal with the difference between our wants and our income? How do we react to people who simply do not share our opinions on an issue? Again, so many little things, but life is made up of little things.

Of course, any discussion of meekness is incomplete without reference to the Savior. In many instances, the Savior stated who He was (the Son of God, Alpha and Omega, the Creator, the Bread of Life), but He very seldom described His own personal attributes. In one of the few instances when He did so, He invited, "Take my yoke upon you, and learn of me; for I am meek and lowly in heart: and ye shall find rest unto your souls" (Matthew 11:29). The creator of the universe, the beginning and the end, describes Himself as meek and lowly.

Why would He describe Himself that way? Because He was willing to submit Himself and His power to the will of the Father. He said, "O my Father, . . . not as I will, but as thou wilt" (Matthew 26:39). Despite His tremendous power, the Savior wanted to do what His Father wanted Him to do. If we emulate Him in this meekness, we can call upon His grace to perfect us in all other ways. "My grace is sufficient for the meek, . . . my grace is sufficient for all men that humble themselves before me" (Ether 12:26–27). The Bible Dictionary points out that, in addition to all else, grace gives us strength and assistance to do good works that we otherwise could not do[8]—including increasing our ability to become meek.

Now, back to the Beatitude, the meek shall inherit the earth. Think of it. The meek will literally inherit this earth when it receives its paradisiacal glory and becomes a celestial dwelling. From Doctrine and Covenants 88:25–26 we learn that "the earth abideth the law of a celestial kingdom, for it filleth the measure of its creation, and transgresseth not the law—Wherefore, it shall be sanctified; . . . and the righteous shall inherit it." Again, keeping laws results in blessings. The earth has kept the law of the celestial kingdom and so shall receive celestial glory. It follows, then, that if we obey celestial law, we will receive celestial glory and inherit this earth. Becoming meek is the first step in keeping all of the other commandments and developing all other celestial attributes. In meekness we accept correction and counsel, love and live the commandments, and create an atmosphere of peace and love wherever we are. In meekness we submit to the will of our Father, which is the only way we will truly be happy in this life and the only way to qualify for eternal happiness and celestial glory.

Let me end with President Howard W. Hunter's powerful words: "And what of the meek? In a world too preoccupied with winning through intimidation and seeking to be number one, no large crowd of folk is standing in line to buy books that call for mere meekness. But the meek shall inherit the earth, a pretty impressive corporate takeover—and done *without* intimidation! Sooner or later, and we pray sooner *than* later, everyone will acknowledge that Christ's way is not only the *right* way but ultimately the *only* way to hope and joy. Every knee shall bow and every tongue will confess that gentleness is better than brutality, that kindness is greater than coercion, that the soft voice turneth away wrath. In the end, and sooner than that whenever possible, we must be more like Him."[9]

Notes

1. Joseph Smith, *Teachings of the Prophet Joseph Smith*, sel. Joseph Fielding Smith (Salt Lake City: Deseret Book, 1976), 256.
2. *Webster's New Collegiate Dictionary*, 9th ed., s.v. "meek."
3. *Harold B. Lee*, [vol. 3] in *Teachings of Presidents of the Church* series (Salt Lake City: The Church of Jesus Christ of Latter-day Saints, 2000), 203.
4. Neal A. Maxwell, *Meek and Lowly* (Salt Lake City: Deseret Book, 1987), 15.
5. J. Reuben Clark Jr., in Conference Report, April 1951, 154.
6. *The Little, Brown Book of Anecdotes*, ed. Clifton Fadiman (Boston: Little, Brown and Company, 1985), 476.
7. Wayne S. Peterson, "Our Actions Determine our Character," *Ensign*, November 2001, 83.
8. LDS Bible Dictionary, s.v. "Grace," 697.
9. Howard W. Hunter, "'Jesus, the Very Thought of Thee,'" *Ensign*, May 1993, 64–65; emphasis in original.

"WHAT AM I
SUPPOSED TO DO NOW?"

꒜

Julie B. Beck

I went to high school with a friend who panicked on graduation day. "My parents have told me all my life that I would graduate from high school and then get married," she said. "Do you realize that I graduated today and I don't have anyone to marry? What am I supposed to do now?" That is the age-old question. When the dream or plan we had for ourselves does not materialize, we demand, "What am I supposed to do *now?*"

Maybe you find yourself graduating from college with no definite goal in mind. You ask, "What am I supposed to do now?" Maybe you find yourself with the responsibility of rearing a family alone. You question, "What am I supposed to do now?" Maybe you have a serious illness that requires you to change your life plans. You beg to know, "What am I supposed to do now?"

Because of our faith in God's plan for us, there are a couple of things we can do now. First and foremost, rather than focusing on ourselves, our inadequacies, our fears, our follies, and our mistakes, we can follow the admonition of the Lord Jesus Christ to the doubting Thomas: "Be not faithless, but believing" (John 20:27). We can develop faith and a personal testimony that helps us maintain the

Julie Bangerter Beck, first counselor in the Young Women general presidency, received her bachelor's degree in family science from Brigham Young University. She is a full-time mother and homemaker and has been very active as a volunteer in her community. She has served as a member of the Young Women General Board and in numerous stake and ward callings in all the auxiliaries and in the Missionary Training Center. She and her husband, Ramon P. Beck, are the parents of three children and the grandparents of three.

long-term vision of where we are going. Second, from a basis of faith, we can develop a personal strategy that helps us adapt as life changes.

Some months ago, a friend of mine discovered she had cancer. When I asked her how she was coping, she said, "The Church is true; everything is alright." That did not mean she was enjoying her cancer treatments; it did not mean it was easy for her. It meant that she knew what to do now. Over the years she had developed a strategy for coping with the unexpected, and I saw how, in these new circumstances, her overall life plan was still working for her. She read scriptures, attended the temple, served in the Church, cared for her family, went to work, and continued to reach out and help others. She also began a new creative hobby that helped her look to the future. She sought in new experiences—pleasant or not so—to learn the lessons tailor-made for her.

The Lord told Adam and Eve to "be fruitful, and multiply, and replenish the earth, and subdue it: and have dominion . . . upon the earth" (Genesis 1:28). He also told them to "dress [the garden] and to keep it" (Genesis 2:15). Those instructions are still in force. They are all about creating life, managing life, and living a full and hopeful life.

Having dreams for ourselves is a good way to replenish, subdue, and keep life fruitful and fulfilling. Dreams give us a direction for what we do each day. They provide a focus for faith. Despite great effort and faith, however, all of our dreams do not materialize. What do we do when we can see that our dreams will not become a reality? In *Standing for Something*, President Gordon B. Hinckley tells us to starve the problems and feed the opportunities.[1]

I have a friend who has not had the opportunity for marriage and a family of her own, yet she lives joyfully and very productively. She has a strategy for her life. She says that if her dream seems not to be the will of the Lord, then she rewrites the dream. She has also developed some personal skills that stand her in good stead whenever she needs to rewrite her dream. Here is her list:

Reach out to others.
Make new friends.

Find the meaning in life beyond the paycheck or other earthly
   measure.
Find joy in the gospel.
Learn in a new environment.
Appreciate current and past blessings.

Another sister I know was left alone to raise a large family. What
should she do now? Moving to a new state, new ward, new neighborhood, new everything, she felt disoriented and found making friends
difficult. Her ward seemed filled with women in her same situation and
people did not reach out to her much. "I didn't need much help," she
told me, "but I did want some friends. So, every time the Relief Society
presidency announced a new baby born or someone ill, I took dinner
to their home. It was not long before I had a ward full of friends."[2]

I know another sister who was stricken with a debilitating illness.
No one gave her hope for a future beyond the walls of her home. She
would be homebound. After a period of grief and discouragement, she
held a meeting with herself and asked, "What is it I *can* do? Where *can*
I contribute?" By starving the problems and feeding the opportunities,
she found ways to replenish in her own sphere. She found ways to contribute to her family and projects she could do in her home that kept
her creative spirit alive. Life began to have meaning for her again.

I loved watching my grandmother in her nineties. Frail and without much hearing or vision, yet with a strong and vibrant faith, she
kept a productive routine. She spoke often with her children and
grandchildren, encouraging them to greatness. She listened to conference talks and books on tape, wrote letters, and crocheted afghans, setting the stitches by touch. She dropped a stitch occasionally, but to her
the effort was what mattered, not a perfect product. When tired, she
would eat, lie down for a short rest, and begin afresh. She wanted to
learn and contribute every day.

One of my best friends cared for a sick daughter for ten years before
that daughter died. A year later, she was struck with the same illness
that took the life of her daughter. What was she to do now? She has
found wonderful ways to serve within the sphere of her influence. I was

among those blessed by her many kindnesses. For the five years I served on the Young Women General Board, she sent dinner to our home once a week. She could not leave home to do what I did, she explained, but she could make it a little easier for me to serve.

A few months ago our current Young Women general presidency visited Sister Ruth Funk, a former general president. She greeted us with a huge smile. Now a widow in need of some help in her daily routines, Sister Funk says she has much to learn and do every day. In her prime, she was a gifted musician, noted for her well-trained choirs and her piano skills. Music was a central focus of her life for many years. Now she cannot see much beyond a blur, her hearing is almost gone, and she has lost the feeling in her hands. That means she cannot see the notes on a sheet of music, she cannot hear the notes well, she cannot even feel the keys to play the lovely Steinway in her living room. When asked about this great loss, she responded, "Oh, I am learning *new* things now. I have a few challenges, but I hope you live long enough to have some challenges like this. It is amazing what I am learning about the Atonement and the Lord's plan for me."

All of these remarkable women have several characteristics in common. They all keep the focus on relationships with others and away from themselves. They all are able to rewrite their dreams, but they never stop dreaming. They all find ways to serve. They all have a hobby or talent to develop and a passion for learning or creating that adds interest to their lives. They all look forward with an eye of faith, keeping a vision of the true end in mind. They all feed their opportunities and starve their problems. They look to the Lord to provide their guidance and their strength. They press forward with a brightness of hope centered in the Lord Jesus Christ, doubting not and fearing not because they know His promises are sure.

Years ago at a family dinner, our son wanted to sit at the table with the "big people." He asked, "Will I ever be a big?" When Adam and Eve left the garden of Eden, they entered the "big" world of trying things out on their own. They were on earth, away from the bright light of heaven. By choosing to follow our Father's plan and come to earth, we were expressing the age-old desire of children to become like the big people in their lives. Also like Adam and Eve, we are discovering how difficult things can be when we have to learn from our experiences. Choices are not clearly outlined. Some experiences undermine our confidence. Will we ever know enough? learn enough? have good judgment? have the strength of character we desire?

When life is unsettling and self-doubt creeps into our minds, how reassuring it is to know that we are not sent here to be punished. Life is not meant to be a lottery or a game of chance where the odds are stacked against us. The Lord has a plan for us; our earth life has a purpose. This life is a time to prepare to meet God, a time to show that we can live by faith, increasing in knowledge and understanding as we go.

When the unforeseen requires us to adjust our plans, we can move forward in faith. For the Lord has promised through his prophet Isaiah, "I am with thee: be not dismayed; for I am thy God: I will strengthen thee; yea, I will help thee; yea, I will uphold thee with the right hand of my righteousness" (Isaiah 41:10).

Notes

1. Gordon B. Hinckley, *Standing for Something: Ten Neglected Virtues That Will Heal Our Hearts and Homes* (New York: Random House, 2000), 172, as adapted from Peter F. Drucker, *The Effective Executive* (New York: Harper & Row, 1993).
2. Personal knowledge of author.

"SEEING I GO CHILDLESS"

❧

Jini L. Roby

I suspect that some of you are reading this article because you have adopted or are thinking about adoption. Maybe some of you are looking for words of comfort for issues relating to infertility. While preparing this material, I have prayed that I might be guided by the Spirit to share something that will help you whatever your circumstances. Probably the most important thing to know about me is that I am an adoptee and that I have adopted. I have experienced the joys and challenges of adoption from both sides.

I was adopted by a family that already had seven children and never considered adopting more. One Christmas they decided to participate in a gift exchange program that was set up by a member of their hometown who was serving in the military in Korea. I was a twelve-year-old child in an orphanage in South Korea who received their Christmas gift, card, and a family picture in a gesture of charity and friendship. Having studied English in school for perhaps one year, I wrote a very rudimentary letter thanking them for the Christmas present. They wrote back and a relationship blossomed, which in time resulted in my becoming a member of their family. They felt that Heavenly Father had led them to adopt me. To my mind, no one in

Jini L. Roby, a native of South Korea, was adopted as a child and has adopted children of her own. A former president of Utah Adoption Council, she has worked extensively with adoptions as an attorney and social worker and serves as a faculty member at Brigham Young University. She and her husband are the parents of three children.

this entire world has been more blessed by adoption than I have. I not only gained an instant family with a loving mother and father and seven siblings but I was also introduced to the gospel. My family and the gospel are my most precious possessions in life.

In college I fell in love with a wonderful young man who was also an adoptee. I was not looking for that background. It just happened. His family had adopted all of their children—three boys. Even before we married, we remarked on how unusual it was that we were both adopted. We, of course, loved and cherished our adoptive families, and as we discussed our experiences, we talked about adopting children ourselves after we were married, although we didn't expect to start out our family that way.

After four years of marriage with no children coming along, we decided that maybe Heavenly Father had planned all along for us to adopt our children. Our decision was easier than many of yours. We didn't have the sense of despair and agony that many people experience when they are infertile. Because we had both been so incredibly loved by our families, we simply thought of adoption as an alternative way of building a family rather than as our last resort.

We applied to adopt and were very fortunate to obtain a referral right away from South Korea. We adopted a wonderful little girl, Micia. Heavenly Father led us to her and confirmed our feelings that she was meant to come into our family. A recent college graduate, Micia is heading for medical school. I always look at her and think, *That lucky girl with her great genes!* Beautiful and intelligent, Micia has personality characteristics, sophistication, and talents that my husband and I couldn't have given her. We are sure that her genetic capabilities far exceed our own and feel lucky to have someone with her traits and attributes in our family.

When we were ready to adopt again, Micia decided that she needed a baby sister—and who were we to propose anything different? So we put in for another girl and were again blessed with a spiritual confirmation and a very special little girl, Mikkel, also from South Korea. As with Micia, I look at Mikkel and marvel at the wonderful qualities she brings to our family. Understanding, compassionate, and gentle by nature, she wants to follow in my footsteps and become a social worker. I'm honored.

Eleven years into our marriage, we were thoroughly content to be raising these two exceptional girls. I was coping fairly well with my first semester in law school, until I started getting nauseated and feeling tired all the time. "I'm not handling law school very well," I told my husband when my symptoms persisted without turning into a cold or flu. "I've never reacted this way to stress, but I'm literally sick. I just don't know what's wrong." Several days later he said, "You know, this is a wild idea, but it would really explain a lot if you are pregnant." I laughed. "Oh yeah, that would really be funny." Thus a wonderful third child came into our family.

Observing certain physical characteristics and personality traits that come from you in a child is fun, but I want to tell you that other than that, there is absolutely no difference in terms of my affection, my attachment, and my admiration for each of my children. Having worked with couples as a social worker, I know that many people who consider adopting question their ability to love children who are not born of their own bodies. Perhaps that could be true, but I have not found a shred of evidence to support that in my own experience. Each one of my girls is very different, and I love, respect, and cherish their individuality. I find that parents, whether they have adopted or given birth, see and love the uniqueness of each child.

This year, I met with government leaders from a country recently ravaged by war. As a faculty member at Brigham Young University, I have been engaged in some international child welfare work, trying to find ways to protect children and to establish some adoption programs. I've been worried about the children of that particular country for quite some time because I know of atrocities we can scarcely imagine here that are commonplace there. This was a great opportunity to meet government leaders and seek solutions to the plight of their children.

"We have over one million children who are on the streets," they informed me. "Some of them have lost their parents. Others still have parents, but the parents cannot support them, so they are out on the streets trying to eke out a living or survive somehow. You'll even see the four- and five-year-olds begging on the streets." Then they added this alarming information: "There is rampant selling of children. Just last week in a village, twelve children were kidnapped. Children are being sold to the international organ market. Children are being sold into the sex trade. There are mothers who have thrown their children into wells and then jumped in themselves because they are starving and they can no longer exist, and the mothers can't stand to see their children starving to death."

I asked, "What about adoption? Is that something that might be an option that you would pursue?"

The answer was very swift: "No."

Strongly held cultural or religious beliefs clearly prohibited that possibility, and our own international government policies dictate that we respect those convictions. I am not in a position to judge people's religious or moral beliefs—but I am worried. What can be done for the children of that country? If it hadn't been for adoption for me, I know that my life would be much less than it is. I know for certain that I wouldn't be enjoying the wonderful, rewarding life that I now have. I am grateful for adoption. I am concerned about the political and policy-making forces around the world in regard to children.

Once at a leadership conference in Korea, I met a leader from China who was the community population control officer. As many of you know, China has had a one-child-only policy for quite a long time. That policy has greatly impacted family life and children's welfare. I asked her, "Now that this policy is in force, what do you as the community population control officer do when you find out that a woman has become pregnant with a second or third child?"

She told me, "We pay a visit to that family and take the woman to the hospital to have a medical procedure to take care of the problem." Obviously she was referring to abortion or partial birth abortion.

I said, "But there must be a point at which you say, It's too late, we must let the child be born."

"Oh no, there is never a point," she answered.

I said, "Well, what about eight months of pregnancy?"

"No, that's not too late."

"What about eight and a half?"

"Oh, no, that's not too late. As long as the child is not born, there is no problem. We enforce the policy."

I was amazed by her equanimity. She seemed a very nice person. So I asked, "How do you do that? Does it bother you?"

She answered, "No, not really. It's the law, and people who break the law have to be brought to justice."

I couldn't help but think, *Why not allow that child to be born and find a loving family through adoption?* China does not prohibit adoption. In fact, in terms of international adoptions, China is the country that supplies the most children for adoption into the United States. In 2001, 4,861 children were adopted from China; 4,297 were from Russia; 1,870 came from South Korea (at one point, South Korea was sending as many as 8,000 to 10,000 children a year); 1,609 from Guatemala; 1,246 from Ukraine; 732 from Romania (although there is currently a moratorium as a result of reported abuses with the adoption process there); 737 from Vietnam; 672 from Kazakhstan; 543 from India; and 407 from Cambodia. In all, 17,237 children were adopted from these countries in 2001.[1] We talk in vast numbers, but these children are adopted one at a time. Each one is a unique and precious child of God. Each one deserves a loving home.

The Family Proclamation reiterates that "children are an heritage of the Lord (Psalm 127:3)." The Proclamation further declares that "children are entitled to birth within the bonds of matrimony, and to be reared by a father and a mother."[2] In certain circumstances, families can be substituted so that children can grow up with a father and a mother and a loving home. That's what adoption is all about. It's a beautiful program.

The *Encyclopedia of Mormonism* states, "The desire to adopt children is strong among Church members, but Church leaders have cautioned them never to become involved in adoption practices that are

legally questionable. In a letter dated April 20, 1982, the First
Presidency urged members to 'observe strictly all legal requirements of
the country or countries involved in the adoption.' It was also stated
that 'the needs of the child must be a paramount concern in adoption.'
Members considering adoption are counseled to work through the
Church's social services agency [now LDS Family Services] or through
others with the 'specialized professional knowledge' necessary to ensure
that the child's needs are met."[3] If you are considering international
adoptions, I hope that you will take that advice very seriously. Unwary
adopting parents might be participating unknowingly in less than ethi-
cal practices. The State Department has a helpful website with information about countries that are open to adoption.[4] They will also alert
you to particular problems to be aware of in some of these countries.
Please work through reputable agencies that know who they are dealing with, what they are doing, and are honorable in their practices.

I want to underscore that the Church is strongly supportive of
adoption. Our Church leaders have repeatedly stressed that when children are adopted into families, they are to enjoy all the blessings of
children who are born into families. When our last child was born to
us, I called the temple and said, "I know that children who are born in
the covenant don't need to be sealed to their parents, but couldn't we
still come to the temple and have some kind of a special ceremony?
That experience with our other two children was so wonderful." A
kind, elderly temple worker very lovingly said, "No, sister." I'm sure she
thought I was a little bit crazy, but we didn't want our third daughter
to miss out on that experience. Sealing ceremonies remind you of what
a special blessing it is to be sealed to one another and to your children
as an eternal family.

Adoption allows us to build eternal families as surely as giving
birth. Adoption is a way to provide a loving home for a child whose
birth parents are unable to raise them for whatever reason. President
Gordon B. Hinckley said of unwed, teenage mothers, "When marriage
is not possible, experience has shown that adoption, difficult though
this may be for the young mother, may afford a greater opportunity for

the child to live a life of happiness." President Hinckley advises, "Wise and experienced professional counselors and prayerful bishops can assist in these circumstances."[5]

I am truly grateful for the birth families who are willing to make that personal sacrifice to ensure their children a better future. When I gave birth to Marika, my youngest one, and I held her in my arms, I couldn't imagine giving her up. My heart was breaking for the mothers of my other children who, after giving birth to them, had them taken away from their arms. For the first time, I really understood the pain that they must have felt. In the eternal scheme of things I feel an affinity and sisterhood with these birth mothers. I strongly feel that I am in partnership with them, even though we may never meet. I feel I have a responsibility to them as well as to their children. Whether born to us or adopted, all of our children are given in stewardship. We are to guide and raise them in righteousness and love and wisdom.

Notes

1. U.S. Department of State, Office of Visa Processing; available at www.childrenshopeint.org.
2. "The Family: A Proclamation to the World," *Ensign*, November 1995, 102.
3. *Encyclopedia of Mormonism*, edited by Daniel H. Ludlow et al., 4 vols. (New York: Macmillan, 1992), s.v. "Adoption of Children," 4:21.
4. See http://travel.gov/adoption.
5. Gordon B. Hinckley, "Save the Children," *Ensign*, November 1994, 53; also *Teachings of Gordon B. Hinckley* (Salt Lake City: Deseret Book, 1997), 673.

SEEKING TO FORGIVE

Heidi S. Jones

As I drove to Provo from Salt Lake City, I glanced over at the Utah State Prison as I usually do, checking, just checking, to make sure things were locked up tight, safe, secure. Because the man who murdered my mother is there. Seventeen years ago Mark Hofmann placed a homemade bomb outside my parents' home—addressed to my father in the hopes of diverting attention away from an elaborate forgery scheme. Hofmann knew he had to kill a man named Steve Christensen, because Steve was on to his scheme. Steve was also a good friend and former business partner of my dad's. Hofmann thought that planting the bomb at my parents' house would divert attention away from him and his forgeries, to focus police attention on the business problems that connected my father and Steve Christensen. My mother picked up the package on that crisp autumn morning. She was killed instantly.

Let's talk about forgiveness.

When I told my third graders that I was speaking at women's conference, we talked about forgiveness. I asked them, "Why is it hard to forgive?"

Chris said, "Because sometimes you just don't want to."

Christine said, "Because you have to look at them straight in the eye."

Matthew said, "Because you're angry, and you don't really like the person."

Heidi S. Jones, an elementary school teacher, serves as a ward Relief Society compassionate service leader. She embraced forgiveness when she forgave the man who took her mother's life. She and her husband, Roger, are the parents of four children.

Then I asked how they feel when they forgive.

Victoria said, "Like hugging someone."

P. K. said, "Like I'm grown up."

Jessica said, "Like I sure did the right thing."

Finally I asked them to write why forgiveness is important.

Staci wrote, "Because you will use it your whole life."

Samantha wrote, "First I would like to forgive Mrs. Jones for not being here for Thursday. Good luck at the women's talk." Then she summed it all up in her nine-year-old way by saying, "Forgiving someone isn't just, 'I'm sorry,' and, 'I forgive you.' It is giving people another chance to fix things because everyone deserves another chance."

So why is it hard for us to forgive?

Our *natural* human inclination is to fight back when we're wronged or hurt. But although seeking revenge may be natural, it isn't what God asks of us: "For the natural man is an enemy to God, . . . unless he yields to the enticings of the Holy Spirit, and putteth off the natural man and becometh a saint through the atonement of Christ the Lord" (Mosiah 3:19).

In his book *Forgiveness*, Brent L. Top says, "Even with a sure foundation of spiritual strength—even then, our ability to forgive others may be our most difficult and demanding test of true discipleship."[1]

Let me share how I visualize forgiveness. Imagine rocks representing the burdens of resentment we carry. Now imagine placing them in a backpack and carrying those rocks around with you all day everyday. Let's start with the small hurts. These are the stones we can practice tossing out—letting go. Forgiving isn't easy. We need daily practice to become a forgiving person. Here are some examples of small things to practice on:

The person who cuts you off in traffic.

The woman in front of you in the express line at Albertson's, because she has seventeen items (not ten). You know. You've counted.

The neighbors with the scroungey looking yard . . . and kids.

The noisy family who sits by you at church.

Your children, because you can't ever find scissors or tape in your
  house.
An insensitive comment made by an aunt.
The coach who cut your child from the team.
Anything done by an ex-husband.

Our backpacks could easily become full of small stones if we let
them. We'd carry around more and more until, eventually, the load
would be so heavy we would have to empty them out (usually so we
could fill them up again). *Unless . . .* we keep letting go of the small
stones every day.

We may have to add to that list the small stones we carry around
when we don't forgive ourselves. When we can't forgive ourselves, how
can we go on to forgive others? So let's also clear all the rocks with our
own names on them out of our backpack. I'll forgive myself for saying
something stupid. I'll forgive myself because I don't like to scrapbook.
I'm okay, even though I'm not enjoying my children right now. I'm still
a good person, even though I didn't get much accomplished today.

So many of us have an "if they only knew the *real* me, they
wouldn't like me" complex. I have news for you: The Lord knows you,
He loves you, and He forgives you. So move on and forgive yourself.

I recently had to get rid of an oddly shaped stone. It was the head
from a Lladro™ figurine of a mother holding a child. A couple of weeks
ago, I heard a crash in the living room and ran to find my ten-year-old
son holding his beach ball. He looked at me, anticipating my reaction,
then instantly ran out the front door, wisely giving me time to start
working on forgiving him. (Some stones can't be tossed until the end of
the day. Just make sure you still toss them.)

With the small stones out of the pack, we're ready to tackle the
regular rocks. Several years ago, when I was new in a ward, I overheard
a young mother in the ward apologizing to an older sister. The older
sister quickly interrupted her and said, "Oh please, don't worry. You
can't offend me." This intrigued me. *I think I want to be friends with her,*
I thought to myself. *Just think, a stress-free friendship.* As I got to know
her, I found that she really didn't take offense—ever. I realized that

saying "You can't offend me" to others would be a commitment not to take offense. I would not be a person who waits around, ready to get upset or hurt by someone else's mistake.

C. S. Lewis looks at it this way: "Do not waste time bothering whether you 'love' your neighbor. Act as if you do. As you do this you find one of the great secrets—When you are behaving as if you love someone, you will presently come to love him. . . . If you do him a good turn . . . you will feel yourself disliking him less. We must wish one another good."[2]

Tracy has been my friend since the eighth grade. We have tossed a lot of rocks over the years working to maintain our friendship. One of Tracy's gifts is relating to young women. A few years ago, she introduced a program to our ward's young women called "The Five Gifts of Christmas." During the month of December, each girl gives a gift to five people: a friend, a stranger, a person in need, the Savior, and an enemy. Each year as I've thought about who this last gift might go to, I've had the chance to think about who has hurt me, who I need to open my heart to and forgive. More often, someone comes to mind whom I've offended, someone I need to ask for forgiveness, and I do that as well. Matthew 5:44 says, "But I say unto you, Love your enemies, bless them that curse you, do good to them that hate you, and pray for them which despitefully use you, and persecute you."

Cami was in my Laurel class a couple of years ago. Because I knew Cami had two classes from a teacher at school who was known to be mean and difficult to get along with, I asked her how things were going. Her answer surprised me. "I decided a few months ago to pray for this teacher," she told me. "As I prayed, my own heart was softened, and I began feeling kinder and more tolerant towards her." Cami also felt that the teacher had begun treating her better since Cami had been praying for her. Cami could have carried a rock in her backpack during her senior year with that teacher's name on it, but she didn't.

Unfortunately, some of us have a hard time wanting to let go of our rocks. Maybe we enjoy the attention we get when we talk about our "rock collection" and how miserable we are carrying them around.

Some rock collectors carry their rocks so long they become rock pol-ishers. They show them off, turn them over and over, and buff them up before they tuck them safely back in their pack, never daring to let them go. If you have rocks in the bottom of your backpack that are looking polished, it's time to get rid of them. Either simply let them go or take the actions necessary to resolve whatever issue you may have to forgive, and *empty your backpack.*

What about the big boulders that come along without warning, often because of the sins of another? These are not problems we have brought on ourselves and often cannot be resolved by our own actions—or unloaded by working something out with the other party. These boulders are just too heavy to remove from our backpacks alone. Are we doomed to carry them forever?

I've been seeing a physical therapist for a foot injury caused by run-ning. After giving me some therapy, examining my running shoes, and even watching me run on a treadmill, the physical therapist told me I had to change the way I run. I'm forty-three; I don't know a lot of dif-ferent ways to run. In fact, I only know one way to run. What he was asking me to do sounded impossible. Getting the big boulders out of our backpacks may seem just as impossible. And they would be impos-sible without the Atonement.

President James E. Faust defines the Atonement as being "at one" with the Savior.[3] Whatever rock is in your backpack, the Savior has carried it. He knows your pain, your anguish, suffering, sorrow, and agony. He is there, ready to support you through this time, to allow you to then heal your wounds.

God commands us to forgive—everyone. That is how important it is to Him that we learn to forgive completely. Doctrine and Covenants 64:10 says, "I, the Lord, will forgive whom I will forgive, but of you, it is required to forgive *all* men" (emphasis added). Heavenly Father knew we couldn't pick and choose whom to forgive; this commandment is actually a blessing, for as we forgive, we are forgiven.

In a parable in Matthew 18:23–35, a king called his servant before him and asked him to repay a debt of 10,000 talents—an amount so great it would take several lifetimes to repay. If the servant could not repay the debt, his wife and his children would be sold to pay the debt. The servant fell down and worshipped the king, saying, "Lord, have patience with me, and I will pay thee all." Then the king "was moved with compassion, and loosed him, and forgave him the debt."

That same servant then went out to find a fellow servant who owed him a hundred pence, a small amount, less that $100 in today's money. "Pay me that thou owest," he threatened, taking the man by the throat. "And his fellowservant fell down at his feet, and besought him, saying, Have patience with me, and I will pay thee all. [But,] he would not: . . . and cast him into prison, till he should pay the debt."

Upset by what they had observed, other servants told the king. He called the first servant and said, "O thou wicked servant, I forgave thee all that debt, because thou desiredst me: Shouldest not thou also have had compassion on thy fellowservant, even as I had pity on thee? . . . [Then he] delivered him to the tormentors, till he should pay all that was due unto him."

Just as the first servant could never repay the debt to the king, we are eternally indebted to Christ for his eternal sacrifice on our behalf. This parable shows the hypocrisy of asking the Lord to forgive our heavy and numerous sins when we withhold forgiveness and mercy from others whose offenses may be small or even petty in comparison.

Corrie Ten Boom and her sister Betsie were Christians living in Holland during World War II. Because they provided hiding places for Jews, they were sent to a Nazi concentration camp at Ravensbruck. Betsie died there, a slow and miserable death. After the war, Corrie spoke to congregations of her experiences, testifying of the loving, forgiving nature of God. After one meeting, a man approached to shake her hand. He was, she recognized with a jolt, one of her former Nazi guards. "He would not remember me, of course—how could he remember one prisoner among those thousands of women? But I remembered him and the leather crop swinging from his belt. I was face-to-face with one of my captors and my blood seemed to freeze."

Her experience came back with a rush: The huge room with its harsh overhead lights; the pathetic pile of dresses and shoes in the center of the floor; the shame of walking naked past this man. She could see her frail sister's form ahead of her, ribs sharp beneath the parchment skin.

"Now, he was in front of me, hand thrust out: 'A fine message, Fraulein! How good it is to know that, as you say, all our sins are at the bottom of the sea!'

"And I, who had spoken so glibly of forgiveness, fumbled in my pocketbook rather than take that hand."

She had spoken of Ravensbruck, and the man, not recognizing her, asked her to forgive him "for the cruel things" he had done there before becoming a Christian.

This was a terrible moment for Corrie Ten Boom. "Since the end of the war I had had a home in Holland for victims of Nazi brutality. Those who were able to forgive their former enemies were able to return to the outside world and rebuild their lives, no matter what the physical scars. Those who nursed their bitterness remained invalids. It was as simple and horrible as that.

"And still I stood there with coldness clutching my heart. But, forgiveness is not an emotion—I knew that too. Forgiveness is an act of the will, and the will can function regardless of the temperature of the heart. ' . . . Help!' I prayed silently. 'I can lift my hand. I can do that much. You supply the feeling.'

"And so woodenly, mechanically, I thrust my hand into the one stretched out to me. And as I did, an incredible thing took place. The current started in my shoulder, raced down my arm, sprang into our joined hands. And then this healing warmth seemed to flood my whole being, bringing tears to my eyes.

"'I forgive you, my brother' I cried. 'With all my heart!'"[4]

A boulder landed in my backpack the day my mother was killed. I hadn't done anything to bring it on, I hadn't planned on it happening, but it was mine, and I had to deal with it.

It took several months for charges to be filed against Mark Hofmann. During those months, I ran into him several times in the small community where we lived. That was hard. I became obsessed with the media, with the news broadcasts, with the newspapers. I read and reread the articles. I felt frustrated and angry because many of the things reported were not true. As I spent more time stewing, fretting, and worrying, I spent less and less time feeling the Spirit and being a good mother and wife. I was miserable, as if my feet were stuck in big buckets of cement. I became tired of carrying the pain and misery around. I wanted them gone, but I didn't know how to get rid of them. I was tired of talking about the crime everywhere I went. It came up in Sunday School classes and every social event I attended. I was desperate to get rid of the burden.

I knew then that I needed to ask my Father in Heaven to take this from me. After I spent much time in prayer and became *willing* to let it go and not take it back, He took my burden so I could be free. That was many years ago. Since then, I rarely think about Mark Hofmann, and I don't dwell on the circumstances of my mother's death. I have a very full and wonderful life. I believe fully in the power of the Atonement. I have seen it work in my own life. I know it can work in yours.

Notes

1. Brent L. Top, *Forgiveness: Christ's Priceless Gift* (Salt Lake City: Bookcraft, 1996), 99.
2. C. S. Lewis, *Mere Christianity* (New York: Macmillan, 1952), 116.
3. James E. Faust, "The Supernal Gift of the Atonement," *Ensign*, November 1988, 12.
4. Corrie Ten Boom, as quoted in Raymond J. Williamson, "Christ Secured Forgiveness of Sins," *LDS Church News*, 1 April 1995.

GRIEF JOURNEY

🙵

Shirley Pauole

Grief is a journey. We each grieve one step at a time, and each person's grief journey is unique. No one grieves the same way, so when someone says to you, "I know exactly how you feel," that's not true. Though they may have experienced a similar sorrow, they do not know exactly how you feel. They have not walked your same path.

Allow me to share my own journey. Thirty-one years ago, my life was going the way I thought it should be. I was a returned missionary and had married in the Oakland Temple. We had a brand-new home with a two-car garage and actually had two cars to go in that garage. My husband and I both had church callings. I was in the Young Women presidency. I was struggling with a backyard flower garden and enjoying a beautiful three-year-old son and one-year-old daughter. We were on our way.

One morning I got my husband off to work, fed my son breakfast, and left him watching *Sesame Street*. My daughter was sleeping in later than usual, so I thought I'd better wake her up. I opened the door to her bedroom and instantly sensed something wrong. My son dashed in behind me and jumped up in her crib like he did every morning, only there was no giggling. There was nothing. She lay very, very still. Thoughts raced through my head, *What do I do now? I have to be logical. I can't panic. I have to keep my head.* I lifted my son out of the crib,

---

Shirley Pauole, a returned missionary, is a bereavement coordinator for hospice in Charles County, Maryland. She serves as a Relief Society teacher in her ward. She and her husband, Allan, are the parents of nine children, including a daughter who died in infancy.

then immediately called the hospital. "We'll get an ambulance out there right away," they responded.

Within minutes I had not only an ambulance in front of my house but a couple of police cars and a very large fire engine. My neighbor ran over to see what was happening. All I remember is my daughter on a stretcher being put in the ambulance and a fireman saying to my neighbor, "We're taking her child to the hospital. Can you please stay with her so that she can call her husband?" My neighbor called my husband; I couldn't do it. "Your daughter's very ill," she told him. "She's been taken to the hospital. You need to come pick up your wife right away." The only thing I could think of was that my daughter needed a priesthood blessing. So I immediately called my dad: "Please meet us at the hospital. Lehua needs a blessing."

When my husband and I arrived at the hospital, my dad and brother were there already. The hospital staff took us to a little room with "clergy" written on the door where we were to wait. Finally, a doctor walked in, sat down, looked me square in the eye, and asked, "How long has your daughter been dead?" In that moment my life changed, totally and irrevocably. I became a different person.

I knew nothing about grieving, but I knew that I needed to talk to somebody—I just didn't know who. My husband was in his own pain and I couldn't deal with his pain and mine too, nor could he deal with mine and his own. My parents believed that if you don't talk about it, it eventually goes away. I tried to find somebody in the ward I could talk to, but no one had experienced a loss like mine. People would say, "You're young. You can have more children." I knew that—and we've had more children—but it didn't replace her. It never has and it never will. After a while, my friends stopped calling me and dropping by the house. When I went to church they began sitting away from me, on the other side of the chapel. I felt totally lost, not knowing where to turn, what to do.

A young couple had moved into our ward not long before my daughter died. To me, the wife seemed kind of stuck-up—or, at the very least, unfriendly—but she had been called to be the secretary in our Young Women presidency. One evening before Mutual, she was sitting in the back of the chapel with her secretarial books. Oddly enough, I felt an impulse to stop and ask her how things were going. She looked at me and said, "Shirley, my husband and I were talking about you the other night. He was saying how well you're doing. You are just doing so well." Then she added, "I know that's on the outside. What's on the inside?" She became my new best friend, because not only did she ask but I soon found out she actually wanted to know.

The weeks, the months—that whole year passed pretty much in a blur. Grieving people have a motto: "Fake it till you make it." You just go from day to day, and you keep going. One of the things I discovered is that I became very confused and disorganized. In the past, my life had been relatively orderly. Certain household tasks were done on certain days. My routine began in the morning: I would make our bed, wash the dishes, vacuum the house. Now I would get up, make my bed, wash the dishes, vacuum the house—then walk back into the bedroom to find the bed only partially made. In the kitchen, dishes were still in the sink; in the living room, the vacuum was still sitting in the middle of the room. I felt dazed. I seemed unable to complete even the simplest tasks.

And I was angry. I was a very angry person. I was angry at everybody, absolutely everybody. I'm surprised my husband stayed with me. I'm certain I took most of my anger out on him.

During this time, I really thought I was going crazy. In fact, I almost hoped I was. Then they would take me to "the home." "The home" would be a really nice place to go. They would feed you pudding. You would make crafts out of Popsicle sticks. That's about all I thought I was capable of doing. Going to the home. That sounded lovely. But I still had a son to raise; I still had a husband, even though I didn't know why he stayed. I was confused, angry, and despairing. That's where I started my grief journey.

Several years after my daughter died, I picked up an *Ensign* magazine that had just come in the mail and noticed an article on grief. As I read through that article, I wept. "Oh yes, yes. That was me, that was me." I hadn't realized that "going crazy" is a normal part of grief. I wish I had had the article sooner. I believe information helps.

In time we had seven other children—wonderful, beautiful children. As the other children came along, it was important for me to let them know that they had a sister. So in a row across our wall we've hung all nine baby pictures. As the kids have grown up, married, and started families of their own, I've added wedding pictures and family pictures—except where my daughter's picture is. The space around her baby picture is blank. I will always ache for her. Not denying that is an important part of my grief journey.

Today I work as a bereavement coordinator with hospice in Charles County, Maryland. My job feels like a calling. I minister to so many wonderful people. The bereavement program in hospice is not just for hospice patients. I have helped people whose loved ones have died in car accidents, sudden heart attacks, murder, suicide, drug overdoses. The grief experience is unique for each situation. In Maryland, where we now live, our county is the home of many of the Pentagon people who were killed on 9-11. Our little town was devastated by a horrible tornado a little over a year ago and our hospice office was destroyed. In addition, the Washington beltway sniper was traversing our county in search of his victims and murder sites. The past year has been difficult for our community.

I have learned that in dealing with those who are grieving, I am the student, they are the teachers. Before I go into a bereaved person's home or start a new support group, I sit in my car and I ask the Lord to please help me learn what it is that those people are going to teach me about their grief. Let me share some practical advice I have learned from them.

First, if you are grieving, please realize that you need to be good to yourself. Nobody else is going to be good to you—really. Pat yourself on the back for the little things that you do. A woman called me once and admitted, "It's 4 o'clock in the afternoon, and I'm still in my pajamas."

I questioned, "Are you still in bed?"

"No, I got up."

"Then give yourself a pat on the back for getting out of bed." That's the hardest thing to do when you are grieving—getting yourself out of bed. Maybe tomorrow you'll get dressed. If not tomorrow, then maybe next week. But give yourself credit for getting yourself out of bed.

Second, you need to eat properly. I know we hate to be told that. In the beginning stages go ahead and eat those comfort foods. I would like to recommend, however, that you add 8-ounce glasses of water and one good vitamin pill. That will help. Eating makes a lot of difference.

You also need to get enough rest, which is very hard when you are grieving. Most grieving people may fall asleep for an hour, but then their eyes just pop open and they can't return to sleep. My recommendation is, please, go see your doctor and get a thorough physical examination. Most grieving people suffer headaches, stomachaches, and a host of other physical illnesses. We're somewhat prepared to acknowledge the mental and the emotional part of grieving, but we are not aware of the physical effects. So get a good checkup. Let your doctor know what has happened. If he prescribes an anti-depressant or a sleeping aid, take it. Use it wisely. You need rest. You cannot continue if you are exhausted and grieving at the same time.

Next—and I know you are going to hate this—is exercise. When I was grieving, my bishop suggested that I go for a walk daily. So every afternoon after my husband got home, I left for a walk by myself. I learned that when you are walking you can talk to the Lord, you can meditate and ponder on your life. I can't do that if I walk with other people, so I like to just walk alone. A word of caution here: walking outside is not always safe. Early one morning, one of our neighbors was stabbed while jogging. "He was just in the wrong place at the wrong time," the policeman said. So I bought myself a treadmill for the family room. I get on that treadmill very early in the morning, between 4 and 4:30. As a former early-morning seminary teacher, I'm awake and ready to go at that hour, and I have to get on the treadmill before my brain knows what I am doing. It's important that you do some kind of exercising. Just walk a little. You don't have to walk a lot. Just walk a little.

Next is hygiene. Do the basics. Brush your teeth every morning, no matter what. You've got yourself out of bed, now brush your teeth. It gets you back into your routine. It's a ritual. It's what your mother would want you to do, and it's what people who come in contact with you would like you to do. Brush your teeth.

Take out the garbage every single day. Just get it out of your house. If you take it out every day, one of those days will be the day the garbage man is actually coming. Get it out of your house.

Last, remember to breathe. People under stress tend to take short, shallow breaths. So several times during the day, take some really good deep breaths. Breathing deeply will help more than you might think.

For those of you who wonder how best to help those who are grieving, I can sum it up in one word: *listen*. If people who are grieving have one good friend who will listen, they are very, very lucky. Grieving people desire and need to tell their story over and over again. Allow them to do that. It helps them grasp that this event has really happened. Sometimes as bereavement coordinators we absolutely insist that grieving individuals use the "D" word: *dead, died, dying*. (Those are good words and you need to use them, especially with your children, so that they understand what they mean.) It takes a long time to truly understand that a death has occurred. Widows expect their husband to walk through the door. Widowers expect to come home and find their wife still in the kitchen. Telling the story over and over helps them realize their loved one really is gone. God gave us two ears and one mouth, so we would listen twice as much as we talk. So just listen. Just listen.

Be careful what you say. As Latter-day Saints, we sometimes say things like, "It was God's will." In my head I knew that, but with my painful, broken heart, it was hard to grasp. Probably the best thing to say is just "I'm sorry," and give them a hug. If you have a memory of the loved one, share it. They would like to know.

If you take some food to someone who is grieving, instead of delivering it in a disposable container, take your very best dish out of the cupboard. Don't put your name on the bottom of that dish, and when you deliver it, say, "Don't worry about returning this dish to me. I'll come back and get it." Two weeks later, when everybody else has stopped calling and coming around, go over to get your dish, and when you do, say, "Would you like to talk about it?"

Not too long ago, a little boy taught me the importance of using terminology that doesn't offend those who are grieving. This little boy's brother had been killed in a car accident. "Now, tell me again," I said to him. "Your brother died in a car accident."

He said, "Don't use the word *died*."

I remembered that when a loved one is a murder victim or a drunk-driving victim, people often prefer the word *killed*. So I said, "Okay, so your brother was killed in a car accident."

"Don't use the word *killed*."

So I asked, "What word would you like me to use?"

"He passed away." Those are the words he preferred. Find out what words people feel comfortable hearing. I still stay, "I lost my daughter." But if I say to a child that I lost my daughter, the child wonders why I'm not out there looking for her.

I might add that children grieve. Anyone old enough to love is old enough to grieve. Children are wonderful grievers because they will grieve in spurts. They will cry and cry, seemingly inconsolable one moment, and then the next moment they're outside playing, as if to say, "I've had enough of this. I'm going out to play now." One little girl was the only survivor of a car accident in which her mother and twin sister had been killed. We were talking one day while she was trying to put her shoe on, and suddenly she threw the shoe across the room and began sobbing, "I miss my mommy. I miss my sister." Picking her up, I sat her on my lap, wrapped my arms around her, and let her cry. She cried so deep down, I felt my own heart was tearing out. Then as suddenly as it had begun, she stopped. She hiccuped a bit from sobbing so hard and long. Then she looked up at me and asked, "Do you have any peanut butter?" And off she went. (I, on the other hand, was exhausted.) Children have taught me wonderful things about the process of grieving.

One of the things that I have learned over the thirty-one years since my daughter died is that I do not know why she had to die. A wonderful Presbyterian minister, who was teaching during my hospice training, said, "Never ask a why question because there is no answer to a why question." Have you thought about that? If you ask your kids why questions, what do they usually say? "I don't know." I believe that if anyone knows what grieving feels like, it's my Father in Heaven, who watched His Only Begotten Son suffer and die. At hospice we share this wisdom: "Grief is neither a problem to be solved, nor a difficulty to overcome. It is a sacred expression of love, a sacred sorrow."

I do not know the meaning of all things. I do not know why. What I do know is that my Father in Heaven loves me, and He wants me to be happy. And that is what I have strived for. I did not want to be miserable all the rest of my life, but there was a time when I thought I would never be happy again. I am now finding that life is good. Life is wonderful. It's great to be alive. I love my job; I'm not a better person because my daughter died—I'm a different person. I would never have become a bereavement counselor—and I find great joy in that work. It's where my grief journey has brought me, and it's a place I'm glad to be.

AN OUTWARD EXPRESSION
OF AN INWARD COMMITMENT

⁂

Mary C. Hales

As I watched the Conference Center fill up with 21,000 people last April, I was impressed by how good everyone looked—cleaned up, covered up, and well behaved, no one's appearance screaming for attention, no strident voices or profanity, just decency, modesty, and cheerfulness. From what we generally see in the world, you might think a modest person is a lone voice crying in the wilderness. But here were 21,000—and, with each succeeding session, 21,000 more until there were 100,000—all great examples of "a quality of mind, heart, and body, . . . an attitude of humility, decency, and propriety . . . evidenced in thought, language, dress, and behavior."[1]

In his book *Stand a Little Taller*, President Gordon B. Hinckley says: "Of all the creations of the Almighty, there is none more beautiful, none more inspiring than a lovely daughter of God who walks in virtue, with an understanding of why she should do so, who honors and respects her body as a thing sacred and divine, who cultivates her mind and constantly enlarges the horizon of her understanding, who nurtures her spirit with everlasting truth."[2] Notice he did not say she walks in virtue, period. He said, "She walks in virtue with an understanding of why she should do so." It is wonderful to be modest, but we also need to understand why.

Mary Crandall Hales, wife, mother, and homemaker, holds a bachelor's degree from Brigham Young University. She and her husband, Robert D. Hales, a member of the Quorum of the Twelve Apostles, are the parents of two children and the grandparents of nine. She serves as a Relief Society teacher in her ward.

Why is the Latter-day Saint view of modesty different from that of the world? Most of the world does not have the truths that came with the restoration of the gospel, nor have they made the commitments we have. Let's look at the truths we know about a mortal body and the value of a soul, and then consider the level of our commitment to the principle of modesty.

People in many religions think the spirit is good but the body is naturally evil; whereas Latter-day Saints regard the body as sacred and divine. Why? In Genesis 1:27 we learn, "So God created man in his own image, in the image of God created he him; male and female created he them." From this we may conclude that the human body is of heavenly design with a purpose planned by God. We also know from other scripture that after resurrection, our spirits will be reunited with our bodies and become immortal souls. Many people in the world—even those lucky enough to believe in a life after death—think we will exist only as spirits. We are fortunate to have the Book of Mormon, which teaches about the resurrection with clarity. Our knowledge of a physical resurrection reinforces the high value we place on the body.

We know why we need bodies. God's plan requires that each spirit experience life inside a mortal body in order to progress. We need to learn how to live His commandments inside a mortal body with its hormones, passions, pains, illnesses, and the trials and temptations of a mortal world. Only a mortal body provides us with the power of procreation.

We know it is a privilege to receive our bodies. Only two-thirds of the spirits from our premortal life received mortal bodies. One-third of the spirits rebelled against God and His plan and so were cast out, never to have the opportunity to have a mortal body. Doctrine and Covenants 29:36–37 describes it this way: Satan "rebelled against me, saying, Give me thine honor, which is my power; and also a third part of the hosts of heaven turned he away from me because of their agency; And they were thrust down, and thus came the devil and his angels."

What is the goal of Satan and his followers today? In 2 Nephi 2:18 we learn that "because he had fallen from heaven, and had become miserable forever, he sought also the misery of all mankind." From Adam's day to ours, the devil has sought to deceive us into joining him in his misery. He has captured many who are now actively participating in rebellion against God. He has, indeed, been very successful.

One of his most successful tactics is in the promotion of immodesty. After a Relief Society lesson on this subject, a sister asked if modesty was an American concept or a gospel concept. It is a gospel concept and has been from the beginning. Recall Genesis 3:21: "Unto Adam . . . and to his wife did the Lord God make coats of skins, and clothed them." In this early day in time, was God concerned about the neighbors or children? No. Simply put, there weren't any. God clothed Adam . . . and Eve because they were no longer innocent and able to remain in Eden; and as such, He wanted them clothed and protected. He wants the same for us. The Lord values the mortal body and even gave specific instructions about its care in our day. In Doctrine and Covenants 89, He warned us against addictions that would diminish our agency. He also wisely counseled us to nourish our bodies with fruits, vegetables, and grains. He wants us to value this gift of a body and keep it clothed, nourished, and protected.

Let's consider the truths we know about souls. The body combined with the spirit makes a mortal soul, each one precious to God. Doctrine and Covenants 18:10 says, "Remember the worth of souls is great in the sight of God." And in verse 13, "How great is his joy in the soul that repenteth!" Then in verse 15, "And if it so be that you should labor all your days in crying repentance unto this people, and bring, save it be one soul unto me, how great shall be your joy with him in the kingdom of my Father!"

I often think God loves us more than we love ourselves. We get discouraged when we see our weaknesses, and we may not feel very valuable; but the Lord knows our potential. He knows we did not join in Satan's rebellion in heaven but remained faithful. We have come here according to God's plan. He gives us commandments knowing we will struggle to master some of them, yet knowing that gaining mastery over them is the purpose of coming. He does not give up on us when we do wrong but has provided a plan of repentance so we can move forward. When we falter in the struggle to live righteously, God still cares about us. He even sends His believers to teach the unbelievers. Knowing the afflictions that missionaries will suffer while preaching to the word, God still sends them to offer the gospel message so that all may choose to accept or reject it.

An example of this is found in Alma 26. Ammon is speaking: "Now do ye remember, my brethren, that . . . when our hearts were depressed, and we were about to turn back, behold, the Lord comforted us, and said: Go amongst thy brethren, the Lamanites, and bear with patience thine afflictions, and I will give unto you success. . . .

"And we have taught them in their streets; yea, and we have taught them upon their hills; . . . and we have been cast out, and mocked, and spit upon, and smote upon our cheeks; and we have been stoned, and taken and bound with strong cords, and cast into prison; and through the power and wisdom of God we have been delivered again.

"And we have suffered all manner of afflictions, and all this, that perhaps we might be the means of saving some soul; and we supposed that our joy would be full if perhaps we could be the means of saving some.

" . . . Now my brethren, we see that God is mindful of every people, whatsoever land they may be in; yea, he numbereth his people, and his bowels of mercy are over all the earth" (Alma 26:23, 27, 29–30, 37).

The Nephite missionaries suffered painful afflictions, and the Lord knew they would. The Lord loved Ammon and his courageous brethren, but allowed them to suffer to save the souls of the unbelievers.

Every soul is valuable to the Lord—so valuable that God sent His Son to redeem them. When His beloved Son asked if this cup might pass but also said, "not my will, but thine, be done," God let the Atonement go forward to save our souls (Luke 22:42). He loves His Son, and He also loves us.

How can we stay focused on that knowledge in a world so full of distractions and temptations? How do we maintain a high level of commitment?

Sacred covenants help us stay focused. Through the sacrament prayer, we renew our commitments to take His name upon us, to always remember Him, and to keep His commandments. Then we are promised we can have His Spirit to be with us. Why do we need to be reminded so frequently—every Sunday? Perhaps because the distractions and temptations of the world are cruel and relentless. When someone is baptized, it is by complete immersion—whole body, not half. In fact, if only a toe comes out of the water, the baptism has to be repeated. Similarly, we can't be partly in the world and partly in the kingdom, not even by a toe's worth. Covenanting to "always remember" means under any and all circumstances.

Temple covenants also bring more knowledge, strengthen commitment, and increase our reverence for our mortal bodies. Temple covenants are of such value that the Lord required the Saints in Nauvoo to build a temple despite poverty and persecution. And build a temple they did, using the best craftsmanship available and considering every detail. Even more astounding to outsiders, the Saints built the temple knowing that after receiving their temple covenants, they would have to leave their temple behind and move west.

Some years ago, before the Berlin Wall came down, the Church in East Germany was in my husband's area of responsibility. Many times we traveled into East Germany through Checkpoint Charlie, past the barbed wire, the search dogs, and the machine-gun-armed guards, to visit the Saints and hold district conferences. The Saints there had remained faithful for many years despite very difficult circumstances. Although they had no temple, they never forgot that in a meeting in Görlitz in 1968, Elder Thomas S. Monson, as a member of the Quorum of the Twelve Apostles, promised them that all the blessings of the gospel would be theirs if they remained faithful.[3] In 1983, after years of faithfully living the gospel, they were granted permission by their government to build a temple—six years before the Berlin Wall came down. I believe this loosening of governmental restriction was a reward from the Lord for their faithfulness. In 1985 we witnessed their joy at the dedication of their temple in Freiberg. They have honored their temple commitments, and their temple has since been enlarged.

With a flurry of temple building around the world in recent years, most of us do not have to sacrifice like the Nauvoo Saints or endure the long years of faithful waiting as did the Saints in East Germany, but the covenants we make are just as sacred and require the same level of commitment. A temple standard of modesty is an outward expression of an inward commitment—not just looking modest but actually being modest in every aspect of life.

What is our attitude toward our commitments? When we promise to always remember Him and keep His commandments, we don't mention any exceptions. That means remaining faithful at home, at work, at school, and even on vacation. There is no way to keep our covenants and fit in with the world. We will never get praise from everyone. That is inevitable, even desirable. Changing our positions to appeal to everyone is futile; in the long run, we please no one—neither the Lord nor ourselves.

Modesty is an attitude of the heart as much as of the mind. It is not enough to keep only the letter of the law, perhaps by choosing clothes that come within a thread of being immodest. It saddens me, for example, to occasionally see on the grounds of the Church offices a young couple, newly sealed in the temple, posing for photographs, the bride in a dress that serves more as a worldly fashion statement than as an outward expression of the covenants she and her husband have just made in the temple. These brides' choice of dress does not show respect for themselves, their husbands, or the Lord. Most brides find happiness in their beautiful, modest dresses. We need to enjoy our lives well within the bounds of the commitments we have made, not on the edge of those commitments, where it might be easy to take a step outside.

Recall for a moment your last drive in the country. You may have seen cows in a field. Some were likely in a shelter; others were roaming, enjoying the wide range available to them; and some were just resting. Others, however, could not help but hover along the fence, trying to put their heads through and nibble the grass on the other side. True, these cows were inside the fence by the width of a one-inch board; but their focus and interests were clearly on the other side.

Our attitudes are all-important. Keeping a law with stinginess (insisting it's okay to poke your head through the slats as long as you remain on the right side of the slats) can hardly merit generous blessings or greater understanding. Living only the letter of the law is difficult over time because there is no joy in it. So burdensome is letter-of-the-law obedience that in time we may begin to look for excuses to get out of it. Seeking a deeper understanding allows us to embrace the concept so it becomes a joyful choice, our natural preference.

The Lord wants us to value our mortal bodies. He has tried to let us know how much He loves us and values our souls. He has entered into covenants with us to keep us focused on what is important. How much we receive of these gifts is up to us. "For what doth it profit a man if a gift is bestowed upon him, and he receive not the gift? Behold, he rejoices not in that which is given unto him, neither rejoices in him who is the giver of the gift" (D&C 88:33).

We have been given a gift of a mortal body so that we may progress according to God's plan. Do we appreciate that gift? Do we give gratitude to God for it? Do we show respect for it through "an attitude of humility, decency, and propriety . . . evidenced in language, dress, and behavior"?[4] I pray that each of us will respect the body we have been given as sacred and divine, that we will keep our covenants with God, and that our modesty will be an outward expression of our inner commitment.

Notes

1. *Encyclopedia of Mormonism*, edited by Daniel H. Ludlow et al., 5 vols. (New York: Macmillan, 1992), 2:932.
2. Gordon B. Hinckley, *Stand a Little Taller: Counsel and Inspiration for Each Day of the Year* (Salt Lake City: Deseret Book, 2001), 189.
3. Dell Van Orden, "Opportunities Unfold in 'Week of Wonder,'" *LDS Church News*, 12 November 1988.
4. *Encyclopedia of Mormonism*, 2:932.

REPENTANCE FROM SEXUAL ADDICTION

David A. Whetten

When I was called to serve as a BYU ward bishop I was surprised by the number of ward members struggling to overcome chronic violations of the law of chastity. More significantly, I was surprised and worried by how ineffective I was in responding to their requests for assistance. I suspect that my initial views on this subject were fairly typical of LDS parents and other leaders in single adult wards. Because a change in my thinking was necessary before I could effectively assist these active Church members fully repent of this grave transgression, I hope my story will be helpful to others.

EARLY EXPERIENCES AS A CAMPUS BISHOP

I invite you to go back with me about three years to when I was first called as a BYU campus ward bishop. My wife and I felt we had been called to serve in the Garden of Eden. Every week we were edified by carefully prepared talks and lessons and inspired by our ward

David Allred Whetten, the director of the Faculty Center, is a professor of organizational leadership and strategy at Brigham Young University. He holds bachelor's and master's degrees from BYU in sociology and a Ph.D from Cornell University in organizational behavior. He received the Distinguished Service award from the Academy of Management in 1994 and served as president in 2000. He also received the David L. Bradford Distinguished Educator award while teaching at the University of Illinois, Urbana-Champaign. He currently serves as a bishop in a BYU student ward. He and his wife, Zina, are the parents of four children and the grandparents of six.

members' constant example of dedication to the Lord and commitment to the Church. But some of these wonderful young Church members struggle with very difficult personal problems, which sometimes require the assistance of a bishop. The most common confession I heard and continue to hear from the male members of my ward involves violations of the law of chastity, including long-standing practices of masturbation and pornography.[1]

As a new bishop, I felt confident that these young men would soon rid themselves of these pesky habits if they strengthened themselves spiritually and exercised greater self-mastery. To that end, I stressed the need for more fervent prayer, more diligent scripture study, and more consistent service. I also emphasized the importance of controlling their desires and avoiding sexual temptations. To my surprise, I observed that while this course of action was effective for first-time or occasional sexual transgressors, it didn't prevent relapses in chronic cases. And, to my dismay, as these active Church members made honest efforts to follow the counsel of their bishop, but saw no consistent change in their behavior, their discouragement and self-loathing often increased, sometimes to the point of despair.

As you can imagine, I was very troubled by what I was witnessing. I cared deeply for these wonderful young elders, and I knew God's love from them knew no bounds. Seeing case after case going nowhere, I realized that these young men were dealing with a far greater challenge than I understood. Slowly, I began to understand Christ's observation to his disciples that some forms of evil don't "come out" except through extraordinary means (see Mark 9:14–29). While I remained convinced that scripture study, prayer, and service were essential prerequisites for change, it became increasingly apparent that sustainable change would require additional measures.

One night, as I was driving home after listening to a series of disappointing progress reports, I began wondering, "Is it possible that sexual addiction is more than a metaphor? When these young men say they feel out of control, is it possible that they really have lost control over their sexual appetites?" Addiction seemed like an apt metaphor for what I was observing—underscoring how difficult it is to break the cycle of chronic sexual transgression—but I wasn't sure if it fit the psychological and physiological profile of true addiction. Furthermore, as a bishop I wondered whether it was appropriate to classify violations of the law of chastity as an addiction. It was, therefore, with mixed feelings that I began my search for more information on this subject.

THE SEARCH FOR ANSWERS

One of the first places I looked for help was lds.org, the Church's Internet site. I knew that President Gordon B. Hinckley had frequently cautioned Church members to avoid the entrapment of Internet pornography, and I wanted to study more carefully the details of his warnings. In reading his talks, it was both informative and reassuring to learn that he had underscored the addictive nature of this practice. For example, in 1998 he cautioned: "Stay away from pornography as you would avoid a serious disease. It is as destructive. It can become habitual, and those who indulge in it get so they cannot leave it alone. It is addictive."[2]

Reviewing other talks by General Authorities and articles in Church publications, I observed the term *sexual addiction* being used more broadly and more frequently. Furthermore, some described sexual addiction in considerable detail. A recent *New Era* article exemplifies this trend. "Viewing pornography triggers sexual feelings. We can easily get hooked on those pleasurable feelings, especially if they seem to relieve stress or anxiety—and we can start a cycle of addiction just as difficult to break as an addiction to drugs or alcohol."[3] In response to the rhetorical question, "Is pornography a new drug?" the authors respond, "Pornography can be powerfully addicting. Scientific research—including new brain-scan technology—is beginning to show that pornography may cause physical and chemical changes in the brain similar to those caused by drugs."[4]

In response to the growing realization that many youth and young adults in the Church are becoming addicted to sexual gratification, LDS professionals, including BYU faculty and staff, have recently produced an impressive array of resources on this subject.[5] These materials and their accompanying bibliographies provide a wealth of detailed information on sexual addiction.

As I read, one story in particular struck a responsive cord. An article in *Marriage & Families* described the work of Dr. Victor Cline, a prominent LDS counselor in Salt Lake City, with a young father in his thirties, active in the Church and a successful businessman. During his first counseling session, the man explained, " 'It's like being on Crack. I can see what it is doing to me and I want to be rid of the habit, but I can't seem to stop. Nothing seems to work.'

"Dr. Cline decided to give this man a powerful incentive not to look at pornography. He asked him for a thousand dollars and explained he would put it in a special bank account and hold it for 90 days. If the young father could stay porn free, he would get his money back. If he relapsed even once, the money would be donated to charity. With a big grin on his face, the man said, 'Fantastic! How did you know that I'm such a tightwad with money? There's no way I will look at porn if it's going to cost me a thousand dollars. You couldn't have chosen a better incentive for me.'

"The therapy sessions that followed were productive, and the man stayed porn free for well over two months. However, on day 87, while on a business trip, he went to a porn shop and literally gorged himself. When he told Dr. Cline of his relapse, he was in tears. Dr. Cline said, 'Look, I know we said you would lose the money if you messed up even once, but if you made it 87 days, you can make it 90. Let's keep the money in the account and start over for another 90 days.' The man recommitted, but didn't even last two weeks. The money went to charity.

"Dr. Cline asked his patient, 'What if it had been ten thousand dollars or twenty?' The man sadly raised his head, looked at his therapist, and said, 'It wouldn't have mattered how much it was. I'd have still lost it.'"[6]

After reading this account I realized that I, too, had assumed that my role as bishop was to help ward members struggling with this problem increase their motivation to succeed. I believed that all they needed was an extra measure of desire to make good on their long-standing, sincere commitment to change. In retrospect, I recognize that this approach is like gunning the engine of a car stuck on an icy incline—the car isn't moving forward because the tires don't have adequate traction, not because they aren't turning fast enough. This insight helped me differentiate between the necessary action of asking an elder who has broken covenants to give me his temple recommend and the unrealistic expectation that the loss of temple privileges will produce the appropriate corrective action.

Early in my search, I puzzled over the question, "Why doesn't everyone who experiments with sexual gratification become addicted? How can we claim that sexual gratification is addictive when not every teenager who experiments with sex becomes hooked?" Upon further reflection, I realized that this problematic observation isn't limited to sexual addiction. After all, not everyone who experiments with alcohol, marijuana, or cocaine turns into a drug addict. I have since learned to restate the question as, "Under what circumstances are those who experiment with an addictive practice likely to become addicted?"

CHARACTERISTICS OF SEXUAL ADDICTION

To address this question we first need to clarify what qualifies as an "addictive practice." Some people always chew gum, but gum chewing isn't, strictly speaking, an addictive practice. Actions that are potentially addictive all have a common physiological effect: they stimulate the brain to produce mood-altering biochemicals, such as endorphin, dopamine, and serotonin. Hence, quibbling over whether sexual gratification, as an activity, is comparable to ingesting cocaine or amphetamines misses the critical point that their biological effects are functionally equivalent. Brain research has produced conclusive evidence that similar central nervous system responses can be produced by mood-altering substances *and* mood-altering behaviors. It is in this sense that sexual addiction qualifies as a drug addiction. Viewed from this perspective, it is monumentally tragic that the "natural high" built into our physical makeup can so easily be corrupted when used in ways and for purposes not intended by our Creator.

Many paths lead to sexual addiction, though two seem to be particularly well-worn by LDS young men. First is the path of *innocent exposure* to salacious material. Turning away from the thrill of new-found pleasures is always difficult, but especially so at a young age. The immature mind of a boy is unable to grasp the significance of these powerful, God-given feelings, including their intended role in marriage. Without a mature understanding of God's purposes, innocent minds are all too easily persuaded to treat sex as a hedonistic pleasure and females as objects of desire.

In addition, individuals with what psychologists refer to as an "addictive personality" find it particularly challenging to resist the allure of sexual pleasure. These individuals, often characterized as thrill seekers, have low impulse control and tend to act and speak without thinking. The trait of low impulse control, especially when coupled with extended, unsupervised computer use, makes these young people prime candidates for sexual addiction.[7]

A second path to sexual addiction involves the use of sexual gratification as a *response to emotional pain*. This type of sexual addiction, which is more difficult to understand and treat, is the one that I will focus on. While the group on the first path struggle with low resistance to the enslaving effects of addictive practices, those on this second path are actually drawn to these practices. Many young men who experience high levels of emotional distress, including loneliness, rejection, or fear of failure, discover that sexual gratification temporarily masks their intense pain. Counselors have long observed that young men have a particularly difficult time coping with painful emotions (the suicide rate for young men is three times higher than for young women). Hence, it is not surprising that male teenagers often turn to various forms of "self-prescribed pain killers," such as alcohol, drugs, and sexual pleasure. Because these coping strategies temporarily relieve pain, but fail to eliminate its causes, they can easily evolve into full-fledged addictions.

Thus we can say that whereas sexual experimentation might be characterized as an *occasional indulgence* (giving in to an alluring temptation), individuals driven by pain use sexual gratification as a *necessary indulgence*. For them, sexual pleasure has become an essential coping mechanism. As one counselor explained to me, "For active LDS men who need a 'drug' to deaden their emotional pain, sexual gratification will likely become the drug of choice." Ironically, when repeatedly used for this purpose, pornography and masturbation tend to lose their significance as sexual activities. Hence, over time these practices have less to do with sex and more to do with addiction. Recognizing this helps us understand why a sizeable proportion of those seeking help for sexual addiction from the BYU Counseling Center are married.

From a spiritual perspective, sexual addiction, regardless of its origin or function, involves the loss of agency. Lehi opens his discourse on moral agency with the premise that "men are free." He then describes how we forfeit our freedom by choosing "according to the will of the flesh . . . which giveth the spirit of the devil power to captivate" (2 Nephi 2: 29). It follows that any path to addiction involves gradually losing the ability to turn away from a particular temptation (see 2 Peter 2:18–19).

Consistent with Lehi's teaching, if a person "gives no thought" to his response to emotional pain, but, instead, "automatically" invokes a pain-relieving, sinful pleasure, he eventually forfeits his agency in this matter. Imagine a scenario in which the auto-pilot function on an airplane becomes jammed, making it impossible for the pilot to control the direction, altitude, or speed of the plane. Having lost control of his plane, the frustrated pilot is unable to respond to warnings from air traffic controllers or pleas from passengers to avert a catastrophe. Until the auto-pilot mechanism is turned off, information and encouragement from others are of little practical value to the pilot. Through my study and experience as a bishop, I have learned that repeated law-of-chastity-confessions often constitute "mayday" distress signals from a pilot who has lost control of his plane.

REPENTANCE AND SEXUAL ADDICTION

With the benefit of this understanding, I began shifting the focus of my counsel as a bishop. President Spencer W. Kimball wisely observed that in matters of repentance the bandage needs to be big enough to cover the sore.[8] I now better appreciate his meaning. When Church members struggling with addictions fail to repent successfully it is because they haven't repented fully—in the sense that their efforts to change have not fully addressed the underlying problems fueling their persistent transgressions. Given that the root causes of habitual sexual transgression typically have little to do with sex, per se, change-strategies focusing exclusively on avoiding sexual temptation are at best ineffective, and very often counterproductive.

Fortunately I have found that when a Church member is willing to admit that he is truly addicted to sexual gratification, he is generally also willing to do whatever it takes to give up his sins. Concerns about embarrassment pale when compared to the corrosive effects of continuing to cover up a sin so enslaving. At that critical moment when they realize that their "problem" is much larger than they had thought, it is important that they receive informed assurances that an equally large set of resources are available to help them regain their agency, and that the outcome will be worth the effort.

To that end, establishing realistic expectations is extremely important. In matters of addiction recovery, there is no such thing as a successful quick fix. Reversing a process that's been going on for years can be done, but not quickly or easily. Clearly, whatever they have done in the past to reform their practices has not been enough. Hence, they need to begin thinking more broadly and deeply—exploring possible connections between their addiction and any and all other facets of their life. The guidance of professional counselors in this process of self-examination is essential. I have gained profound respect for the skills of professional counselors and deep gratitude for their willingness to help with these difficult cases.

To complement the benefits of professional counseling, my goal is to help these spiritually troubled Church members enhance their spiritual understanding and strengthen their spiritual capacities. Although our discussions vary, two subjects seem to be particularly important. First, understanding the difference between temptation and transgression, and, second, restoring hope in the cleansing and sanctifying effects of the atonement of Jesus Christ.

Temptation and Transgression

To help young Latter-day Saints distinguish between temptation and transgression, I point to the Lord Jesus Christ, who was tempted in all things but remained sinless. "For we have not an high priest which cannot be touched with the feeling of our infirmities; but was in all points tempted like as we are, yet without sin. Let us therefore come boldly unto the throne of grace, that we may obtain mercy, and find grace to help in time of need" (Hebrews 4:15–16).

The following scenario illustrates how failure to distinguish temptation from transgression can undermine the repentance process. Beginning with an honest and sincere confession to his bishop, a young man resolves to overcome this sinful habit and earnestly begins a thoughtful plan to change. He prays more and does so more sincerely, he reads his scriptures more diligently, and he becomes more involved in ward service projects. Then one day, for whatever reason, his mind is flooded with sexual thoughts and memories. Because he associates this sexual temptation with his deeply etched pattern of sexual transgression, he assumes that nothing has really changed—that *he* really hasn't changed. Believing—falsely—that the mere presence of sexual impulses proves he has no self-control, he concludes that he has no choice but to give in to temptation.

How can someone who has forgotten how to make choices in response to a temptation begin to reclaim his exercise of agency? From my study I have gleaned three guidelines.

1. *Normalize the impulse*. Counselors point out that emotionally intense struggles to "control sexual temptation" significantly increase the likelihood that sexual transgression will follow. This is consistent with the general observation that the more a person dwells on a feared outcome, the more inevitable that outcome becomes. Instead, counselors encourage their clients to dispassionately dismiss sexual temptations as normal but unwanted distractions. For example: "I'm experiencing sexual feelings and thoughts. But it's probably not that unusual for a guy living in a sexually saturated world to be pestered by these kinds of thoughts and feelings."

2. *Choose your response*. When an impulse to act routinely results in the same response, it becomes difficult to tell the difference. In the person's mind, the impulse comes to stand for, or symbolize, the seemingly inevitable outcome or response. A person trying to regain his agency needs to "loosen" the connection between impulse and automatic response. Making decisions is the practice of agency, and stopping to think is the first step in making a decision. As simple as it sounds, the key to regaining agency is learning to think before responding—to consider options before the auto-pilot control kicks in. For example: "I'm experiencing a sexual temptation. So, what are my options? Of the consequences associated with these choices, which do I want to experience?"

3. *Interrupt old patterns*. Wise choices before a test increase the likelihood of making good choices during the test. In this case, if the habituated response to temptation has been placed out of reach, it is easier to reach for a better alternative. It seems self evident that a recovering alcoholic should not continue his part-time job as a barkeeper, recognizing that he cannot resist the temptations associated with spending three hours a day in an alcohol-saturated environment. By analogy, it seems prudent for a person recovering from sexual addiction to make lifestyle choices consistent with his desire to adopt new, more constructive, responses to emotional pain. Think of these changes as responsible, preventative measures that increase the likelihood that a reasonable desire to change can begin to override years

of thoughtless action. Naturally, artificial barriers cannot substitute for a genuine commitment to change—crutches don't mend a broken leg. Instead, lifestyle changes should reflect a person's deep-felt desire to live in a different kind of environment—one that is consistent with the type of person he is striving to become, and, importantly, one that would not offend God, upon whose strength he must rely on. These actions are consistent with the principle that the Lord magnifies our *best* efforts—no matter how small or insufficient they might be. In moments of wavering faith, we readily empathize with the father of a demonized son who, believing, brought his child to the Master Healer, but who, when asked by Jesus if he truly believed a miracle could occur, "cried out, and said with tears, Lord, I believe; help thou mine unbelief" (Mark 9:24).

HOPE IN THE ATONEMENT

If I were asked to identify the single largest spiritual roadblock to the progress of individuals burdened by sexual addiction, I would point to their loss of hope. These despairing young men readily relate to the pitiful lament of the unforgiven King David, "Why standest thou afar off, O Lord? Why hidest thou thyself in times of trouble?" (Psalm 10:1). They feel abandoned by God because they have lost hope of ever feeling worthy of His forgiveness and approbation. I have observed that until they truly believe that they are not unpardonable sinners, they are unable to begin the return journey from their self-imposed spiritual exile.

Hope is one of the three defining virtues at the heart of Christ's teachings: a steadfast *faith* in His atoning sacrifice, a perfect brightness of *hope*, and *charity*, an abundance of God's love for one's neighbors (see Moroni 10:20). Counseling individuals struggling with addiction has helped me appreciate the central importance of the middle virtue, hope.

What is hope? It is "desire and expectation, combined," according to the Oxford dictionary.[9] The *Encyclopedia of Mormonism* entry on *hope* indicates that the core scriptural meaning is trust, or confidence, in God.[10] These definitions suggest that when filled with hope, what we desire to happen we expect will happen because we trust God's promises. If a person believes that he can be helped, *personally*, by the atonement of Jesus Christ, then his faith is energized and his charity is quickened. However, if through repeated transgression a person concludes that he has forfeited the right to be rescued from sin, the resulting despair undermines his faith and dilutes his charity. Moroni describes this woeful spiritual state: "And if ye have no hope ye must needs be in despair; and despair cometh because of iniquity" (10:22).

To better understand the devastating effects of despair, it is useful to step back and contemplate two key elements of our mortal experience: transgression and repentance (see Alma 36, 42). The Light of Christ, given to all men, helps us discern the difference between good and evil. One way we learn that transgressions, or violations of the laws of God, are evil is that they trigger feelings of guilt—a sense of alienation from God's spirit. Guilt, in turn, prompts feelings of remorse (deep regret, or Godly sorrow). Remorse prompts us to make different choices—to repent and seek forgiveness through Christ the Redeemer who is able to reverse the alienating effects of sin in our lives. In this process of spiritual transformation, remorse is the critical step. It is God's invitation to turn back toward His light—to feel its warmth on our face and to use it as a beacon to guide our feet.

In contrast, repeated failure to overcome a particular transgression leads to deep discouragement, as positive remorse is smothered by negative shame. Sunk in shame, a sexual addict loses sight of the Good Shepherd's outstretched arms and turns, instead, to the familiar embrace of his addiction—once again welcoming the momentary relief from pain. This "vicious cycle" is reflected in the commonly observed "addict's binge." BYU counselor Marleen Williams illustrates the self-perpetuating nature of addiction, using the analogy of a dog: (1) When I feel stress, I chew shoes. (2) When I chew shoes, I am scolded. (3) When I am scolded, I feel stress. In this manner, Satan the Accuser short circuits God's plan for spiritual transformation. Shame is substituted for remorse as such thoughts arise as: "I don't deserve the blessings of the Atonement." "God is ashamed of me." "I can't stop sinning—I must be too far gone to save." Thus our adversary shifts the target of a sinner's disdain and disgust from his actions to himself—where remorse abhors the offending sin, shame condemns the sinner.

Shame suits Satan's purposes because it alienates a person from God (I'm unworthy of His love), from his family and loved ones (I'm unworthy to serve or be loved by others), as well as from himself (I'm unworthy of self-respect). In this manner, Satan drives a wedge between the shame-filled sinner and a merciful God—because shame cannot comprehend mercy. I testify that the surprising realization that what one assumed was Godly guilt is actually Satan-inspired shame helps those burdened by despair consider the restoration of hope as a realistic possibility. And, importantly, with this possibility comes the feasibility of full and complete repentance.

The LDS Bible Dictionary observes: "The Greek word of which [repentance] is the translation denotes a change of mind, i.e., a fresh view about God, about [ourselves], and about the world."[11] I particularly like C. S. Lewis' account of this process. "We may, indeed, be sure that perfect chastity—like perfect charity—will not be attained by any merely human efforts. You may ask for God's help. Even when you have done so, it may seem to you for a long time that no help, or less help than you need, is being given. Never mind. After each failure, ask forgiveness, pick yourself up, and try again. Very often what God first helps us towards is not the virtue itself but just this power of always trying again. For however important chastity (or courage, or truthfulness, or any other virtue) may be, this process trains us in habits of the soul which are more important still. It cures our illusions about ourselves and teaches us to depend on God. We learn, on the one hand, that we cannot trust ourselves even in our best moments, and, on the other, that we need not despair even in our worst, for our failures are forgiven. The only fatal thing is to sit down content with anything less than perfection."[12]

One objective of repentance is to help a person filled with shame begin viewing himself through God's eyes. In practical terms, this means recognizing that sexual addiction is one, and only one, aspect of a person's behavior. Hence, it should not be given disproportionate weight in his self-assessment. Until a young man can see that his sexual addiction is not all of him, or for that matter, even typical of him, encouragement to seek God's help is likely to fall on deaf ears. In most cases, those who seek my counsel for overcoming this problem are very active, dedicated members of the Church. They faithfully attend their meetings, they accept and fulfill their callings, they pay their tithes and offerings, they look out for the needs of others, and they engage in regular prayer and scripture study, but they haven't been willing to give themselves credit for these good works. Hence, they live segmented lives—one that is filled with sin and self-condemnation, the other that is filled with good works but no self-*commendation*. The more they can recognize the significance of their righteous choices in other aspects of their life, the easier it is for them to consider the possibility that a tree that bears this much good fruit couldn't have a rotten core or dead roots.[13]

As the smallest cracks begin appearing in the isolating wall of shame, I offer the following challenge: "Do whatever it takes for you to feel the spiritual presence of a nonjudgmental Father in Heaven. Go home and become reacquainted with the God of Hope—the God from whom you have become estranged." To that end, I encourage them to reflect on what they have done in the past to nurture an intimate relationship with their Father in Heaven and then to renew those practices. Effective initiatives have included reading personally meaningful verses of scripture, walking in the woods at dawn or looking at the nighttime sky from a mountain top, reading the parable of the prodigal son from the father's perspective, listening to inspirational music, studying their patriarchal blessings, thinking more deeply about repentance and forgiveness.[14] Importantly, I encourage them to continue these practices regularly, even if they "slip up"—otherwise they never learn the meaning of Godly mercy and they never experience the miraculous effects of God's power. In every case where I've observed a young man make significant progress in overcoming sexual addiction, the critical turning point has been a breakthrough, heartfelt experience with his Father in Heaven.

I testify of the supportive influence of God's tender mercies and the transformative effect of God's mighty power. I know that hope can, indeed, overcome despair—the shackles of shame can truly be broken. With the Apostle Paul, I add my witness that, "Hope maketh not ashamed; because the love of God is shed abroad in our hearts by the Holy Ghost which is given unto us" (Romans 5:5). Buoyed by this conviction, I pray that we will be more determined to better understand, so we can better share, the burdens carried by the discouraged in our midst.

Notes

1. Although sexual addiction is obviously not limited to males involved in habitual masturbation and pornography, I have chosen to focus on these practices because this form of chronic transgression is particularly difficult to overcome. Females can also become ensnared in these practices, and sexual addiction for both males and females can be manifest as chronic violations of the law of chastity in dating relationships. I have also learned that although chronic eating disorders, like bulimia, are not considered to be transgressions, they should be treated as addictions.

2. Gordon B. Hinckley, "Living Worthy of the Girl You Will Someday Marry," *Ensign*, May 1998, 49.

3. "Danger Ahead! Pornography's Trap," *New Era*, October 2002, 35.

4. "Danger Ahead!" 39.

5. I recommend the proceedings of recent BYU conferences on Internet pornography, called Cyber Secrets, available through the BYU Women's Services and Resources (www.byu.edu/wsr). In addition, on the BYU FamilyLife web site you can also download a copy of the August 2002 issue of *Marriage & Families* devoted to this subject (http://familylife. byu.edu). One of the most widely cited books is Patrick Carnes, *Don't Call It Love: Recovery from Sexual Addiction* (New York: Bantam, 1992).

6. Victor Cline and Brad Wilcox, "The Pornography Trap," *Marriage & Families* (August 2002): 12.

7. These characteristics are also key indicators of attention deficit disorder (ADD), a neurological disorder often associated with addictive behaviors. Teenagers and young adults with ADD are particularly likely to be

exposed to Internet pornography because they are attracted to attention-absorbing activities, such as computer games and Internet surfing.

8. Spencer W. Kimball, *Faith Precedes the Miracle* (Salt Lake City: Deseret Book, 1972), 178.

9. *Oxford English Dictionary*, s.v. "hope."

10. *Encyclopedia of Mormonism*, edited by Daniel H. Ludlow et al., 4 vols. (New York: Macmillan, 1992), s.v. "hope," 656.

11. LDS Bible Dictionary, s.v. "Repentance," 760.

12. C. S. Lewis, *Mere Christianity* (New York: Macmillan, 1952), 93–94.

13. I have observed that individuals struggling to rid themselves of sexual addiction sometimes attempt to overcompensate—they try to make up for their weak performance in one area by striving to become "perfect" in several other areas overnight. Hence, the purpose of this counsel is to help these individuals recognize and value their current good works, not to make them feel any more inadequate by encouraging them to set unrealistic new goals.

14. Talks by Elder Richard G. Scott, Stephen E. Robinson's *Believing Christ: The Parable of the Bicycle and Other Good News* (Salt Lake City: Deseret Book, 1992), and Elder Lynn A. Mickelsen's "The Atonement, Repentance, and Dirty Linen," *Ensign*, November 2003, 10–13, have been mentioned as especially helpful.

SLOW TO ANGER

༄༅

David G. Ericksen

Everyone struggles with anger at one time or another. The gospel teaches us that our Father is real, has a physical body, and is a being of "passions." Though the scriptures overwhelmingly portray Him as a God of love, they also reveal that He experiences the full range of passions and emotions that His children do, including anger. Just as God is "well pleased" in some passages, others refer to His anger or wrath, almost always in the context of His dealings with His disobedient children. I bring this up at the outset to acknowledge that anger is a normal emotion, experienced by all of us in this earthly existence and, apparently, experienced from time to time by our Heavenly Father as well.

The phenomenon of anger is not, in and of itself, a sin. This does not mean that anger is a good thing, or something we need not worry about, just that it is an emotional experience common to all of us. How we deal with the anger we experience is what is important. In the Beatitudes we read: "But I say unto you, That whosoever is angry with his brother *without a cause* shall be in danger of the judgment" (Matthew 5:22; emphasis added). Proverbs 15:18 states, "He that is slow to anger appeaseth strife." It does not say, "He that never feels angry—or resentful or bitter or any of a number of other negative emotions—shall be exalted." Again, the issue is not that we should never feel or experience anger—we all do. Rather, we should ask ourselves

---

David G. Ericksen received his doctorate in clinical psychology from the University of Utah. He maintains a clinical and consulting practice in Salt Lake City. He has been a branch president and currently serves on the high council of his stake. He and his wife, Irene, are the parents of two sons.

how easily we are brought to anger, and what do we do with anger once we feel it. Dealing with anger is one of the ways in which we contend with what the scriptures call the "natural man." We can deal with our anger as an enemy to God would, or we can strive to yield to the enticings of the Spirit.

Understanding that anger is a "secondary" emotion is also helpful. That is, anger tends to *follow* other feelings, such as fear, embarrassment, shock, pain, rejection, or powerlessness. When we feel anger, it should be a cue to us that something else troubling our spirit needs to be dealt with.

Anger levels vary widely from one individual to another, or within the same person at different phases of life. In clinical practice we occasionally see those whose anger is almost literally out of their control. Uncontrollable rage is often the result of neurologic injury, such as head injury, seizure disorder (especially temporal-lobe seizures), stroke, meningitis, or an episode of insufficient oxygen to the brain. An injury of this type sometimes results in, among other things, easily triggered anger and aggression that can be controlled only by physical restraint and/or psychotropic medication. The behavior we see is impulsive aggression, because the person has a diminished capacity for reflection or considering alternatives or consequences. A physically strong individual with this type of injury can cause significant harm to others if unrestrained. Behavior at the extreme end of the anger scale can indicate a difficult, physiological problem requiring intensive clinical attention. For the vast majority of us, however, how we act once we feel anger is largely a decision, a choice, and even a habit.

Are there other times when anger might require professional help? Yes. Let me offer a brief overview of a hierarchy of anger seriousness. Most commonly, anger results in a verbal interchange between two people. Anger intensifies when that interaction becomes quite heated and those involved shout, name-call, swear, and so on. The next step up would be hitting, kicking, or throwing something, not at the other person, but in anger. Next would be grabbing or pushing another person, then slapping, then striking with force, then threatening with, or actually using, a weapon. Clearly, professional help is needed when anger begins to escalate, and definitely when people begin to get physical with each other. Once anger escalates, if underlying problems are not addressed, the cycle will continue, resulting in possibly serious emotional (and sometimes physical) damage.

Even if no physical threat is present, when shouting, name-calling, put-downs, and swearing become *habitual,* it is time to stop the pattern and get help. This pattern of losing control signals a relationship in trouble, whether between husband and wife or parent and child.

At the other end of the scale are those who constantly suppress their anger. Those who never acknowledge strong negative feelings that should be addressed are also trapped in a harmful pattern. One of my goals here is to emphasize that anger is not an "all-or-nothing" phenomenon—it varies and it can be regulated. This said, I want to discuss the "normal" kind of anger that most of us struggle with in our day-to-day lives.

In my office people often say: "Dr. Ericksen, I need you to give me the tools to manage my anger," or "I need tools to communicate with my wife (or husband)."[1] Nearly every time I probe for further information, I find that the person does indeed have quite well-developed "tools" for communicating and controlling anger in almost every situation—except at home. People rarely if ever fly off the handle or show inappropriate anger at work, with friends, at the store, or at church. But something happens once they get home. Does this sound familiar? I can find some understandable reasons for this phenomenon. For one thing, our behavior and speech are much less controlled and cautious at home than when we are in public, or even with friends. A familiarity and emotional intimacy at home allows us to express a wider range of emotion and behavior than we would feel comfortable showing in public. Also, over time we tend to take family members for granted, causing us to be less civil, courteous, and kind toward the people that we would be quick to say we love the most.

Instead of dwelling on times when you handled a situation poorly, expressing anger in a way that damaged a relationship, please think about a time when you felt an initial inclination to get angry and didn't—when a situation could have gone one way or the other, and you caused it to go in a good direction. When I ask my clients to relate such a "success story," they usually describe a time when they focused on the "big picture" instead of the issue of the moment. They didn't succumb to the "tunnel vision" of anger, which occurs when we focus on something that hurts or irritates us and forget the rest of the picture. Anger dissipates if we can put the smaller, less important things of the moment in the context of what really means more to us—our relationship with a loved one.

Let me relate an example. A father told me about how he had decided his angry interchanges with his son partly boiled down to his own need to be "right" and not let his son "take over." To put it simply, he had felt it was important to "win" when his son questioned him or went against his wishes. But he had begun to realize that while he was "winning" these confrontations with his son, their relationship was slowly eroding. What was his "tunnel vision"? "My son is questioning my authority and arguing with me, and I can't have that. I must clearly establish who is in charge here." What did he begin to do instead? He began to consider the cost of his narrow approach to the relationship. He began to feel that winning all of their small, daily battles was costing too much and that his long-term relationship with his son was more important. That shift in perception allowed this father to begin to reduce the number of angry interchanges with his son, and when conflicts between the two of them did arise, he was able to keep the "big picture" more in mind.

Next, let us consider what tends to trigger our anger. All of us could make very long lists, but anger typically arises for one or more of a rather small handful of reasons. Perhaps the most common reason is, simply, because *we care*. Caring is wonderful, and I am not suggesting we should not care. But when something or someone we care about is threatened or ridiculed, we tend to get angry. Realizing this fact can help us choose our response. Sometimes expressing anger isn't the best solution. Another common trigger is the pain of feeling *rejected*, *disrespected*, or *powerless*. We sometimes use anger to numb that pain of feeling rejected, disrespected, or powerless. This anger represents an attempt to regain our power or to control others. When we become loud and angry, we get what we want. In this case, anger has the unrighteous goal of attempting to diminish the freedom of others. One other very common reason for anger is that old devil *unrealistic expectations*. Church members may be even more susceptible than most to being cut by the double-edged sword of high expectations. Our inspiring vision of human potential can lead us to have high expectations of ourselves, our children, our spouses, and our leaders, to name a few. This can be a good thing, helping most of us grow beyond what we otherwise would. We have to be careful, however, to weigh those expectations and striving for perfection with the counsel to "not run faster . . . than [we] have strength" (D&C 10:4).

Let me share how I see women struggling with this common cause of anger and frustration. Frequently in my office I hear women talk about the high expectations they have for their families. In my experience, women often have a more focused sense of responsibility for the spiritual and emotional well-being of their families than do their husbands. This intense focus leaves many mothers and wives with disappointed hopes and expectations. They are sure that everyone else has achieved the ideal family: everyone else's children are less contentious, more cooperative and obedient, and so on. As one mom put it: "Our family home evenings would be wonderful if the kids weren't there!" Another mom said, "I knock myself out trying to achieve the ideal of the righteous, dedicated LDS family, and my kids keep messing up the whole plan!" She added, half kidding, half not, "Sometimes I feel my kids were put on earth just to torment me!"

We've grappled with this in our family, and we have had to modify our expectations over time. My wife has repeatedly tried to have the perfect model family home evening complete with opening song, profound spiritual lesson, activity, treat, and prayers. Some of those expectations died a slow, agonizing death in our home, as our boys found ways to make every aspect of home evening fun—*for them*. The opening song degenerated each week into a circus of howling coyotes, and then it was hard to get the boys back down to earth so we could have anything like a lesson. We don't bother going to the piano for a song anymore (and I think our neighbors are grateful!). We have had to come to terms with what works for our family and how to share a meaningful few moments of love and spiritual insight with each other. While we held to those "ideal expectations," we were angry at our children at the end of almost every home evening. We all need to consider our expectations and see where they needlessly set us up to react with anger.

Now let us consider what we can do to better manage our anger. Changing the way we think about and interpret what is happening can help. The triggers I just mentioned do not *force* us to react with anger. An angry response is a choice, even though sometimes we might feel pulled very strongly toward that choice. Cognitive Therapy, an approach to counseling that has been quite effective for a number of problems, including anger management, helps people slow down and correct their distorted interpretations of what is happening when their anger is triggered. Many of the distortions involve faulty assumptions. For example, how often do we assume we know what another person is thinking or feeling, or expect them to understand how we are feeling, without either of us explaining those feelings? This happens a lot in marriage, especially early in a relationship. It also happens often as we deal with our children, and even with our friends.

Here is a typical example: A church member passed in the hall another ward member whom he had known for years. He tried to greet his friend but felt brushed off. During the rest of the Sunday block, the one who felt slighted developed a long list of assumptions about the other person's behavior and intentions: he must have felt superior, been mad at him, not appreciated him as a friend, or maybe just turned into a plain jerk. The initial hurt, fueled by these thoughts, began to escalate into anger. Later that day, the slighted man's wife said, "Oh, did you hear that Jim's company is moving out of state and he is going to lose his job?" Suddenly, the slighted brother was able to see the whole situation in a different light, and his anger immediately subsided. The cognitive approach involves getting out of our tunnel vision of assumptions about what is happening. We can ask ourselves, for example, "How likely is it that what I'm assuming is correct? What other possible explanations are there? How is my assumption fueling my anger, when the assumption may not even be correct?" The goal is to catch the emotion before it escalates into behavior and/or words we will regret.

Other helpful stress- and anger-management activities include calm breathing exercises and deep muscle relaxation. Let me briefly describe them to you. Breathing slowly and deeply from the abdomen helps you relax. There is little movement in the chest area but the stomach slowly moves in and out as you breathe. Slow, deep abdominal breathing is restful because the diaphragm does the work, other muscles relax, and your heart and lungs do not need to work as hard. This is a surprisingly good antidote to stress and growing anger.

Deep muscle relaxation is another form of relaxation that helps distract you from angry thoughts. The procedure is to progressively tense and then relax the major muscle groups of your body, starting with the feet and moving up through the body to the face and head. Concentrate on how the states of tension and relaxation feel; notice the contrast between these two states. Many adults have become accustomed to feeling chronically tense and stressed, which can put us in a state of readiness to feel angry. Muscle relaxation does not just help us calm down; it also helps us catch ourselves when we are becoming tense or angry so that we can consciously work on relaxing and diffusing our anger.

What counsel do we receive from gospel sources? Let me mention a few. We are counseled to be forgiving with each other. This attitude can be a very effective antidote to anger, but it requires us to expand beyond our "tunnel vision" of pain and desire for justice, and see those who have harmed us as struggling, imperfect human beings in need of the Lord's help, just as we are. Doctrine and Covenants 121 is a useful guide to managing how we deal with potentially angering situations. Although the section specifically addresses priesthood holders, the counsel applies to everyone. Verse 41 states: "No power or influence can or ought to be maintained by virtue of the priesthood, only by persuasion, by long-suffering, by gentleness and meekness, and by love unfeigned." Verse 43 adds: "Reproving betimes with sharpness, when moved upon by the Holy Ghost; and then showing forth afterwards an increase of love toward him whom thou hast reproved, lest he esteem thee to be his enemy." This is good advice not only to help us manage our own anger but also to keep us from inciting others to anger.

Above all, we need to look to the Savior and make the Atonement effective in our lives. We learn of His desire to help us do just that in a passage from Alma: "And he shall go forth, suffering pains and afflictions and temptations of every kind; and this that the word might be fulfilled which saith he will take upon him the pains and sicknesses of his people . . . ; and he will take upon him their infirmities" (7:11–12). A tendency to become angry is a common infirmity. I'm grateful that the Savior understands what you and I struggle with, and that He is compassionate and stands ready to help us.

Note

1. One book that I recommend to clients is Glenn Schiraldi and Melissa Hallmark Kerr, *The Anger Management Sourcebook* (Chicago: Contemporary Books, 2002).

"AN EFFECTUAL STRUGGLE":
RELIEF FROM FINANCIAL BONDAGE

꜅꜀꜅

Kristin H. South

A few years ago, a young woman I know wanted to go on a mission. She sent in the appropriate papers to Church headquarters and was delighted to receive a call to serve. When she and her bishop sat down to discuss her mission, he discovered that she had a rather large load of credit card debt. Rather than sending her out on a mission with unpaid debt, he arranged for her call to be delayed until she paid off all she owed.

In contrast, a few weeks ago my husband and I visited friends who had recently been called to preside over a mission. They described their nervous anticipation as they went to be interviewed by Elder Neal A. Maxwell regarding their worthiness and preparation to serve. To their surprise, the first question he asked them addressed the amount of debt they carried. They were very pleased to be able to report that they were free to go, and they will leave for New York next month.

Why would freedom from unreasonable debt be a prerequisite to worthy service in the Church? Why have all of the modern prophets emphasized wise management of resources and provident living? In Luke 16:11, Jesus remarked, "If . . . ye have not been faithful in the unrighteous mammon [or worldly riches], who will commit to your trust the true riches?"[1] The way we discharge our temporal stewardship

---

Kristin Hacken South is the mother of three boys and the wife of Mikle South. They have lived in Connecticut, where Kristin received her education at Yale University; California; Cairo, Egypt; and in Utah. She has served in many callings, but her favorites have been ward and stake Relief Society president and Gospel Doctrine teacher.

reflects our commitment to gospel principles and is a training ground for developing spiritual riches.

When we overspend our resources, we fall into the bondage of debt. The word *bondage* is not too strong here: as the Proverbs note, "The borrower is *servant* to the lender" (Proverbs 22:7; emphasis added). Jesus taught that no one can serve two masters. When we are in debt, we have a master other than God (see Matthew 6:24).

An American folk song reflects this same thought. It tells the story of coal miners who were forced to borrow money from their employers to buy needed tools. Despite hard toil, they could never earn enough to repay their debt or even keep up with the interest.

> *You load sixteen tons and what do you get?*
> *Another day older and deeper in debt.*
> *Saint Peter, don't you call me 'cause I can't go,*
> *I owe my soul to the company store.*[2]

I have been impressed by two closely related stories in the Book of Mormon, found in Mosiah 7–24, that teach clearly the perils of materialism and the way to escape its bondage. Zeniff had been sent as a spy to the land of the Lamanites. When Zeniff arrived, he saw much that was good, so much, in fact, that he became "over-zealous to inherit the land of [his] fathers" (Mosiah 9:1–3). He convinced other Nephites to return with him and settle among the Lamanites. Zeniff worked out a treaty with the king of the Lamanites so that Zeniff and his people could live in a part of the Lamanites' land. Without further concern, they began to till and plant and build.

Only after settling in and making the land very productive did they learn of the cunning of the Lamanite king: he planned to bring the Nephites into bondage so that he and his people could "glut themselves with the labors of [their] hands" (Mosiah 9:12). At first the people of Zeniff were able to repel the Lamanites attacks because they called on God for protection and He heard their prayers. When the people stopped trusting in God, however, they were left to their own strength and fell prey first to the greed and idolatry of their own wicked

King Noah, then to the Lamanites (Mosiah 9:17–18; 10:10; 11:2, 6–7, 17; 19:15).

In the midst of this, the prophet Abinadi was sent to warn the people to repent. At first, only Alma believed, but he fearlessly taught the gospel message to 450 others. Together these righteous people fled from the wicked King Noah. Those who remained came under the rule of the Lamanite king, who exacted one half of all their goods and set guards day and night to prevent them from escaping. Under the relentless misery, and with their wicked King Noah dead, the people began to repent and to desire a means of escape: "And they did humble themselves even to the dust, subjecting themselves to the yoke of bondage, . . . and they did cry mightily to God. . . . And it came to pass that they began to prosper by degrees in the land" (Mosiah 21:13–14, 16).

Now properly humbled and aware of their dependence on God, the people under their new king, Limhi, were ready for deliverance. They achieved freedom in several steps. First, they had a strong desire to be delivered (see Mosiah 21:36). Next, they all came together, discussed various alternatives, and agreed upon the one most likely to succeed (see Mosiah 22:1). This was a very important step, because achieving freedom meant a sharp change to their lifestyle; they would need to leave behind many of their material possessions. They all recognized the need for these sacrifices and agreed that the goal of freedom was worthwhile (see Mosiah 22:2). The people of Limhi accordingly made and carried out a specific plan, by means of which they escaped (see Mosiah 22:6–13).

Several aspects of this story are relevant for us today. It was the material desires of Zeniff that landed him and his people in bondage. He was tricked by the Lamanite king because he was willing to believe that the king would give him what he wanted without asking for anything in return. Our equivalent might be those credit card offers that promise a "low introductory rate," then charge exorbitantly high interest and hidden fees as soon as a payment is missed or even delayed. Tragically, Zeniff brought a lot of people into bondage with him. His son, King Noah, loved the hedonistic lifestyle so well that he led his whole people into spiritual darkness and bondage, and he killed the prophet sent to warn them. It took many years for the people to recognize their error and to gain the faith to be freed. Three generations of bondage resulted from the folly of one. Can we suppose that the consequences are any less severe when we overreach our income and attempt to live on borrowed means? We must think about what our children will learn about priorities, about how long it takes to dig back out, before we run to buy the latest luxury or fad.

The second thread of this story concerns the people of Alma who had left just before the bondage of Limhi's people. They traveled many days to a new land. After telling of their escape, the record of Mosiah reminds us of this important truth: "Nevertheless the Lord seeth fit to chasten his people; yea, he trieth their patience and their faith. Nevertheless— whosoever putteth his trust in him the same shall be lifted up at the last day. Yea, and thus it was with this people" (Mosiah 23:21–22).

A passing band of Lamanites discovered Alma and his people in their new land and took them captive. The people of Alma immediately turned to God for deliverance, and immediately He responded. First "the burdens which were laid upon Alma and his brethren were made light" (Mosiah 24:15). For us, a lightening of our financial burdens might mean that our needs become simpler, or we are able to lower our material expectations; it might mean a raise in pay for a current job, or finding ingenious ways to stretch the money a little further.

After the people of Alma displayed their continued faith, bearing their burdens cheerfully and with patience, the Lord spoke again to Alma: "I will . . . deliver this people out of bondage" (Mosiah 24:17). Notice how they escaped: after spending the night gathering together their flocks and their food, the people simply walked away in the morning while the Lamanite guards slept a "profound sleep" (v. 19) sent upon them by God. In broad daylight, they simply walked away. It was God who allowed them to come into bondage, and it was He who delivered them in a miraculous manner.

I have dwelt on these stories at some length because I see a valuable lesson in comparing the two different ways people can find themselves in bondage or, to apply it directly to ourselves, in *debt*. In the first instance, Zeniff and his people reaped the bitter fruit of their own actions. In the second story, the bondage of Alma's people was outside their control, a product of the need for every person's faith to be tested. Both groups of people were sufficiently humbled before they could be released. Both groups were delivered from their bondage, rejoiced, and recognized the hand of God in their deliverance. The escape of the people of Alma was particularly miraculous. To the degree that each group of people was able and willing to trust in God, He was able to help them (see Alma 38:5). To the degree that they were responsible for their own bondage, they were expected to work to that same degree to free themselves.

Whatever the reason for our bondage, God wants to deliver us, but the means and the timeline of deliverance may vary. We will need to work through the consequences of our actions if our debt is the result of imprudent, improvident living. Elder Robert S. Wood clarifies the reason for this: "[There is] a tendency to which we all are subject—the tendency to desire some miraculous delivery from the consequences of our actions . . . with little effort on our part.

" . . . [But] being free requires being responsible. The very word *freedom* connotes the ability to judge rationally between alternatives and the willingness to accept the consequences of one's decisions. . . .

"God has paid us the ultimate compliment: He holds us responsible and respects us as free, rational beings. He has given us this freedom through the Atonement of Jesus Christ. The concepts of individual freedom and personal responsibility are at the very center of the Atonement. . . .

"Note this great truth: once we have accepted responsibility for our own actions, the grace of God is extended to us. For freedom implies not only accountability but also the ability to repent."[3]

How is it possible to "repent" of financial mismanagement? Although debt might seem to be "only" a temporal matter, God has said that to Him all things are spiritual (see D&C 29:34). The laws of temporal and spiritual repentance are the same, including feeling remorse for your actions, making things right to the extent possible, and changing your habits and future ways. These universal principles of repentance and change apply as directly to debt or other temporal concerns as to sins. Remember, repentance is not a freedom from all consequences; instead, it is the God-sent ability to change, not to labor eternally under guilt and the consequences of actions that you often can't fix. For Alma, who had lived wickedly under the influence of King Noah, repentance was not an easy, automatic process; he describes it as "sore." But "after much tribulation" the Lord did hear his cries (Mosiah 23:9–10). The same happens with temporal deliverance, both in financial matters and in other areas.

The laws of temporal and spiritual stewardship are also the same. The scriptures are filled with promises that those who ask in righteousness will receive (see, for instance, Matthew 7:7; 3 Nephi 27:28; D&C 4:7). According to Doctrine and Covenants 46, the keys to receiving spiritual gifts include desiring the gift, asking only for what the Spirit confirms is a righteous desire, having gratitude for what is given, putting the gift to good use, and using it for the good of others as well as one's self (D&C 46:8, 9, 30, 32). Temporal gifts are given on these same principles, but we must be willing to make the sacrifices necessary to achieve them, which will certainly include time as well as mental and emotional energy.

Taking care of our temporal stewardship trains us to develop spiritual riches. Don't be deceived: many people are rich in temporal things but have lost the ultimate riches, as "he that hath eternal life is [truly] rich" (D&C 6:7). Too often a sincere, honest desire to provide for one's family turns to a cankering hunger for more and more, far beyond the necessities. Financial bondage is not limited to those who are in debt. We can all find ourselves in bondage if we let a preoccupation with temporal affairs deter our spiritual growth. The nineteenth-century English poet William Wordsworth voiced it this way:

> The world is too much with us; late and soon,
> Getting and spending, we lay waste our powers:
> Little we see in Nature that is ours;
> We have given our hearts away, a sordid boon![4]

A healthy antidote to this type of bondage includes taking an honest look at the true value of money. Successful money manager and writer Suze Orman has written about money from this perspective: "It isn't how much you have that creates a sense of freedom. It's how you feel about what you have, or don't have, that either keeps you prisoner or sets you free. . . . The quality of our lives does not depend only on how we accumulate, save, and spend our money. True financial freedom lies in defining ourselves by who and what we are, not by what we do or do not have. You are the person you are. . . . We cannot measure our self-worth by our net worth."[5]

The way we handle our finances displays our level of commitment to gospel principles. Do we truly believe that the worth of every soul is great, regardless of the worth of that soul's bank account? I would like to suggest some principles that can help each of us develop a more healthy relationship with our resources.

Principle number one: *It's better to have money in the bank than to have "stuff."* People who are committed to financial health live well below their means. They recognize that financial security means having money that hasn't been spent. They value money in the bank more than they value things, and they generally have an ethic of thrift and self-discipline.[6]

Number two: *People with healthy attitudes enjoy their wealth quietly.* At the end of spring break one year, I sat down to dinner with some roommates who were discussing their vacations. One mentioned casually that she and her parents had gone boating. I thought that sounded nice but unremarkable. Later I was amused to learn that her "boating trip" had actually been a trip to the Caribbean on a private yacht! Her modesty helped me not to judge her unrighteously based on her wealth, and I am grateful that she similarly did not judge me for my lack of it.

Number three: *People who know the true value of money give and serve, often anonymously, and without keeping track or expecting favors or gratitude.* Many of you undoubtedly know that secret feeling of satisfaction that comes when you are able to help someone else anonymously. Doesn't it make you feel rich when you are able to share what you have with others?

Number four: *People who understand money teach their children how to handle money.* Money management is not a taboo topic in healthy households; instead, it is taught alongside other important skills. One wise father, an accountant, sat down with his fourteen-year-old daughter, explained the basics of budgeting, then gave her a monthly allowance. The amount she received was far more than she was accustomed to having. She called her best friend, and together they went out and spent the whole sum the next day. I'm sure they had a great time! A week later, she had an urgent need, but her money was all spent. When she told her mom that she needed some money, her mother pointed out that her month's allowance was gone. She very quickly learned the importance of saving and of careful spending.

Number five: *People with a healthy attitude toward money have internalized the axiom, "Waste not, want not."* Amy Dacyczyn, a self-proclaimed "frugal zealot" and author of *The Complete Tightwad Gazette,* has made her life a testament to the possibility of raising a large family on one modest income through conscious choices to cut back on unnecessary spending. She observes simply, "Frugality has enabled me to live the life I wanted."[7]

I would like to put in my own comment on frugality. My husband and I purchased our first home just six months ago. We found the perfect house in the perfect neighborhood, and it was perfectly within our price-range only because it was perfectly run-down. We have scrubbed, sanded, weeded, hauled, and overhauled most of the house and yard. A few weeks ago my husband tackled the bathroom plumbing. He had gained some experience by redoing the plumbing in the sinks, so he was ready for the ultimate test: the bathtub. He took out all of the old pipes, put in new, and miraculously, they all worked. I gleefully counted up the hundreds of dollars we must have saved by doing the work ourselves. The drain was having a little problem, but we figured that would be easy enough to fix.

The day after we "fixed" that "little problem" was a Sunday. After

I took my shower and drew a bath for the kids, I heard what sounded like "the rushing of mighty waters" downstairs. I quickly judged that this was an earthly, not a heavenly, sound; after a cry to my husband for help, I ran down to find the whole tub of bath water pouring from our basement ceiling onto our food storage on one side of the wall and the clean laundry on the other (I knew I should have folded that laundry)! I in my Sunday dress and my husband in pajamas grabbed garbage pails and with every towel in the house mopped up the best we could until the deluge finally ended. Thanks to expert packing in sealed cans at the church cannery, the food storage survived, and the laundry was fine once it dried again. I even concluded that it was all still worthwhile to have done it ourselves. We learned a few things about plumbing and saved a lot of money. I was reminded, however, of a wise proverb: "It is not economical to go to bed early to save candles if the results are twins."[8]

Self-reliance comes through acquiring and using practical skills. A friend of mine gives beautiful hand-knit gifts on special occasions, instead of store-bought items. I have found that I have learned many valuable skills at Home, Family, and Personal Enrichment meetings, including how to preserve foods through canning and drying, how to do laundry right (though I have not yet mastered this skill!), how to make bread and cook with dry beans, how to garden, crochet, and fix a flat tire. Self-reliance *is* an important principle of the gospel. The value—both personal and financial—of such knowledge cannot be overemphasized. It can also be a lot of fun!

In addition to self-reliance, we must not lose sight of the importance of self-sacrifice. In many instances, the present wealth and happiness of one generation is due to the sacrifices of a previous one. A current example of this principle is the Church's Perpetual Education Fund. As one generation invests in a moderate amount of debt to gain an education, the cycle of poverty will be broken, and many generations into the future will be blessed.

I have also been impressed recently to read about sacrifices that were an essential part of the American war of independence. John

Adams, a stalwart of the American Revolution, played a major role in crafting the concepts that guided the Declaration of Independence and the Constitution. His devotion to the cause of his nation meant that he had to spend a great deal of time in Philadelphia, while his wife, Abigail, remained at home in Massachusetts, bearing and raising children and running the family farm.

John and Abigail were apart for seven of the first fourteen years of their marriage. A modern biographer has written of one particularly trying time, "Rampant inflation, shortages of nearly every necessity made the day-to-day struggle at home increasingly difficult. A dollar was not worth what a quarter had been, Abigail reported. 'Our money will soon be as useless as blank paper.' Bread, salt, sugar, meat, and molasses, cotton and wool had become dear beyond measure. Farm help, help of any sort, was impossible to find. Yet she managed— scrimped, saved, wove her own wool, made the family's clothes— determined not only to stay free of debt, but to make improvements."[9]

In March of 1777, Abigail Adams wrote, "Posterity who are to reap the blessings will scarcely be able to conceive the hardships and sufferings of their ancestors."[10]

I admire Abigail Adams. Her persistence and faith in the face of great trials show that she was fully confident that the cause was right and the suffering worthwhile for the sake of future generations, who would benefit from her sacrifices regardless of their own personal merit. It would be easy for many of us in those later generations to think that we somehow "earned" our standard of living, our ease, and our freedom. It is good to remember that we have not. It is a gift freely given, though dearly bought.

When I think about any gift freely given, though dearly bought, I think first of the Atonement of Christ. We often talk of the Atonement as a ransom, Christ's selfless payment that frees us from the bondage of sin.

"Ye are bought with a price," declared Paul to the Corinthians (1 Corinthians 6:20). In this sense, all of us are literally in debt to Christ. He has paid the price for our everlasting freedom from death and hell. Unlike earthly creditors, Christ wants to lighten our load, to help free us from our sins, our sorrows, our debts.

Christ wants to deliver us from *all* of our burdens. If you are in financial bondage, regardless of how you got there, God wants to deliver you, if you are ready. Ours is a God of deliverance. In His Old Testament persona, God led His people out of bondage in Egypt into a promised land. At the beginning of the Book of Mormon, He led his people out of harm and into a promised land (see Alma 36:27–29). In the course of human history and in each of our individual lives, Christ leads us all out of all manner of bondage. His atonement pays an infinite debt.

It may take years of struggle before you can be freed, or it may seem to happen overnight. Whatever the case, trust in God. Consider the words of Limhi: "I trust there remaineth an effectual struggle to be made" (Mosiah 7:18). Your struggle will be no longer or more strenuous than his people's, but your escape will be equally miraculous and joyful. Remember that the Lord will sometimes try our patience and our faith, but that if we "submit cheerfully and with patience to all the will of the Lord" (Mosiah 24:15), we will be delivered. It takes fasting, prayer, faith, sacrifice, time, and self-discipline, but what a small price to pay for the freedom to offer our whole souls to Him. He has promised eternal abundance in return.

Notes

1. See also Jack M. Lyon, "How Many Loaves Have Ye?" *Ensign*, December 1989, 36.
2. Merle Travis, "Sixteen Tons," original recording Capitol Studios, Hollywood, Calif., 8 August 1946.
3. Robert S. Wood, "On the Responsible Self," *Ensign*, March 2002, 28–29; emphasis in original.
4. William Wordsworth, "The World Is Too Much with Us," in *A Treasury of Great Poems*, compiled by Louis Untermeyer (New York: Simon and Schuster, 1942), 650.
5. Suze Orman, *The Nine Steps to Financial Freedom* (New York: Crown Publishers, 1997), 272, 281.

6. See, for instance, Thomas J. Stanley and William D. Danko, *The Millionaire Next Door: The Surprising Secrets of America's Wealthy* (Atlanta: Longstreet Press, 1996).

7. Amy Dacyczyn, *The Complete Tightwad Gazette* (New York: Villard Books, 1998), xiv.

8. Dacyczyn, *Complete Tightwad*, 17.

9. David McCullough, *John Adams* (New York: Touchstone Books, 2001), 171.

10. McCullough, *John Adams*, 169.

A CROSSWORD OF JOY

※ ⟨⟨

Susan L. Gong

I am an inveterate crossword puzzler. I'm compulsive about it. I pick up the morning paper at about 6:40 and start the puzzle. I've learned to set a time limit so that the puzzle doesn't take the whole morning. But the day just isn't underway until I've given the crossword my best shot. My children know that if, when they read the comics after school, they find the puzzle unfinished or, worse yet, untried, Mom has not had a great day. I do the puzzle before I take a shower. Before I read the scriptures. There, I've confessed. You know my disreputable early morning priorities.

When you do the crossword every morning it gets easier week by week because the puzzle makers have favorite clues they use over and over again. They become like free spaces on a bingo card. Example: three-letter word; clue, "subject for a church sermon." This one always annoys me. The word that fits the puzzle is always the same, *sin*, but the answer I always want to give is *joy*. Joy should be a part of every church sermon. After all, "Men are, that they might have joy" (2 Nephi 2:25).

Wouldn't it be wonderful to live in an all-joy-all-the-time world? A world like the one depicted in buy-this-product advertising: we would all be perpetually young, beautiful, rich, fit, talented, smart, and

Susan Lindsay Gong is a mother, homemaker, and student. She and her husband, Gerrit Gong, are the parents of four sons. She served as a member of the 2003 Brigham Young University Women's Conference Committee and is a counselor in her ward Relief Society presidency.

thin. We'd always have high self-esteem, never have any worries or doubts or fears or pain. We would all have husbands and they would all be perfect: attentive, kind, generous, handsome, witty, and spiritual. Our children would be perfect too: low maintenance, high achieving, obedient, soft spoken. They would never embarrass us. Our lawns would be green and our gardens weed-free.

Would it really be wonderful to live in such a world? The Book of Mormon tells us that there must be opposition in all things.[1] In this existence, happiness and misery are intertwined. In fact, C. S. Lewis wrote that joy itself reminds us of another world and so carries with it "the stab, the pang, the inconsolable longing."[2] Joy speaks of something greater. It necessarily includes within it a desire for something longer ago or further away or still "about to be."[3]

Thinking about joy has been like doing a crossword puzzle. I've followed many clues and pieced together some new ways of thinking about it. Let me try to capture some of the things I've learned with a few stories about times I've felt joy.

Spaghetti and the Iguana: God's Love

I had long admired a single mother in our ward with whom I had worked in Cub Scouts. Working full-time and raising four active children on her own, she certainly had her hands full. But she was giving and good despite her hectic schedule. She never complained. I asked her about that once. "Oh, you know, people don't want to hear that," was all she said. Her birthday was coming, and her sons wanted to do something special for her. We plotted together. They gave me a key to their townhouse so I could go in and tidy up a bit while they were in school. Then they'd make a special spaghetti dinner to have ready for her when she came home.

The day of the birthday came. I picked a bouquet of flowers from my garden and drove over to their home. I let myself in, tidied the kitchen, and set the table. Things were going exactly according to plan when I turned to the sink to make a salad. I heard a strange, slow, clicking noise on the open stairway behind me. I was not alone in the house! I turned just in time to see a two-foot long, bright green iguana jump from the stairs to the table I had just set. I let out a scream that would have put Faye Ray (the girl in the *King Kong* movie) to shame. Eventually, I recovered my composure, found a broom, and coaxed the lizard upstairs and into a bedroom, where I closed the door. Firmly. Then I washed all the dishes from the table and set it again, then tidied and swept the living room. It really wasn't much. If it had not been for the "attack of the lizard," it would have been a very straightforward affair. But as I was leaving, I felt impressed to kneel and pray that the boys' plan, and my small part in it, would convey the love with which it was given, that this sister would know that she was appreciated and that the house would be filled with the love of the Lord. Kneeling there, a joyous feeling washed over me. I cried, grateful for the blessing that the boys' plan had brought to me. Joy is an intimation of the Lord's great love for us.

A Soggy Miracle: God's Glory

When my oldest son was just a toddler, we were in the front yard of our little house in Falls Church, Virginia, one glorious, late spring afternoon. Something unusual on the porch caught our attention, and we moved closer to see. As we watched, a newly emerged monarch butterfly, its wet wings still furled, slowly took shape before our eyes. It was magic. The vivid, rich rust-colored wings opened to the light and warmth of the sun. The butterfly moved its wings slowly up and down while we watched transfixed. It was exquisitely beautiful. I put out my finger and, on long black legs, the monarch crawled up. I transferred him gently to my son's little finger. The insect, still drying his wings with graceful, slow up-and-down motions, turned around and then, when he was ready, lifted into the air and flew away on the breeze. My son and I shared a joyous moment when the wonder of nature and the glory of creation seemed to unfold before us.

Joy spreads what C. S. Lewis calls the "bright shadow of holiness" on even the most mundane things.[4] Once while canning peaches, I was captivated by the bright colors of the fruit, a glowing round sunset in my hands. "I think," says Lewis, "that all things, in their way, reflect heavenly truth, the imagination not least."[5] Joy is an echo of God's glory.

SURPRISED BY ANNA: GOD'S GOODNESS

Several years ago I was called to be the Relief Society president in a ward in Virginia. The very day the bishop extended the call, I returned home from an afternoon walk with my husband along a wooded path in our neighborhood to find a message on my answering machine. It was from one of the sisters in the ward, a very dear friend, who was expecting their fourth child. Her calm voice on the recording explained the situation. Her husband had gone into the office to finish up some paperwork so that he would be free in the coming week to be with her for the birth of the baby, which was still a few days away. Or so they had thought. It was the weekend. No secretaries were in her husband's office to answer the telephone so she couldn't reach him. She'd left messages but her labor had started, and could I please come over and be with her until her husband returned home?

I called her back immediately, then drove over. When I arrived, she was sitting on the floor in her bedroom, her back against a dresser, breathing with great concentration through a contraction—a marvel of self-control. Her eleven-year-old son was kneeling beside her with a watch timing it. "About two or three minutes apart," he said with the seriousness of a surgeon. We timed the next one, definitely under three minutes.

"Maybe you'd better drive me to Columbia Women's," she conceded bravely between contractions; the hospital was half an hour away.

"Why don't I call the paramedics?" I suggested. She moved to the bed.

Her husband arrived just minutes ahead of the ambulance and the fire truck. Can anyone tell me exactly why they send a huge hook-and-ladder truck to deliver a baby? Several large, burly men in uniforms squeezed into her bedroom. I went looking for the children—besides the son, there were two younger daughters, one a redhead and one a brunette. I found them in the backyard praying for their mother and the baby.

Meanwhile, the paramedics had timed another contraction—five minutes. According to their protocols, they still had time to get "the lady" to the hospital before the baby came. They lifted my friend onto a gurney, covered her with a blanket, rolled her out of the house, and bumped her down the stairs and across the lawn. Her husband ran to the front of the ambulance to take his seat beside the driver while her children and I watched from the front porch. Through it all, the expectant mother remained calm, even dignified. The paramedics lifted the stretcher into the ambulance, and as one of the men closed the doors, I saw his eyes suddenly widen and all the color drain from his face. Somewhere between the bedroom and the ambulance, my friend had given birth to beautiful little Anna.

As you can imagine, the next several minutes were full of some confusion and rush. But not many minutes later, father first and then the brother and sisters climbed into the back of the ambulance, still parked in front of the house, to greet their new sister. Soon after, I was invited to join them. I peeked in through the open door. The new mother cradled her infant close and tenderly. The father, a little ashen, rested his arm around his wife's shoulders protectively. Brother and sisters with smiles of wonder clustered close to the little miracle who had just arrived, caressing her, loving her at first sight. That little scene in the back of an ambulance was a diorama of heaven: joy in a box. The promise of life, the love of a family, the goodness of God was radiating in all of their faces. What a pleasure to be witness of it. Joy is a whisper of His goodness.

The Marian Kellner Fan Club: God's Peace

The oldest member of the McLean First Ward in the year 2000 was Sister Marian Kellner. She was born on the fourth day of the fourth month of the year 1904. Do the math, and you'll realize she was that spring a full ninety-six years old. Marian was born and raised in a

Pennsylvania Amish family. I loved to hear her tell about her growing-up years with a houseful of hardworking brothers and sisters. Her mother rose every morning at about four o'clock to start the bread for the day. Before going to the kitchen, however, she walked down the upstairs hallway, stopping at the door of each bedroom to kneel and pray for protection and guidance for children still asleep in their warm beds.

Marian, like her mother, was also a remarkable, hard-working woman. She valued education and was the first woman to graduate from the Wharton Business School. She married outside her faith, her beloved Hank, and for many years her community and even her close-knit family shunned her. Hank and Marian were never able to have children so when Hank passed away, Marian was alone. Two delighted stake missionary sisters found her while tracting one day. She listened to their lessons and recognized the good news of the gospel. Baptized in her mid-seventies, she was active, intelligent, supportive, independent, faithful, and fun. I was a member of the Marian Kellner fan club.

One night, during a violent Virginia downpour, Marian called. She had a pain in her stomach and didn't want to be alone. When I arrived, she was too weak to come to the door. We called her conscientious doctor, who knew Marian well. She quietly told me that Marian's body was deteriorating, shutting down; there wasn't much medicine could do for her now. The doctor recommended we call hospice the next morning and engage their services. I thanked her, hung up, and called Marian's home teachers, who came to administer a blessing of comfort. After they had laid hands on her head, they visited for a while and left her to rest on the sofa in her living room. The storm still raged outside. Unexpectedly, the electricity went out, and we were alone in the dark. We talked quietly, of happy memories, her good life. She looked forward, she said, to seeing her husband and mother again. Here was a soul at peace. I was reminded of the account in Mosiah 4:3: "And . . . the Spirit of the Lord came upon them, and they were filled with joy, having received a remission of their sins, and having peace of conscience, because of the exceeding faith which they had in Jesus Christ."

"I just want to stay here in my home," Marian said. "Don't let them move me."

"We'll do all we can, Marian," I promised. A joyful tranquillity settled around us in the dark.

Marian lived for several more months. Sisters took the daytime turns in four-hour shifts. New friends from hospice helped. At night, college students home for the summer kept her company, watched over her, and brought their boyfriends for her approval. We were all blessed by our time with Sister Kellner. In the last two weeks of her life, Marian's condition required professional care, and she was moved to a hospice facility. The day before Marian passed away, her friend Wilma visited. Marian told Wilma that her husband, Hank, had come to get her, but she'd told him she had someone she had to see before she could leave. "Marian," Wilma gently chided, "the next time your Hank comes, you just go."

The next day, Marian's younger sister, whom she had not seen in years, came to visit. A few hours later, Marian slipped away in her sleep, a conscience at peace.

SIN AND JOY

So far, we have learned that joy is an intimation of God's love, an echo of His glory, a whisper of His goodness, a reflection of a conscience at peace. All these are, I think, manifestations of "the enticings of the Holy Spirit"—glimpses of the divine, always pointing to something beyond, something, as C. S. Lewis says "other and outer."[6] Joy helps lift us outside the natural man and point us toward "becom[ing] a saint through the atonement of Christ the Lord" (Mosiah 3:19).

That scripture brings us back to King Benjamin's great address. Let's consider the context of this beautiful and moving passage from Mosiah 4:3: "The Spirit of the Lord came upon them, and they were filled with joy." King Benjamin, having been commanded by an angel, has been teaching these good, obedient people the plan of salvation, the plan of happiness. He lays it out clearly. God, our Father, created us "from the beginning" and "preserv[es] [us] from day to day, by lending [us] breath, that [we] may live and move and do according to [our] own will, and even supporting [us] from one moment to another" (Mosiah 2:21). We depend on Him for everything. We owe to Him all that we have and are.

But, as natural men, we estrange ourselves from Him. King Benjamin's words are: "If ye should transgress . . . , ye do withdraw yourselves from the Spirit of the Lord, that it may have no place in you to guide you in wisdom's paths" (Mosiah 2:36). He warns them that they must obey the Holy Spirit that they may not transgress the law of God contrary to their own knowledge (see Mosiah 2:33). We cannot be happy in sin, yet as natural men we cannot help but be sinners.

For those who die without repenting, "the demands of divine justice do awaken his immortal soul to a lively sense of his own guilt, which doth cause him to shrink from the presence of the Lord, and doth fill his breast with guilt, and pain, and anguish, which is like an unquenchable fire, whose flame ascendeth up forever and ever" (Mosiah 2:38).

But, King Benjamin explains, there is a way out of this terrible predicament. "Jesus Christ, the Son of God, the Father of heaven and earth, the Creator of all things from the beginning . . . [shall come] unto his own, that salvation might come unto the children of men even through faith on his name" (Mosiah 3:8–9). These indeed are "glad tidings of great joy" (Mosiah 3:3).

Through King Benjamin's careful teaching, his people come to see themselves in a new, not very favorable, light. "The fear of the Lord had come upon them. . . . They had viewed themselves in their own carnal state, even less than the dust of the earth" (Mosiah 4:1–2). That wasn't what we would call a high self-esteem moment. "And they all cried aloud with one voice, saying: O have mercy, and apply the atoning blood of Christ that we may receive forgiveness of our sins, and our hearts may be purified; for we believe in Jesus Christ, the Son of God, who created heaven and earth, and all things; who shall come down among the children of men." What happens next is truly a miracle, a gift. "And . . . after they had spoken these words *the Spirit of the Lord came upon them, and they were filled with joy,* having received a remission of their sins, and having peace of conscience, because of the exceeding faith which they had in Jesus Christ who should come" (Mosiah 4:2–3; emphasis added).

The key insight for me in this passage, and probably the most important discovery I made while studying this topic, is that the good people of King Benjamin did not find joy by seeking it. They found joy by seeking forgiveness, by seeking the Savior. To attain joy they had to have a deeper understanding of their relationship to Heavenly Father than is celebrated in the sweet song of innocence, "I am a Child of God."[7] They needed also to acknowledge their unworthiness before Him and their great need of His mercy.

Paradoxically, sin and joy are related. Of course, we understand that "wickedness never was happiness" (Alma 41:10), but to be filled with joy we must also come to understand that we are all sinners. Even those who have "no more disposition to do evil," sin in ways we hardly understand (Mosiah 5:2). We are preoccupied when our children need us. We are impatient with an imperfect spouse. We harbor unkind feelings toward a neighbor. We fail to forgive an offense. We judge another, or ourselves, harshly. We live our lives inwardly or frantically, not seeing or easing the pain and loneliness of those around us. We are ungrateful and fail to acknowledge His hand in all things. We are proud or short-tempered or uncharitable.

These failings may seem like little things, but the best of us have caused pain we cannot ourselves heal. A wise friend of mine once said, "If gossip (or pettiness or criticizing church leaders) smelled like tobacco smoke, how many of us would be embarrassed even to come to church?" In Anton Chekov's play *Uncle Vanya*, Elena says, "Ivan Petrovich, you are an educated, intelligent man, and I should think you would understand that the world is being destroyed not by crime and fire, but by . . . all these petty squabbles."[8] These kinds of sins and sorrows certainly make the Savior weep.

We need the Lord not just to "lead [us], guide [us], and walk beside

[us]" but to free us, change us, purify us, forgive our many sins.⁹ A friend
who teaches a Book of Mormon class at Brigham Young University asks
his students every semester to consider which song is more central to
the doctrine of the Church, the Primary song "I am a Child of God"
we all so love to sing because it makes us feel loved and purposeful, or
the powerful hymn "I Stand All Amazed." Certainly both speak to
important gospel principles. Alma teaches that when we come to know
Christ's mercy and long suffering toward us, once we realize that he has
broken the bonds of death and the chains that encircle our hearts, we
will feel to "sing the song of redeeming love" (Alma 5:26). "I Stand All
Amazed" is just such a song.¹⁰

> I stand all amazed at the love Jesus offers me,
> Confused at the grace that so fully he proffers me.
> I tremble to know that for me he was crucified,
> That for me, a sinner, he suffered, he bled, and died.
> . . . . . .
> I marvel that he should descend from his throne divine
> To rescue a soul so rebellious and proud as mine,
> That he should extend his great love unto such as I,
> Sufficient to own, to redeem, and to justify.
> Oh, it is wonderful that he should care for me
> Enough to die for me!
> Oh, it is wonderful, wonderful to me!

He has paid dearly for our souls. Through His plan of redemption
we are saved by His infinite sacrifice when we sincerely accept it. So
here is the final word in my crossword puzzle—the one word that
makes the turning of our sorrows to joy possible: *Atonement*. Christ's
Atonement makes possible our encounters with joy in this life and a
fullness of joy in the next. "It is by grace that we are saved, after all we
can do" (2 Nephi 25:23). Only in Him is our joy is full.

Therefore, if we want joy, we will find it not by seeking to recreate
some sensation, however wonderful, we have felt before. We find it by
seeking Him of whom joy itself testifies, our Savior, Jesus Christ. We

find it by serving Him and expressing gratitude for all He has done for us. Joy cannot be manufactured or controlled. Joy is a gift. It is a form of the "enticings of the Spirit," an echo of God's glory, a whisper of goodness, an intimation of His love. It comes in fullness with the peace of conscience that accompanies the remission of sin.

I am grateful for parents who live life joyously, for a husband whose love and support are an echo of something divine, for sons who are growing into honorable men, for the glories of creation, for holiness in all things, for chances to learn and serve. And most especially for the sacrifice of our Savior which, if we repent and call upon His name, can turn even our weaknesses to strengths, our sorrows to joy.

Notes

1. See, for example, 2 Nephi 2:11–15.
2. C. S. Lewis, *Surprised by Joy* (New York: Harcourt Brace Jovanovich, 1956), 72.
3. Lewis, *Surprised by Joy*, 78.
4. Lewis, *Surprised by Joy*, 179.
5. Lewis, *Surprised by Joy*, 167.
6. Lewis, *Surprised by Joy*, 168, 238.
7. "I Am a Child of God," *Hymns of The Church of Jesus Christ of Latter-day Saints* (Salt Lake City: The Church of Jesus Christ of Latter-day Saints, 1985), no. 301; see also William Blake, *Songs of Innocence and Experience* (New Rochelle: Peter Pauper Press, 1935).
8. As cited in Gary Saul Morson, "Prosaics: an Approach to the Humanities," *The American Scholar*, Fall 1989, 523.
9. "I Am a Child of God," *Hymns*, no. 301.
10. "I Stand All Amazed," *Hymns*, no. 193.

"A Time to Laugh"

❧

Louise Plummer

When I lived in St. Paul, Minnesota, my good friend Lanay called on the phone and made this request. "Teach me how to have fun," she said. "I don't know how to have fun."

"You don't know how to have fun?" I asked. Lanay was my friend; I thought she was plenty fun. Besides, who didn't know how to have fun?

Lanay was adamant. "I was raised to be serious and hardworking, and I don't know how to have fun."

"You mean, you want me to plan a fun activity of some kind?" I asked.

"Yes," she said. "I need to learn to have fun."

Like a dope I said, "Okay."

It took me a few days to come up with something unusual . . . and fun. I decided we should rent roller skates and skate around Lake of the Isles in Minneapolis on Saturday morning. The lake had a smooth, concrete path that ran the three miles of its circumference. It was a picturesque lake with elms and stately mansions surrounding it, all of which appealed to my aesthetic senses. The fun part would be for a bunch of us in our forties to don skates for the first time since

Louise Roos Plummer, a talented creative writer and conference speaker, received her master's degree in English from the University of Minnesota. She teaches writing classes as an associate professor of English at Brigham Young University. She has published four young adult novels and a book of essays as well as numerous stories and articles with Young Miss, Lake Street Review, New Era, and Ensign. She has served in all the auxiliaries, taught seminary, and been "the story lady" in Primary. She and her husband, Tom Plummer, are the parents of four boys.

childhood and try to make it upright around the lake on little metal wheels. It made me snigger just to think about it.

Lanay liked the idea, so she and her husband and my husband and our friend Jane drove on down on a spectacular spring day. We rented the skates, put them on, and stood up, arms flailing for balance. There was lots of laughing. *This is fun*, I thought with a swell of self-congratulation. *Really fun*.

When Lanay stood for the first time alone on those skates, she teetered back and forth and dropped awkwardly on her tush. Did I laugh, I wonder now? I probably wanted to and may have snorted involuntarily. A splat like that is the bread and butter of physical comedy.

"Are you all right?" we asked.

She was up on her feet in an instant. "Fine," she said smiling.

"You're sure?"

"I'm ready," she said. And so off we all skated, heads bent, not having an idea of how to stop except to roll into the grass. I'm sure I laughed a good deal. Laughing comes easily for a fun person like me. We all felt very smug when we finished the whole three miles. Olympic gold for everyone.

Later that afternoon, Lanay called and invited us over to watch a video. Tom and I walked down the street to their house. Lanay greeted us at the door with a big cast on her arm.

"What's this?" I asked.

"You know, when I fell down?"

"Yeah."

"I broke my wrist."

My jaw dropped. "Didn't it hurt?" I asked.

"A little. But I just held it while I was skating." So there you are. Lanay went at having fun the same way she did everything else— responsibly, reliably, seriously, and completely. She was going to have fun if it killed her.

For this reason I am a little hesitant to advise anyone on how to have more humor in life. Humor, like fun, can be dangerous. I don't want to break any wrists.

The ability to see what is comical or funny makes us laugh even in times of stress. It makes us work better together, frees us to be more creative, pulls us up, and lightens our burdens. We make humor with meaning, with movement and gesture, and by combining odd associations. Humor is a kind of dissonance. Jonathan Swift said, "Humor is odd, grotesque, and wild."[1] It can be all those things. It can also be insensitive, malicious, exclusive, and sarcastic. It can ridicule, slander, and belittle. But we're not going to go there. Whether humor is healing or hurting may depend on the presenter of the humor (in this case, me), the reader (you), and the situation. Will I be appropriate? Will you choose to be open, or will you be easily offended? We may not all agree.

At one end of the spectrum, I have met people who see any kind of humor as "light mindedness" and a blow against virtue. At the other end are people who laugh and giggle at everything and have no conscious sense of the underlying pain that permeates all of our lives. Ogden Nash said it best in this verse:

> In this foolish world there is nothing more numerous
> Than different people's senses of humorous.[2]

But you aren't reading this to discover my theories on humor. You are reading, I think, with the hope that I will actually *be* humorous.

The safest humor in the world is self-deprecating humor. So I am going to share some stories from my own life, using myself and close family members as grist. Writers are notorious for cannibalizing their own families, and I am no different.

I've been married for thirty-nine years to Tom Plummer, and it has been only recently that I've realized we have irreconcilable differences. The first one, and the most serious, has to do with bedtime, where we each sleep, and the television. It sounds like three items, but they are all part of the same problem. Tom likes to go to bed between ten and eleven, and more important, he wants to go to sleep. I like to go to bed between ten and eleven as well, but I don't want to go to sleep. I want to watch television until I am actually sleepy. This might take several hours.

We have worked it out that the TV is turned off at eleven o'clock on the nights before a workday since we need to be up early on those mornings. I can then watch *As Time Goes By* or *One Foot in the Grave*, my favorite TV show on channel 7 at 10:30. Tom is sometimes awake for it, but more often than not he dozes through it. Irreconcilable differences occur on nights when we have no reason to get up early in the morning. On these nights, I want to watch television until 1 A.M. Sometimes Tom is asleep and doesn't know that I'm still watching, but often he goes to sleep only to wake up to the television and then is unable to go back to sleep. He doesn't like this. When we are being reasonable, he'll say to me, "If you want to watch television, I'll go sleep in the other room."

Or I might say, "I want to watch television so I'll stay down here in the family room and come up later." Both of these solutions work.

The problem is that we are not always reasonable. Sometimes we are both too tired to give anything to the other, and we each want our way. This happened on a Thursday night not long ago. We came home late from work and fell into bed at 9 o'clock. Tom played backgammon on his laptop; I watched television. Perfect. Then he says in a voice that has a slightly whiney cast to it, "Are you going to watch television much longer because I'm really tired?"

And I say, in an annoying voice, "Why don't you go in the other room then?"

And he says, "I don't want to go in the other room. Why don't you go downstairs?"

And I say, "I don't want to go downstairs. I want to be in my beddie."

"Well then," he says, "Can you just turn it down a little? It's shattering my ear drums."

"If I turn it down," I say, "then I can't hear it. What's the point in having it on if I can't hear it?"

"Turn it down," Tom says.

I turn it down a notch or two, and he turns over and falls asleep. I see action, I see lips moving, but I hear one in four words. So I turn up the sound a notch or two. Tom sleeps for an hour and wakes up. "What time is it?" he asks.

"12:15," I say.

He makes a huffing and puffing noise, gets up and goes to the bathroom, gets back into bed still huffing and puffing, and turns away from me with the blanket covering his ears. "Turn it down," he says.

"No," I say.

We now hate each other's guts. I don't care if we have been married thirty-nine years and share four wonderful sons. I don't care if I've known him since he was a deacon passing the sacrament in the Emigration Ward. I don't care if he still likes to dance with me. I'm sixty years old, and I'm tired of needing permission to watch TV like a twelve-year-old. I want to do what I want to do. He feels exactly the same way. Do we duke it out at 12:15?

Never.

He lies awake and I turn the TV off after a while. We go to sleep—mad. We learned years ago to go to sleep with our anger. Talking about irreconcilable difference when you're both tired turns a silly disagreement into an unrecognizable, mutant conflict. It's easier to talk in the morning.

Will this ever happen again? Yes, I believe it will. I like late night television and he doesn't. Most nights we can handle it, but I'm pretty sure there will be another night when like a couple of two-year-olds we will each want our own way and neither one of us will be willing to budge.

We did buy two pairs of earphones that will plug into our laptops. So I can watch a movie sitting in the dark with surround sound; Tom can go to sleep. Unfortunately, the first movie I watched was *Signs*, about an alien invasion. I was fine until near the end, when we think the aliens have disappeared, and the family comes out of hiding, out of the basement, and then we see an alien reflected in the television, and

I screamed when I saw it. Tom woke up mad as a bear. I apologized quickly, enthusiastically, so I could see the end of the movie.

Perhaps the oddest night was when we sat in bed, each of us with a laptop and earphones, watching two different movies. This, then, is the mature marriage.

The second irreconcilable difference has to do with our height. Tom is five-ten and I am five-nine-and-a-half. This was a problem for him when we first began dating. He would look in a plate glass window as we walked together downtown, trying to assess whether I was taller than he was. I was a skinny girl, and I didn't think it mattered. Now I am an older, fatter girl, and I feel big—too big.

Actually I prefer to blame Tom—he is too short. I can see it would have been better to have been married to a tall man who makes me feel petite and feminine. Tom can do nothing about this and we have so much in common otherwise that I have pretty much stuffed down this shortcoming of his. But it was brought to my attention recently when we bought a little book called *The Art of Kissing* by Hugh Morris, first printed in 1936. I realized what a serious problem our equal height was when I read the following under the heading, "Kisses Are But a Prelude to Love."

"Man and woman are born to love, marry, and beget children. Woman is so physically constituted that she is the one who bears the child. Man, on the other hand, is given the duty of being the protector of his wife, and after they are born, of his children. Therefore, he must always be the one who takes the initiative. He must be strong. He must be willing. He must be physically able to take care of his charges. He must be the aggressor. It is therefore necessary that the man be taller than the woman.

"The psychological reason for this is that he must always give the impression of being his woman's superior, both mentally and especially physically. The physical reason with which we are more concerned is that if he is taller than his woman, he is better able to kiss her. He must be able to sweep her into his strong arms and tower over her, and look down into her eyes, and cup her chin in his fingers, and then bend over her face and plant his eager, virile lips on her moist, slightly parted, inviting ones. All of this he must do with the vigor of an assertive male. And all of these are impossible when the woman is taller [or equal heights] to the man. For when the situation is reversed, the kiss becomes only a ludicrous banality. The physical mastery is gone. The male prerogative is gone. Everything is gone but the fact that two lips are touching two other lips. Nothing can be more disappointing."[3]

Now Tom stands on a stair when we kiss. And Mr. Morris is absolutely right. Kissing is better when he towers over me and plants his eager, virile lips on my moist, slightly parted ones.

"In heaven you will be six-three," I tell him. "You will be perfect."

"Or," Tom says, "you'll be five-three. You'll be perfect."

In either case, in heaven we will be perfect.

For this next story you need to know that my mother is in the last stages of Alzheimer's. Is this funny? No. It's grim. But even this terrible disease has given our family some laughs, and I look forward to the time when she gets her memory back and can laugh with us, because she surely will.

Forty-some odd years ago when I was a teenager, I made extra pocket money by baby-sitting. One young couple with a new baby hired me on an almost weekly basis. They were not Mormons. I knew this because my mother was an ad hoc membership clerk of our ward, and they were not on her list. Even more telling was a pack of Salem filtered menthol cigarettes in front of the toaster in the kitchen. They had no television, but they did have a wall of bookcases filled with the latest novels. This was better than TV. And if I got tired of reading, I pulled out a Strathmore premium sketchpad I had brought along and drew long leggy women in beautiful clothes. And if I tired of that, well, then there was always the bathroom mirror.

Theirs covered the whole upper half of a wall. It was nothing like that little medicine cabinet mirror that we had in our bathroom at home, which had to be shared with nine other people. This mirror was a stage for great performances. I made all my faces in it—the haughty face, the laughing face, the sexy face, the distraught face. I strutted, primped, pranced, minced, and tap danced in front of that mirror. I sang, "Saint Louie woman with your diamond ring," in a sultry, alto voice. I was a star.

One night I decided to have a smoke in front of the mirror. I pulled one of the Salems out of its pack, my fingers fluttering nervously. I had never smoked before. I was not planning to be a smoker, but on this one night I wanted to be Bette Davis for five minutes. I lit up in front of the mirror, raised my eyebrows, looked down my nose, and inhaled. It was then that I remembered a talk that I'd heard in sacrament meeting. It was about a woman who was traveling in Asia and had been in a devastating automobile accident. Her injuries were massive, and she needed thoracic surgery. The surgeon asked her if she smoked. "No," she said.

"I need to know if you have ever smoked even one cigarette, because if you have, I cannot perform the surgery." The woman had never smoked even one cigarette and because she hadn't, her life was spared.

I blew smoke through my nose. Too late. If I was ever in a car accident in Asia, it would be the end of me.

I was a grand Bette Davis saying, "But dahling, you're being absurd," while holding the cigarette at what I thought was an elegant angle.

The next morning I confessed to my mother. "I tried smoking last night," I said. I sat in my nightgown at the kitchen table while she cleaned up the breakfast dishes. I told her how I had watched myself in the mirror.

Mother never overreacted. "Well," she asked, "did you like it?"

"I liked holding the cigarette," I said. "I don't know if I actually like smoking all that much."

"I tried smoking once," Mother said.

I perked up. "You did?" Suddenly it wasn't all about me. Mother had taken center stage.

She nodded. "I worked as a maid for the mayor of Nieuwersluis. They had ladies' cigarettes in silver dishes. They were long and thin and colored light pink and green. I took a couple home with me and smoked them as I rode my bike back to Breukelen."

I had seen pictures of my mother in her maid uniform, a crisp full apron over a dark dress, and I pictured her on her bike with two pastel cigarettes in her mouth at the same time. I laughed. "You smoked!" We were co-conspirators now. "Did you like it?"

She shrugged. "I just wanted to try it."

It was a gift, her sharing her own smoking story. I thought she was thoroughly generous. I thought she was an amazing mother, not like other mothers at all. Not like mothers who might have said, "Louise, how could you!" or "You're never baby-sitting for them again!" or "We'll have to talk with your father about this." No, it was a bonding moment between mother and daughter. It has always been one of my favorite stories of her. In fact, I reminded my mother of this about seven years ago. She and my dad were at our house for Sunday dinner, and I was retelling the whole story, my point being how generous she had been. I can still see my mother, her hair now white, sitting on my sofa.

"I never smoked," she said. Her indignant reply almost knocked me down.

At the same time my father said, "Your mother has never smoked in her life!"

"You did! Don't you remember the pastel cigarettes? You smoked them on the bicycle on the way home?"

Mother was genuinely shocked. "I never did!"

"Your mother never smoked. You made it up," my father said.

This is what anyone in my family uses as a stock answer to anything I say that they don't want to believe: "You made it up. That's what you do. You make up things." How could I make up pastel lady cigarettes? Even I couldn't make that up.

"I never smoked," my mother said. "Never."

"She would never smoke," my father said.

Tom, my husband, yelled from the kitchen, "Give it up, Louise."

Memory is wily. It hides in the dark and rises to the surface with a smell or a taste of a cookie dipped in milk, a turn of phrase, a melodic line of a Gershwin tune. Where did it come from and who can distinguish it from imagination, which also surfaces, mixed with old photos and faded, pressed flowers. In my heart I know my mother told me that story, and she never told my father. I could not make up pastel cigarettes.

On the other hand, shouldn't I be thrilled if I *did* make up pastel cigarettes? If I invented them deep out of my core where imagination dwells? Ladies' pastel cigarettes. Wouldn't that be a significant sign of my genius? It might be best, as Anthony Hope writes, "to aim at being intelligible."[4] Now that my mother is loony with Alzheimer's, I feel loony too, almost unintelligible.

One Sunday evening a couple of years ago, my father called to say that Mother was sitting on the kitchen floor and couldn't get up. He suffered a degenerative disease and was not strong enough to help her. "She's acting funny," he said.

We were baby-sitting our grandchildren, so Tom drove over to help. He called to tell me that Mother seemed unusually disoriented and physically weak. "She can hardly walk," he said. "I'm taking her to the hospital. I'm afraid she's had a stroke. She also has a bad cough. Maybe it's pneumonia."

Later he called again. "They've done a head scan and a chest x-ray and taken blood, but they can't find anything. She can hardly sit up, and she's very disoriented." He stopped for breath. "This strange thing happened. I was sitting next to the gurney where she was lying, and she looked at me and said, 'No, no one deserves to be abused.'"

"Mother said that?" I was surprised, not only by the content but by the fact that she could even conceive of such a sentence.

"Yes," Tom said, "and I said to her, 'No one deserves to be abused, especially someone as nice as you.' She just lay there for ten more minutes. Then she turned to me and said it again, 'No, no one deserves to be abused.'"

"Oh, my gosh, do you think someone abused her?" My mind filled with ugly visions of abuse that might suddenly become part of our family's history. *Please don't let it be true,* I prayed silently.

Tom broke into my thoughts, "Well, I asked her if anyone had abused her."

"What did she say?"

"She shook her head," Tom said, "and then I said, 'Well, why are you saying, "No one deserves to be abused"?'"

"And?" I interrupted.

He chuckled. "She pointed at the wall behind my head," he said, "and there was a sign that read, 'No one deserves to be abused.'"

The next day, my sister Judy was startled to see Mother so changed and took her right back to the hospital. She spent all afternoon there, and just like the day before, the emergency staff could not find anything wrong other than the already diagnosed Alzheimer's. That same Monday night, after the two emergency room visits, my father discovered that the Robitussin bottle that someone had bought for my mother's cough a couple of days before was empty. It wasn't hard to figure out that my mother had taken a swig of cough syrup every time she coughed, since she obviously couldn't remember how often she had medicated herself. Mother had been drunk as a skunk. She was drunk as a fiddler, drunk as a lord, drunk as an owl.

My son said, "Grandma Roboed."

Humor releases us, however briefly, from our deepest fears and shame. It is a collision of what we desire with what we get. If you don't get the joke, if everyone around you laughs but you sit mystified, don't worry about it. I think it's like spelling: you either know how to spell or you don't. You either have a sense of humor or you don't. Don't worry about it for three seconds. In the hereafter, we'll all be perfect.

Notes

1. Jonathan Swift, 1718.
2. Ogden Nash, "Very Funny, Very Funny," available at www.humboldt.edu/~etg3/OgdenNash.html; accessed 30 October 2003.
3. Hugh Morris, *The Art of Kissing* (1936; reprint, Garden City, N.Y.: Dolphin Books, 1977).

4. Anthony Hope, quoted in Robert Andrews, Mary Biggs, and Michael Seide et al., *The Columbia World of Quotations* (New York: Columbia Press, 1996), no. 28904.

FEASTING UPON THE WORD

✣

Susan Griffith

I am not a scriptorian, though I'm working on it, and I do not have the most regular scripture study habits. *But* when I read the phrase "feasting upon the word," I take heart. Feasting is something I know about! In fact, I am somewhat of an expert at feasting.

Nephi tells us in 2 Nephi 32:3 to "feast upon the words of Christ." Jacob instructs us to "receive the pleasing word of God, and feast upon his love; for ye may, if your minds are firm, forever" (Jacob 3:2). Nephi also pleads, "Come unto the Holy One of Israel, and feast upon that which perisheth not, neither can be corrupted, and let your soul delight in fatness" (2 Nephi 9:51). That last beautiful phrase was borrowed by Nephi from Isaiah.

The words *feast* and *feasting* must have raised all sorts of images to Nephi's original audience. The Lord connected the celebration of feasts to spiritual values. Feasts in the Old Testament, and, therefore, for the people in the Book of Mormon, were more than just times to eat huge quantities of good food; they were times of spiritual renewal, confession of sin, reconciliation with God, acknowledgment of God as the Provider, and gratitude and joy for His love. These feasts had various names: the Feast of Unleavened Bread, or Passover; the Feast of Weeks; the Feast of Tabernacles; the Day of Blowing of Trumpets; the Day of

---

Susan Griffith, a convert, serves as a Gospel Doctrine teacher in her ward. She taught early-morning seminary for four years, taking her three preschool children with her. She recently returned to school after twenty-five years and is majoring in family history. She and her husband, Tom, are the parents of six children.

Atonement; and the Feast of Purim. All used an earthly expression of celebration—that is, feasting—to express religious joy.

The Savior himself used this symbol when He instituted the sacrament at the Last Supper, which was the Feast of the Passover. He instructed His disciples to eat and drink in remembrance of His body and blood. In 1831 the Lord described the Restoration as the preparing of "a feast of fat things . . . unto which all nations shall be invited" and will come and "partake of the supper of the Lord" (D&C 58:6–11).

Obviously, not all of these scriptures pertain directly to scripture study; they are describing the process of coming to Christ. Scripture study is one of the ways that we can do that. So let's go back to Nephi's injunction to "feast upon the word." Eating is a basic need; without food we will eventually die, and if we skip just one meal, our stomachs can start to hurt. This process can also be true of scripture study; it feeds our souls, and without it our souls can die. If we go too long without reading the scriptures, our souls start to hurt.

But eating is more than just a basic need. It is also a pleasure. The Lord created a world where there is delicious food in abundance, as well as people with bodies that can appreciate the multitude of incredible flavors. The abundance of truths in our scriptures is delicious to our souls, which were created in such a way that we hunger for truths and receive pleasure by partaking of them. And here is one instance where we *can* delight in fatness, because this kind of fatness is healthy for our souls. Spiritual obesity is a goal we can all strive for!

A few months ago, my husband and I went to an elegant buffet in a fine restaurant. This was a feast of feasts—the food so good it made you sad that you had just one stomach. I have developed some rules to maximize my experience at sumptuous buffets like that. First, I select items that I know I like, but I also try to be a little adventurous, trying something new. Translating this to our scriptural experiences, read 3 Nephi all you want, but try to nibble on Isaiah every once in awhile. You may find that it, too, will fill your soul and satisfy you in new ways.

Another rule that I have at buffets is to eat slowly. No gulping is allowed, and I try to savor every bite. When applied to the scriptures, gulping is reading just to get through the pages as quickly as possible. How do we slow down and savor every bite?

There is certainly value in reading the scriptures straight through, as one would read a work of fiction for pleasure. You get a feel for the flow of events and recognize patterns that you may not recognize when you read more slowly. For the most part, however, I prefer to read the scriptures slowly and carefully. A friend of mine reads one or two verses a day and then spends the remainder of his devotional time writing in his journal the thoughts that come to him, both as to the meaning of the scripture and its application to his life. He has filled volumes with the things he has learned from the scriptures.

Another way to savor every bite is to ask questions. Before you swallow and go on to the next bite, ask yourself, "Why did the author feel this was important to mention?" "Why did he select the words he used, and what do they mean to me today?" "What is the principle being taught here?" One of the first things I noticed and appreciated about the Book of Mormon was the way that it often follows a story with the words, "Thus we see that . . ." After struggling with stories in the Bible, particularly in the Old Testament, which seemed strange, with no easily recognizable moral or principle behind them, it was very refreshing to have the lesson pointed out to me by the author. If the author doesn't do it for us, we need to do it for ourselves. A very useful exercise after reading a scriptural passage is to write your own, "Thus we see that . . ." It will help in answering the question, "What is the principle being taught here?"

The more I read the scriptures, the more I am convinced that the Lord loves symbols, and if we are to savor the scriptures, we need to be comfortable playing with symbols. Parables are obviously symbolic, as are metaphors ("I am the light of the world"). But symbols are found throughout the scriptures (even in real-life stories or the names of prophets) that require us to dig more deeply to understand.

I will never forget one experience I had teaching seminary. A passage of scripture in the next day's lesson was fairly straightforward. After feeding the five thousand, Jesus withdrew to a mountain to pray and sent His disciples across the Sea of Galilee to wait for Him on the other side. While they were crossing, a fierce storm arose and tossed their ship around. In the midst of the storm, the disciples saw Jesus walking on the water. At first they were frightened, not knowing who it was, but Jesus said, "It is I; be not afraid" (Matthew 14:27). The account in Matthew then records that Peter attempted to walk on the water (Matthew 14:22–33); the accounts in Mark and John simply say that Jesus entered the boat and the sea was immediately calm (Mark 6:46–51; John 6:17–21). In fact, John says that when Jesus entered the ship, they immediately reached the land on the other side.

Now, this is a simple passage of scripture about one of the many miracles that Jesus performed. And yet, something was bothering me; I knew I was missing something that I needed to teach the next day. I thought and thought about it and got nowhere. Finally, I started to think symbolically about the event. What if we are the disciples, and the journey across the sea is a symbol of our journey in life? We start our journey and, in the middle of it, we run into major problems, problems that could potentially be fatal (as life would be fatal for all of us without the Savior.) Jesus was in the mountains praying; symbolically He was with Heavenly Father. Because we needed Him, He came down from the mountain (perhaps the condescension of His birth) and walked across the water to reach us. As soon as the disciples willingly received Him into the ship (a symbol of us allowing Him to enter our lives and accompany us on our mortal journey), they immediately reached the other side (symbolic of successfully completing the journey.) This wasn't just a story of the disciples' travel adventures; this was a parable of the plan of salvation—in six verses! I was blown away.

Since that experience, I have tried to look for symbols and pick the text apart to see if I have missed another layer of meaning. No matter how many times we have read a scripture or how often we have heard the same lesson on the same topic, we can always find more.

Another way to savor the scriptures is to have a theme in mind as we read, such as faith, family, obedience, service—the possibilities are endless. One topic surpasses all others in importance, the atonement of our beloved Savior. Elder Boyd K. Packer said, "This truth [that is, the Atonement] is the very root of Christian doctrine. You may know much about the gospel as it branches out from there, but if you only know the branches and those branches do not touch that root, if they have been cut free from that truth, there will be no life nor substance nor redemption in them."[1] If we cut our scripture study from the truth of the Atonement, what we learn will hold neither life nor substance nor redemption. These connections will fill us; without them we will come away hungry.

In my ward, I teach a Gospel Doctrine class, and Elder Packer's quotation has sobered me. Am I handing out living branches or dead sticks? So at the beginning of the year, we started something new. At the end of each lesson, we discuss three questions: What does this scripture passage teach us about Heavenly Father and His Son, Jesus Christ? What does it teach us of the Atonement? How does this affect or change my life? If we cannot answer these questions after reading a passage of scripture, then we have missed the mark. These questions, I believe, are the key to filling our scripture study with life, substance, and redemption. I know it has made a great difference in my own personal scripture study.

I would like to mention three scriptures that have touched me deeply, even changed my life. I am a convert to the Church. When I was in high school, I received a testimony that Jesus was the Christ, but I was no longer happy in the church in which I had been raised. I started to visit different churches, searching for one where my knowledge of and love for the Savior could grow. I started dating a young man who was a member of the LDS Church, and he invited me to attend sacrament meeting with him. Since I was searching, I readily accepted.

At that first Church meeting, I had every reason to feel uncomfortable. I was not dressed like everyone else. (Do you remember the debut of mini-skirts?) The meeting was very noisy with lots of children, an experience foreign to me. I was put off by the use of a microphone. (Though admittedly, the presence of the children made it mandatory if one was to hear anything!) In short, things were new and unfamiliar. Yet, I felt strangely at home, warm and good. I had not yet learned to identify this feeling as the Holy Ghost. Still, I walked away from that meeting feeling in my heart that this was where I belonged.

My mind was still skeptical, though. I was invited to have the discussions, and I eagerly accepted. I truly wanted to know more. There again, things new and unfamiliar troubled me. The idea of angels speaking to men in modern day disturbed me. (In my defense, this was before the time of *Touched by an Angel*.) The story about gold plates sounded farfetched. And the idea that a man today was considered to be a prophet was downright scary.

I continued to pray and read the Bible, feeling torn between my mind and my heart. Then one day, I was reading the Sermon on the Mount in Matthew. I had read this sermon many times; I was very familiar with it (or so I thought), and I was reading it more for comfort in the midst of my confusion than for direction. But on this day, a scripture I had often read jumped out at me: "Beware of false prophets, which come to you in sheep's clothing, but inwardly they are ravening wolves" (Matthew 7:15). A black feeling came over me—could this be a warning for me? I put down the Bible and started to ask questions. Why did the Lord include this warning? Why did He use these words? If what I had been taught from childhood was correct, that is, if there were no more prophets after Christ, why didn't He just say, "Don't follow anyone after me, because I will send you no more prophets"? But He didn't say that; He just said beware of the false ones. The more I thought about it, the more I saw that, in this warning, He was actually affirming that there would be prophets after Him, good and bad. I continued to read: "Ye shall know them by their fruits. . . . Every good tree bringeth forth good fruit; but a corrupt tree bringeth forth evil fruit" (vv. 16–17). Not only did this confirm to me that there would be good prophets sent but it also told me how I could tell the good from the bad—by their fruits. I had immediately sensed the joy of the Saints on my first visit to Church, and now I understood where that joy came from: it was the fruit of following a living prophet. Through reading and savoring this scripture, my mind, as well as my heart, was turned, and I was soon baptized. Obviously this scripture changed my life irrevocably, and I am so grateful for it.

I am also grateful for Alma 7:11–12, which has deepened my appreciation for the Atonement. "And he shall go forth, suffering pains and afflictions and temptations of every kind; and this that the word might be fulfilled which saith he will take upon him the pains and the sicknesses of his people. . . . He will take upon him their infirmities, that his bowels may be filled with mercy, according to the flesh, that he may know according to the flesh how to succor his people according to their infirmities." Recently I realized that most of the effects of the Atonement on which I have focused will take place in the future: the Resurrection and the possibility of someday returning to the presence of my Heavenly Father. This scripture emphasizes how the Atonement is also helping us right now. Our Savior suffered every pain, affliction, and temptation that we have experienced or will experience. In a way I do not understand, He experienced the pain of childbirth, as well as the pain of children going astray, as well as everything else we can experience in life. He did this all for the simple reason that He wants to understand our pain so that He can help us deal with it.

We have all gone through experiences that can be understood only by those who have experienced the same anguish. When I suffered my first miscarriage, the most comforting visit I received was from a woman who had experienced two miscarriages herself and could understand my pain. We wept together. She also happened to be bouncing her healthy baby boy on her knee. What hope that gave me.

In a similar way, the Savior doesn't take the pain away from us. We still have the miscarriages; otherwise, the purpose of this life would be negated, as we would have no need for faith. Still, He understands *completely* what we are going through and weeps with us. What a difference this understanding has made in my life. I no longer feel alone with whatever pain I go through. The Atonement, here and now, is helping me deal with life. Of course, the Savior also promises us eventual "beauty for ashes" and "the oil of joy for mourning" (Isaiah 61:3), which gives me great hope—like seeing that healthy baby boy—that someday all our pain will be gone and our joy complete.

A corollary to this lesson comes when we try to follow the Savior. If one of the purposes of His pain is to care for us in our pain, so one purpose of our painful experiences must be to prepare us to take care of each other. I can think of no higher use for our suffering than to allow it to increase our understanding of and sympathy for others. By sharing in the grief of others, we become co-workers with the Savior in easing their pain. What an honor to be on the same team with the Savior.

Another remarkable scriptural passage about the Atonement is Doctrine and Covenants 19:16–19, a first-person account given in our day of the pain the Savior suffered. He tells us how He trembled because of pain, bled from every pore, and suffered both body and spirit. Several years ago, while reading this passage that I had read many times before and had memorized while teaching Seminary, a word jumped out at me. Verse 19 says, "Nevertheless, glory be to the Father, and I partook and finished my preparations unto the children of men." *Preparations*. Why did the Savior refer to the Atonement as His "preparations"? If I were to create a timeline of the Savior's life, there would be His premortal existence, His birth, His life and ministry, and then the main event: the Atonement. Of course, He still leads His Church today, but, certainly, the main event was the Atonement. And yet, this one word taught me that the Savior did not see it this way. He saw the Atonement as a preparation. If the Atonement was His preparation, then what is the main event? I thought about this long and hard and came to a wonderful conclusion: the main event for the Savior is bringing to pass our immortality and eternal life (see Moses 1:39). That is His work. The Atonement opened the gate to immortality and eternal life (the preparation); the main event, however, occurs as each of us come forward one by one to touch His side and feel the prints in His hands and feet (see 3 Nephi 11:15). He then takes each of us by the hand and walks us through the gate. The main event is therefore still going on.

This idea was exciting to me, and I stored it in my head, but the real help came later in answer to great need. Fast forward several years, and I was at the darkest period of my life. My family was facing some heartbreaking problems, and I was questioning whether it was all worthwhile.

I had tried so hard to live the gospel and teach it to my family, and everything was turning to ashes. Why go on trying? What was the point? On my knees one night, I thought I would die from the pain. Then that scripture came to my mind with great force, as if the Savior was saying to me, "Didn't I already teach you that the main event is still going on? It is not over yet. I am working with you, and together, we will do all we can to bring each one through the gate. Trust me." Realizing that the Savior shared my concern and was working hard to solve my problems broke through my pain. I was not working alone; in fact, the Savior headed my team. The burden was lifted, and I was able to carry on. Clinging to that experience and to that hope isn't always easy; yet even recounting it now brings back the hope and solace.

May I offer two words of caution about reading the scriptures: I have gone days and even weeks of reading the scriptures without any particular insights or enlightenment. These periods of famine, I believe, are a normal part of studying the scriptures. We just need to keep plugging away, and the feast will return and be all the sweeter for the famine. The second caution is that feasts give us feelings of guilt as well as feelings of pleasure. I find it counter-productive to dwell on the guilt with thoughts like, "I haven't read the scriptures all week! I'm such a horrible person!" Much more motivating, and therefore productive, is to concentrate on the pleasure that feasting has given you in the past and will give you in the future. You will find yourself grabbing your scriptures, blowing the dust off, and closing your bedroom door for a few minutes of feasting.

So come and partake of all that the Lord has to offer us in His holy scriptures, a feast that is free, "milk and honey, without money and without price" (2 Nephi 26:25). And the best part is that it is one feast that we, as sisters, don't need to spend hours in the kitchen preparing. The only requirement is that we come to the table hungry.

Note

1. Boyd K. Packer, "The Mediator," *Ensign*, May 1977, 56.

OH, WHAT SONGS
OF THE HEART

Jeff Parkin

A few times in life, if you faithfully attend all your meetings, you will be present for a sacrament meeting that you shall never, ever forget. Some years ago, we experienced such a meeting in our student ward at the University of Southern California. In spite of (or maybe because of) our diversity as engineers, filmmakers, dentists, physicists, and lawyers, we enjoyed a Zion-like unity. It may have been Easter Sunday when a certain brother stood to give the final talk. He was attending USC's renowned music composition program, where his work was receiving some nice acclaim. In a previous Fast Sunday, his curly, bleached-blond hair pulled back in a ponytail, this skateboarding composer had described himself as "holding onto the iron rod with a bungie cord." We loved him for his honesty, exuberance, and good heart.

That day he placed a boom box on the pulpit and pressed play. We heard Bach's "Jesu, Joy of Man's Desiring." The music was gorgeous—spiritual, even. Then he pulled from his backpack another CD. When he pressed play this time, we heard Black Sabbath's "Iron Man." Yes, this truly happened in *sacrament meeting!*

Saying we were shocked nowhere near describes our reaction. In that moment, we went from the sublime to the profane, and we all felt

---

Jeff Parkin is a writer and filmmaker, with a master's degree from the University of Southern California. In addition to serving as ward choir director, he has been a counselor in a bishopric, a young men president, Elders Quorum president, and a mostly faithful home teacher. Married to Jana Winters, they are the parents of three children: Joshua, Jordan, and Jeremiah, and live in the Pasadena California Stake.

something dramatic. The entire tenor and spirit of our meeting was different. Instantly. Typically, our bishop would have leaped from his seat, stopped the meeting, and publicly disfellowshipped the brother. But, to everyone's surprise, including his own, the bishop simply sat there and let the talk continue. Later, this goodhearted brother told me that his intention had been to demonstrate the power music has to influence our spirits, but once *the* Spirit was gone, he didn't know how to bring Him back to our sacrament meeting. Later, when the bishop asked our composer what he had learned that day, he replied: "I learned what I was trying to teach."

THEN SING AGAIN IN LOFTY STRAIN

Have you ever wondered how the very same notes—eighty-eight on a piano—merely organized in different combinations and rhythms can elicit a myriad of distinct feelings and diverse responses? On a purely logical level, even the suggestion that mere sounds—noises, really—can affect our feelings is completely ludicrous. And yet we have musical styles named "the blues," "rock and roll," the "tango," the "waltz," and so on. Aren't these names simply attempts at articulating in words how the sounds makes us feel and act?

I am constantly perplexed that there are intelligent people who completely understand music's unseen, unquantifiable influence and yet—because they cannot see it—will not acknowledge or even hear the still small voice, which operates the same way.

Nearly seven years ago, after having been released as Young Men president, I was enjoying my first two days of hiatus when the bishop called to ask if he could visit with my wife and me that evening. Like many of you, I've learned that any time your spouse is invited to such a "visit," you should be very afraid. It was a warm August night when Bishop Michael Hansen arrived; we made the requisite small talk until the conversation up and died, awaiting the news. Like me, Bishop Hansen could get emotional singing "Popcorn Popping on the Apricot Tree,"[1] and so I was not surprised when tears filled his eyes. Then he announced he'd like to call me to be the ward choir director.

No tears came to *my* eyes. Frankly, I would have been less surprised to be called as the Relief Society general president, but those tears said he was absolutely serious. "Of course, Bishop," I answered, adding with the faith of Jonah, "but you do recognize that I haven't even sung in a choir since high school fifteen years ago?" He shook his head. "And that I've never directed a choir before—ever." He shrugged.

"And that there are three *professional* choir directors and an opera singer in our ward who are infinitely more qualified than I am?" He nodded.

"Oh yes," I added, "and—minor detail—that we don't even *have* a ward choir?" He smiled. And I couldn't think of any other excuses. So I said, "Hey, it's your ward."

At the sacrament meeting following my being sustained, I announced a first choir rehearsal. I then stated that I was calling in my chips, and if I had ever done a favor for anyone, I expected them to be at choir practice with us that afternoon. We had a good turnout.

Almost immediately I was inspired as to the three specific elements our choir needed to be successful: First, choir had to be fun. This meant balancing work and laughs and including everyone who wanted to join. Second, the music had to be glorious to sing; finding great selections was an unending quest, but, without exception, I was led to pieces that resonated with us as a choir, as well as with those we sang for. Third, and most important, choir had to be a spiritual, testimony-building experience, a way to both express and obtain a deeper appreciation and understanding of the gospel. After a couple of weeks, I realized we needed three tools to help achieve these goals: (a) snacks—nothing fancy, but something to tide us over; (b) baby-sitting; and (c) a president and a secretary/librarian. A weekly sign-up sheet resolved the snacks, and callings from the bishop resolved the baby-sitters and leaders.

While my conducting that first year was all elbows, my soprano range limited, and my mastery of cut time pathetic, I came to intimately grasp Elder Neal A. Maxwell's observation that "God does not begin by asking us about our ability, but only about our availability, and if we then prove our dependability, he will increase our capability!"[2]

So began a nearly seven-year odyssey of challenge, inclusion, growth, friendship, inspiration, conversion, but, more than anything, immeasurable joy. Few experiences in life compare with singing your testimony at least once a month, three times at Easter, and seven or eight times at Christmas—not to mention at stake conferences, a wedding, several baptisms, innumerable missionary farewells and homecomings, and a special stake concert thrown in for the heck of it.

We experienced a singular sense of unity and love—of Zion. Everyone who wanted to join, tone deaf or perfect pitched, new move-in or long-timer, active or less so, member or not, was not only welcomed but embraced. And each week, we eagerly sought out new singers. The fruits of this unity were both miraculous and humbling: less active members returned to church; members on the fringe found a place to fit; nonmembers felt the beauty and truth of the gospel (several were even baptized!); unendowed members went to the temple; the ward's grasp of sacred music deepened in unexpected and wonderful ways; we grew closer as a choir and more articulate in the language of the Spirit. Some brought well-developed technique and trained voices, others a will to contribute. Some brought brownies. Yet in the end, all were edified.

We learned how the combination of hard work and faith allows miracles. Countless times we rehearsed a piece with all our might but were still not ready to perform it. Then, we would discuss the nature of faith and works and would place our performance in the Lord's hands because, quite frankly, we had nowhere else to turn. I testify to you that, except for one sacrament meeting when pride got the best of us, we sang far better than we had ever practiced. Afterward, we would look at each other and know with a surety that we had been joined by a heavenly choir. Truly *knowing* that you can fall into the hands of the living God and that He will catch you is a priceless blessing (see Hebrews 10:31). Who knew we'd learn *that* in the ward choir? Such experiences have convinced me that ward choirs have measureless potential to transform lives, but they are too frequently overlooked.

How can a ward choir change lives? Listen to the words of some of our choir members recounting their experiences: "Singing in the choir has been a lifeline to me during the most difficult time of my life. I probably wouldn't have remained active in the Church nor kept my testimony if not for the fellowship and sense of belonging that was afforded me from the leadership and membership of the choir. I thank God and all those who prayed for me and wanted me in the choir for that lifeline."[3]

"I had never sung in any ward choir before and I honestly don't remember or know why I decided to join ours. I just know now that I was led by the Spirit to become part of a wonderful group of people who love the gospel and love expressing their feelings through song. Practicing the songs every week . . . lifts my heart and reinforces what I have learned that day."

"I don't read music. My voice is untrained. I have a desire to learn. These are the qualifications I had when I joined our ward choir. The music our director selects for us is not routine and challenges even those with musical training. So who am I to think that I can take part? I am a child of God who believes what it says in Ether 12:27 . . . that our weaknesses will become our strengths. I am encouraged by my choir family that I can do this. I am surrounded by beautiful, celestial voices that bring tears to my eyes and peace to my soul. Sometimes, mine has been one of those voices. I am blessed. I still don't read music. I still have a desire to learn. This is my testimony."

I could believe such statements about serving a mission. But about the *ward choir?*

Thy Spirit, Lord, Has Stirred Our Souls

When I think of those years as ward choir director, I can scarcely believe I was so lucky—so blessed—to be a participant in an extension of heaven. The simple yet stunning fact that we were bound together by sound, by music, leaves me mystified. I ponder music's power and repeat the awe-struck question of Enos after his sins and guilt were swept away, "Lord, how is it done?" (Enos 1:7). How does music work?

Why has the Lord given it to us? Why its soul-reaching beauty and transforming powers?

It is said that French filmmaker Jean Renoir, when asked why he made movies, replied that there was no other way to say what he wanted to say. He was the son of the great impressionist painter, Auguste Renoir, who believed the same thing about painting. Indeed, music is a medium that transcends words; certain ideas, feelings, concepts, emotions simply cannot be expressed any other way. In fact, words are probably the most inefficient way to communicate. Consider, after all, how the Spirit communicates. It is rarely with words.

Listen to how the Lord explained to Oliver Cowdery the way to recognize truth: "If it is right I will cause that your bosom shall burn *within you*; therefore, you shall *feel* that it is right. But if it be not right you shall have *no such feelings*." (D&C 9:8–9; emphasis added). In explaining how to receive a testimony, the Lord said: "I will tell you in your *mind* and in your *heart*, by the Holy Ghost" (D&C 8:2; emphasis added). The converse is also true, as Nephi reminded his brothers: "Ye were past feeling, that ye could not *feel* his words" (1 Nephi 17:45; emphasis added).

Because we *feel* music more than anything else, it becomes an unparalleled route to our hearts, and therefore to action. "Be filled with the Spirit," Paul wrote the Ephesians. How? By "speaking . . . in psalms and hymns and spiritual songs, singing and making melody in your heart to the Lord" (Ephesians 5:18–19). Isn't it fascinating that Paul connects being filled with the Spirit and music?

That music affects us for good or ill is no surprise. "The hellholes of Satan are always made very attractive," said Harold B. Lee. "[They feature] enticing music of the kind that appeals to the lower senses. Now, there may be good rock music—I don't know what it is—but there's damnable rock music that appeals to the lower senses of man, where the offbeat is just as vile and abrasive to human thought as it can be. We say it to you, *we plead with you to listen to the beautiful things*, if you want to be on the right side."[4]

The astounding irony of music's power for evil is this: when

Babylon falls, *its inhabitants will have no music*.[5] Yet that is typical behavior of the adversary: luring us into captivity with the very thing we shall lose once we're in his snares. I remember being fifteen or sixteen and attending a multi-stake youth dance. Appropriately, the leaders had explained Church standards to band members, who were also LDS. That night they played a very popular song. Attempting to keep within the guidelines, the band simply omitted the title word every time it came up. And soon, five hundred revved up young men and women of Zion were filling in those blanks, shouting: "Cocaine!"

LORD, I WOULD FOLLOW THEE

When I was Young Men president, one of my priests had an enormous CD collection filled with "damnable . . . music." His parents allowed him his agency. But they also studied the scriptures together, taught the difference between right and wrong, and let the power of true doctrine work on their son. In his senior year, he felt and followed the promptings of the Spirit and began developing a better relationship with his Heavenly Father. One day, this young man's mother saw him carrying stacks of CDs out to the garbage. Because this took multiple trips, she finally asked what he was doing. He explained that as he drew closer to the Lord, his desire for such music had waned. Being a practical Latter-day Saint woman, and recognizing the money gushing out her door into the trash bin, she asked, as nonchalantly as she could, "Why don't you sell these CDs and recover some cash for your mission?"

The son stopped and said, "Mom, I don't want *anybody* to listen to this music."[6]

There are righteous rock songs and evil classical compositions; genre does not determine value. We don't need lists of do's and don'ts, of approved artists, or sanctioned singers, for "it is not meet that I should command in all things," says the Lord (D&C 58:26). So despite our unlimited musical choices, choosing the good from the bad should not be difficult. Mormon reminds us that "the Spirit of Christ is given to [everyone], that [we] may know good from evil; wherefore, I show unto you the way to judge; for every thing which inviteth to do good, and to persuade to believe in Christ, is sent forth by the power and gift of Christ; wherefore ye may know with a perfect knowledge it is of God. But whatsoever thing persuadeth [you] to do evil, and believe not in Christ, and deny him, and serve not God, then [you] may know with a perfect knowledge it is of the devil . . . for he persuadeth [no one] to do good" (Moroni 7:16–17). All things, not just our music, should pass this test if coming unto Christ is our ultimate goal.

ONE EXULTANT HYMN

I'm a big fan of musical films and plays. Although some people have a problem with a character breaking into song, most of us accept this convention. Why? Because some feelings become more powerful when combined with music. At some time or other, haven't we all felt like breaking into song with unbridled exuberance? I remember the night before my wedding day when I dropped off my wife-to-be at her parents' home and then caroled a whoop of joy out into the cold December air because this was our last dropoff. Had a catchy tune with rhyming words entered my mind right then, I would have swung on a lamppost, singin' in the snow.

Each of our children, at two or three years old, has gone through a short but unprompted stage of singing their evening prayers. Their little voices lilt through a melody we've never heard before—or at least don't remember—expressing thanks and requesting blessings. My wife and I have treasured these sacred, veil-parting moments. Apparently, Heavenly Father has no problem with breaking out in song.

Some of my most treasured spiritual experiences have occurred through music. As a high school senior, on a choir trip to Canada, a group of us gathered in a hotel room on Sunday for a testimony meeting. I shall never forget singing in a cappella four-part harmony "Come, Come Ye Saints," "There is a Green Hill Far Away," "The Spirit of God." At each of our children's births, we have handpicked music to welcome a new life into our family. Singing certain sacrament hymns never ceases to pierce my very heart with the reality of the Atonement, of Jesus' undying love, of the Father's unfathomable sacrifice. I have directed my ward choir with tears streaming down my cheeks in awe and gratitude, as we've sung "Come Thou Fount of Every Blessing," "Jesus, the Very Thought of Thee," and "What Shall We Give to the Babe in the Manger."

> *What shall we give / To the Lamb who was offered,*
> *Rising the third day and shedding His Love?*
> *Tears for His mercy we'll weep at the manger,*
> *Bathing the Infant come down from above."*[7]

I pray you've had similar experiences, where the sheer enormity of a song or a hymn has filled you with insight and gratitude, awe and transcendence.

GLORIOUS THINGS ARE SUNG OF ZION

The purpose of all music is the same: to take us to someplace new and then unite us—if only for a moment—with the very essence of that place, be it Zion or Babylon. For if it cannot transport our hearts, music holds no power.

When I consider those Zion societies of the past, I find two seemingly conflicting principles at work: every individual member develops his or her unique gifts—a voice—if you will; yet the society is completely unified, being of one heart and of one mind. How is this done? Music shows us. Imagine an orchestra made up solely of drums. Now imagine that they must all play the exact same notes at the exact same time in the exact same way. How would that sound? How would it look? How would it *feel?*

Now, imagine a full symphony orchestra with first and second violins, violas, basses, oboes, flutes, bassoons, clarinets, tubas, French horns, trumpets, and so on. Each is playing a different, unique part, yet doing so with *one purpose*, following *one leader*. How does *that* sound? How does that *feel?* In musical terms, we call that *harmony*, which is formally defined as "agreement in feeling or opinion; accord; . . . a pleasing combination of elements in a whole."[8] Sounds like Zion, doesn't it? Or the

Godhead, or the Church, or the family. It is the uniting of distinct voices for one glorious purpose. If you've ever played in an orchestra or sung in a choir, you know this feeling. And it is a transcendent experience, a foretaste of our Father's house, the celestial kingdom.

How can we apply this celestial concept of harmony to our families, wards, work places, and even the world? How can we rejoice in our divine individual gifts *while* becoming of one heart and of one mind? (see Moses 7:18). Music testifies that diverse voices united paradoxically bring us closer to one heart and one mind. And still I ask, Lord, how is it done?

Now Let Us Rejoice

Have you noticed how frequently the scriptures speak of *exaltation* and *music* together? Listen to these descriptions of that great day when we will unite with our Elder Brother to harmonize together: "And it shall come to pass that the righteous shall be gathered out from among all nations, and shall come to Zion, *singing with songs of everlasting joy*" (D&C 45:71). And "all shall know [the Lord], . . . [and we] shall see eye to eye, and shall lift up [our] voice, and . . . together sing" (D&C 84:98). Then we "shall . . . stand on the right hand of the Lamb, when he [stands] upon Mount Zion, . . . and [we] shall sing the song of the Lamb, day and night forever and ever" (D&C 133:56). And what is this "song of the Lamb?" It might be the "new song" laid out in Doctrine and Covenants 84:99–102, which begins: "The Lord hath brought again Zion; / The Lord hath redeemed his people."

I have heard and sung beautiful music before, music that has moved me to my very core. But I am completely incapable of imagining what that New Song will be like, for we know that, "Eye hath not seen, nor ear heard, neither have entered into the heart of man, the things which God hath prepared for them that love him" (1 Corinthians 2:9).

Maybe no encounter with music has touched my life like the one that occurred a few weeks after I was released as ward choir director. Our bishop and dear friend, Bing Leung, was dying of lymphoma. Even with the hospital's best treatments, he was not improving.

Finally, the staff asked the family to provide 'round-the-clock vigilance; I volunteered for an all-night shift. Bing's wife, Susie, was there, and we talked and reminisced as he slept. Around 4:00 A.M., Susie began to feel that Bing would not live much longer and that she needed to go home and get their twelve-year-old daughter, Akemi.

After Susie left, I told Bing that she and Kemi were on their way, and if at all possible, he should wake up and talk to them. I had been prompted to bring a hymnbook, so I started to sing. With the threat of nurses marching through my performance, I was a little self-conscious. Initially Bing showed no acknowledgement of my squawking. But soon enough he was looking at me like, "Who let this guy into my room in the middle of the night?" Gratefully, he didn't recognize me, so I told him again about Susie and Kemi's visit and that he should try to wake up for them. But he was exhausted. So I sang some more—hey, it had worked this far! By the time Susie and Kemi walked in, Bing said hello as if he'd just arrived from a day at the office. As mother and daughter pulled up on either side of Bing's hospital bed, I witnessed a sweet reunion that was only a foreshadow of reunions to come. After that night of singing, we enjoyed several more miraculous days interacting with the good old Bing. (Now, before you call me in the middle of the night, I want to stop all rumors that my singing can wake the dead.)

Days later, another call came. It was Susie. Could I come immediately? I grabbed two hymnbooks and hurried over. I was the first to arrive. Realizing this was it, I didn't care about the nurses coming and going as I stood singing:

> Why should we mourn or think our lot is hard? / 'Tis not so; all
>   is right.
> Why should we think to earn a great reward / If we now shun
>   the fight?
> Gird up your loins; fresh courage take. / Our God will never
>   us forsake;
> And soon we'll have this tale to tell—All is well! All is well![9]

True to form, Bing surprised us again: tears coursed down his cheeks as he squeezed my hand. Soon another close friend arrived, and he and I sang some more:

> Oh what songs of the heart / We shall sing all the day
> When at last we've assembled at home . . .
> As we greet with a kiss, / And with joy we caress
> All our loved ones that passed on before . . .
> As the heart swells with joy, / Oh, what songs we'll employ,
> When our heavenly parents we meet![10]

Bishop Bing died the next morning. I shall always be grateful for the sweetness of singing him home. At the memorial service, Bishop Michael Hansen, issuer of the choir calling, was there from Oregon. In tears again, he testified that my calling had come from God. And now I, also in tears, had to agree.

How Can I Keep from Singing?

Maybe more than anything else, music causes me to brush against the veil. I am overcome with eternal perspectives I cannot articulate but can feel through my soul. I am filled with longings for home. I marvel at the depth of gratitude I feel for innumerable blessings. And as these feelings wash over me, I cannot help thinking of an early American hymn:

> My life flows on in endless song; above earth's lamentation,
> I hear the sweet, though far-off hymn / That hails a new creation.
> Through all the tumult and the strife, / I hear the music ringing;
> It finds an echo in my soul: / How can I keep from singing?[11]

The day shall come when we won't be able to keep from singing. When that song of redeeming love shall envelop our souls and—if we can sing through the tears—our voices will soar as we transcend mortality to be united with our eternal family. Our choir then will be full of more distinct and individual voices than any ever heard; and with such

an array, its harmony will also be the most beautiful. Like our ward
choir, which became a little piece of Zion through music, may we in
our hearts and our homes, our wards and our world, harmonize together
in preparation for such singing.

Notes

1. *Children's Songbook of The Church of Jesus Christ of Latter-day Saints* (Salt
   Lake City: The Church of Jesus Christ of Latter-day Saints, 1989),
   242–43.
2. Neal A. Maxwell, "It's Service, Not Status, That Counts," *Ensign*, July
   1975, 7.
3. This and the following two experiences are from the author's personal
   correspondence.
4. Harold B. Lee, *Teachings of Harold B. Lee*, ed. Clyde J. Williams (Salt Lake
   City: Bookcraft, 1996), 104; emphasis added.
5. See Revelation 18:22; also Brigham Young, *Journal of Discourses*, 26 vols.
   (London: Latter-day Saints' Book Depot, 1854–86), 9:244.
6. Told to author by young man's mother.
7. Traditional Catalonian (French) carol, paraphrase by David Warner,
   "What Shall We Give to the Babe in the Manger?"
8. *American Heritage Dictionary*, 3d ed., electronic version, s.v. "harmony."
9. William Clayton, "Come, Come, Ye Saints," *Hymns of The Church of Jesus
   Christ of Latter-day Saints* (Salt Lake City: The Church of Jesus Christ of
   Latter-day Saints, 1985), no. 30.
10. Joseph L. Townsend, "Oh, What Songs of the Heart," *Hymns*, no. 286.
11. Traditional nineteenth-century song, "How Can I Keep from Singing?"

Preparing to Be an Influence

❦

David B. Haight

At the end of the Gospel of Matthew, in the last verse, we learn of
the resurrected Lord and Savior meeting the Apostles and some disciples on the Mount just before His ascension into the heavens to be
with His Father. Matthew wrote that the Savior spoke to them, saying,
"All power is given unto me in heaven and in earth" (Matthew 28:18).

Let me say that again, as you try to imagine it in your mind: "All
power is given unto me in heaven and in earth. Go ye therefore, and
teach all nations, baptizing them in the name of the Father, and of the
Son, and of the Holy Ghost: Teaching them to observe all things whatsoever I have commanded you" (Matthew 28:18–20).

He's talking to us. This is The Church of Jesus Christ of Latter-day
Saints, restored to the earth through the faithfulness and obedience of
a young lad, Joseph Smith, fourteen years old. We all know the account
of heavenly messengers meeting with the Prophet Joseph Smith on different occasions and what transpired, including the coming forth of the
Book of Mormon.

The Prophet Joseph called some of his trusted men to go to
England in 1838 (see D&C 118). In that group were Heber C. Kimball,
John Taylor, Wilford Woodruff, and George A. Smith. A little later

---

David B. Haight, described by President Gordon B. Hinckley as a "grand old war-
rior," at age ninety-seven is the oldest Apostle in this dispensation. A commander in
the Navy during World War II, he attended the University of Utah, worked as the
district and regional manager of a large retail store chain, was elected mayor of Palo
Alto, California, and served as assistant to the president at Brigham Young
University. He and his wife, Ruby Olson, are the parents of three children.

Brigham Young joined with them, as did Orson and Parley Pratt.[1]
When they arrived in Liverpool, they needed to tell the people why
they were returning to the homeland of many of them. They had come
to attempt to teach the new principles of the gospel, principles that
had been revealed to a group of people in the United States. Imagine
these men from the United States traveling to solid, old, staid England
to teach the people there. They had to prepare the way, to let the
people know that what they were going to teach was new and different—that the heavens were open and they could pray to a Heavenly
Father and receive answers to their prayers. Elder Parley P. Pratt wrote
these words:

> The morning breaks [a new day, a new dawn, a new event in
> life], the shadows flee;
> Lo, Zion's standard is unfurled! [that's running the flag up the
> pole and having it wave in the breeze]
> The dawning of a brighter day
> Majestic rises on the world.[2]

The Apostles began explaining the restoration of the gospel, and
almost immediately they began having some success. New converts
gave the Church some strength and extra support and manpower, and
people started to come to America to learn more because what they
had heard sounded good to them. Their hearts were touched, and they
were moved spiritually to know that they were hearing something that
would be important to them.

Be conscious of impressions that you have. Be mindful of them.
Sometimes you'll get an impression of such power that you know you
need to pay heed to it. That happened to me a few years ago one
evening when the *Deseret News* was delivered to my desk. An article
in it told about a young man who was to be honored by the governor of
the state of Utah for rescuing a man and two girls who had capsized in
a canoe on the Jordan River near Salt Lake. This young man was in a
canoe, too, and he helped them to shore. After he had saved the lives
of these people, he was leaving in his own canoe heading back into the

Jordan River when he had an accident and drowned. The governor of Utah was going to present a hero's award to him posthumously. I saw the name of the young man, but I didn't pay much attention to it and tossed the newspaper aside. Instantly, I received the impression I should re-read the article. I took it out of the wastebasket, put it on my desk, and read it again. That very evening, at that very moment, in the Deseret Mortuary in Salt Lake City, a viewing was being held before the burial of this young man. I had a strong impression that I should attend. I didn't know the people—in fact, I didn't know anything more about it than I've told you—but I called Ruby on the telephone and told her to put the beans on the back burner, that I'd be a little bit late because I was going to the mortuary.

At the mortuary I stood in line—there were a lot of people—and up near the front I could see a casket and the parents standing beside it. A young man, probably in his twenties, was standing beside them. As I was standing in line, the young man walked down to me and said, "Who are you?"

I said, "My name is David Haight."

He asked, "Are you something in the Mormon Church?"

"Yes."

"Well, what kind of position do you have in the Church?"

"I'm a member of the Quorum of the Twelve Apostles."

"What are you doing here?"

"I came here to honor a brave young man and to pay my respects to him."

The young man said, "Please come up and meet my parents," and he took me out of the line. (I don't like to do that sort of thing, but that is how it was.)

As I met the father standing by the casket, I said, "I hope our bishop has been kind to you and helpful during this serious tragedy you've had in losing your son."

The man said, "Humph! I said to him, 'What a hell of a way to meet my bishop.'"

As we stood there visiting, I looked at the young man lying in the casket. It was like a high school picture: he was in a tuxedo, he had a little beard, and his hair was a little on the long side. He had a kind of lei around his neck, and he was holding something in his hand. I said to his mother, "Could you tell me the significance of the lei around his neck?"

"He belonged to a naturalist group," she told me, "and they liked the out-of-doors—different flowers, wildflowers, and kinds of weeds—and they made one for him from some wildflowers." That was the dry lei he had around his neck.

I noticed that his hands were folded over his chest, and he held a feather in them. "Could you tell me the significance of the feather your son is holding?"

"Our son belonged to the Audubon Society. He loves birds. When this happened, we looked all around for something that we might give to John, and we found this long feather and put it in his hands. We wanted John to have something to hold on to when he passes over to the other side."

I looked at that twenty-year-old young man, not in temple clothes but in a tuxedo, a feather in his hands so he would have something to hold onto, given to him by parents who had drifted away from the Church and become inactive.

I shook hands with the parents and said, "I'd like to ask you to come to my office one of these days after you've gone through this time of mourning and sadness. Bring whatever family you would like. Why don't you come to my office and let's talk about John?"

"Well, maybe we could do that," the mother replied.

We followed up with them on the telephone later, and they came to my office, the father and mother, the young man who invited me to leave the line, and other members of the family. We talked about John, gospel principles, and eternal life. I gave them a paperback copy of the Book of Mormon, signed it for them, and told them I would stay in touch with them.

Through our ongoing friendship of many years, I was privileged to seal the family a few years ago in the Salt Lake Temple—the parents together and then their three sons to them, including their deceased son. It happened that the son who had recognized me at the viewing of his brother was the paramedic who came to my rescue a couple of years later when I had a ruptured abdominal aortic aneurysm. He gave me a priesthood blessing at the hospital.

This experience became a great testimony to me of the importance of following through on impressions we may receive. The majesty of this work that we're in is really beyond much of our comprehension.

When I was an assistant to the Quorum of the Twelve Apostles, I was having a meeting one Thursday morning in my office. It was a serious meeting, so I told my secretary that if there were any phone calls, just to take a message and I'd call them back.

In a few minutes, she opened the door of my office and said, "Elder Haight, I thought you would like to know President Kimball's on the phone."

Well, that changes your plans pretty fast. I picked up the phone and said, "Hello, President."

He said, "Is that you, David?"

I said, "Yes."

He said, "I'm on the fourth floor of the temple. I would like you to come over and see me right now." Then he repeated, "Right now? Can you come right now?"

"President," I said, "I'll come just as fast as I can." The fact that he repeated the summons twice—"Right now" and "Can you come right now?"—told me I was in some sort of difficulty. I walked the block as fast as I could, through the garage into the temple and up to the fourth floor. As I stepped off the elevator, there was President Kimball with that warm, wonderful personality. He shook my hand and invited me into a little room I had never been in before. We sat down in two chairs facing each other, and he wanted to know about my personal life. It was interesting for me to attempt to tell him of my personal life. What would you say to the prophet of the Lord if you were being interviewed in a room in the temple and he asked you about your personal life? What would you say? "Oh, it's just dandy"?

I explained to him as best I could that I thought I was living the commandments of the Lord. Then he asked me to stand up, and he took hold of both my hands and said to me, "With all of the love that I possess, I'm calling you to fill a vacancy in the Quorum of the Twelve Apostles."

I almost fainted. I couldn't imagine that happening to a kid like I am—a kid out of southern Idaho—with all of the talent we have in the Church. He put his arms around me and told me he loved me, and as I put my arms around him, I knocked his glasses off. I thought, *Well, here I am, not only standing here dumbfounded but feeling awkward because I knocked off his glasses and he beat me in picking them up off the floor.*

He said, "Let's go meet the Brethren." We crossed the room, he opened a door, and there were eleven of the Twelve. There was one vacant chair, number twelve. President Kimball said to me, "Would you go over and take your seat in that chair?" As I walked across the rug to that chair to sit down—thinking of the hymn, "I Stand All Amazed"³—no one could have been more amazed than I was on that day. I wondered how I would ever, *ever* be able to measure up to those people that I have admired all of my life, to hold that position of responsibility or be able to answer in some way the challenge and the opportunity and the responsibility to be a witness to all of the world.

We had a testimony meeting, and each of the Brethren told me that he loved me and bore testimony. I had an opportunity to speak briefly, and then they assembled in a circle and President Kimball ordained me an apostle of our Lord Jesus Christ. After that, he said to me, "Would you like to contact Sister Haight and tell her what has happened?"

"Yes, I would." I said.

"There's a phone right over here," someone else said.

I stood in this amazed shock looking at the phone, and Boyd Packer asked, "Don't you remember Ruby's name?"

I said, "Yes."

"Do you remember your number?"

I said, "I think so."

So I called Ruby.

She said hello, and I said hello.

She asked, "Where are you?"

I said, "I'm in the temple."

"Well, what are you doing in the temple?"

Then I told her what had happened to me.

She started to cry. Later she told me that when I said hello on the telephone, she knew by my voice that some change had happened to me, some great spiritual experience.

I'm grateful for my ancestors who crossed the plains: on my father's side (Haight), my grandfather, fourteen years old; and my grandmother, age eleven, in another company. On my mother's side (Tuttle), my grandfather and grandmother. They were married in a little waystation on the way to Winter Quarters. They had fallen in love on the wagon train and were later sealed in the Endowment House in Salt Lake. They were wonderful people who worked hard, who had the spiritual experience of hearing the gospel, of believing it was true, and of committing themselves to move forward with their friends and others to help establish the kingdom where they could worship as they would please, where the Church could establish itself and grow and move on in the marvelous way that we see happening today.

When I speak in conferences, I know that my time is up if the light is flashing. LeGrand Richards used to have trouble seeing the clock. Because he couldn't read the time, a little light was put on the rostrum in the old Tabernacle in Salt Lake. The next time he spoke, LeGrand hadn't quite finished and that light came on. He said to the audience, "Someone turned on a silly red light up here. I don't know what's it for, but I'll just put my hand over it." So now when the red light is flashing at me, I have wonderful memories of LeGrand Richards.

When Ruby and I were married in Salt Lake City and going on our honeymoon across Nevada to a new job in Berkeley, California, we had all of our earthly possessions in the rumble seat of a little Model A Ford. Those early possessions were our clothes and some wedding gifts. The rest was an opportunity. And so we go out in the world, we watch what people do, we associate with good people, we learn how to get along and to get things done, and along the way Ruby and I have had seventy-three wonderful years. As I gave her some yellow and red roses on her birthday, I said, "Every year gets better," and that's true.

I testify to you that this work is true. I've been involved in it all of my life, and I've watched the world—the corporate world, the military, and all of the other institutions—and there isn't anything to compare with what we do and teach and say. The gospel is true. And so I say to you women in your roles of all kinds, we are part of the royal army to help people and take advantage of opportunities to help people understand that the gospel has been restored and is on the earth. You can thrill them as you share your own testimony and tell them what has happened in your life.

I want you to know that we wrote the Proclamation on the Family[4] in the temple. Every word of it is correct regarding women and marriage and families and children. The gospel is true. It is the hope of the world. God lives. I know that He lives and He loves us. We are His children.

May you all be blessed in all of your activities. Take advantage of every opportunity that you have, enjoy life, and be a happy, joyful person in helping someone else step onto a little higher plane than he or she might now be on. I bless you, your homes, and your activities, and pray that you will be blessed with the spirit of this work, that your prayers will be answered, and you'll be able to accomplish great things. You do it by living the gospel and keeping its standards. Just live the principles, and they will take you where you want to go.

Notes

1. James B. Allen, Ronald K. Esplin, and David J. Whittaker, *Men with a Mission: The Quorum of the Twelve Apostles in the British Isles* (Salt Lake City: Deseret Book, 1992), 67–83.

2. Parley P. Pratt, "The Morning Breaks," *Hymns of The Church of Jesus Christ of Latter-day Saints* (Salt Lake City: The Church of Jesus Christ of Latter-day Saints, 1985), no. 1; see also Joseph Fielding Smith, *Church History and Modern Revelation*, 4 vols. (Salt Lake City: The Church of Jesus Christ of Latter-day Saints, 1946–49), 4:51.

3. *Hymns*, no. 193.

4. "The Family: A Proclamation to the World," *Ensign*, November 1995, 102.

WHO WILL BE GREATEST?

⋞ᛒᵔᵔ

Katherine Boswell

As a Sunday School Gospel Doctrine teacher, I've spent a lot of time thinking about discipleship. What does it mean to be a disciple of Christ? What were the lessons He taught those beloved disciples who were close to Him during his earthly ministry? In preparation for a lesson some weeks ago, I was struck by an interchange between Christ and His disciples that must have made quite an impression, because it is recorded in Matthew, Mark, and Luke.

Here is how Mark recorded the incident as translated by Joseph Smith: "And he came to Capernaum: and being in the house he asked them, why was it that ye disputed among yourselves by the way? But they held their peace, being afraid; for by the way they had disputed among themselves, who was the greatest among them. Now Jesus sat down, and called the twelve and said unto them, If any man desire to be first, the same shall be last of all, and servant of all. And he took a child and sat in the midst of them; and when he had taken the child in his arms, he said unto them, Whosoever shall humble himself like one of these children, and receiveth me, ye shall receive in my name; and whosover shall receive me, receiveth not me only, but him that sent me, even the Father" (JST Mark 9:33–37).

What a wonderful gem—a glimpse into the human pride and frailties held even by Christ's closest associates. "Who [will be] the

---

Katherine Boswell, a Gospel Doctrine teacher, received her Ph.D. from the University of Texas at Austin. As president of the Education Policy Associates, she consults with governors and legislators across the country on public policy issues.

greatest in the kingdom of heaven?" was their question (Matthew 18:1).

This interchange caused me to stop hard and think, "What is greatness? Who are the greatest men and women that I have ever known? Would they be the greatest in heaven?"

If we were to generate a list of those whom the world considers great, any number of successful scientists, powerful politicians, and captains of industry would spring to mind. But as I thought long and hard about Christ's response to his disciples, only two names, other than family members', came to my mind.

Bill Phelps was second counselor in the bishopric when I was a teenager. He was a humble man, lived in a modest home, and made his living, I think, as a truck driver. I remember Bill coming to our Mia Maid class. He gave each girl a dime and told us always to carry that dime in our shoe for a telephone call (obviously, I'm not in my thirties). If we were ever in trouble we were to telephone him, he said, no matter what the place or time, day or night, and he would come and get us, no questions asked. And we knew he meant it. We knew he loved us and would do anything for us. I carried that dime for years. His offer wasn't mere rhetoric either. More than one of my friends, finding herself in a situation she didn't know how to control, called Bill for help. When Bill died of cancer some years later, his funeral was extraordinary. Mourners filled every room in the entire building—the chapel, the halls, and even the lawn outdoors. Many of them weren't even Church members. Bill had quietly touched hundreds, perhaps thousands of lives, yet in the world's eyes he was uneducated, rough-edged, unimportant. I consider him probably the greatest man I have ever known.

When I was a young girl, Inez Tracy was my mother's visiting teacher. My mother, struggling in an unhappy marriage with an alcoholic husband, had been inactive for a number of years and was fighting serious depression and bitterness. Inez didn't lecture or patronize her; she just loved her. She became Mother's best friend and was ultimately instrumental in helping her gradually find her way back to church. Inez had a glorious soprano voice and was offered an opportunity to sing with the New York Metropolitan Opera when she was younger. She was good enough she might have had a brilliant career, but she chose instead to marry a schoolteacher and raise four great kids. She used her exceptional talent and love of music to lead church choirs and to teach her choir members, starting at age eight, to read and lead music. She encouraged us to learn to play the piano. Her choirs were angelic. Because she never once complained, none of us knew that she was suffering from a terrible degenerative disease that made it agonizing for her to raise her arms above her waist. She died at a relatively young age. I was only twelve, but to this day I can't sing in a choir or lead music before the congregation without thinking of Inez and the priceless gift of music she gave to me and to everyone else in our ward.

Throughout my professional life, I've had unusual opportunities to meet and interact with some of the most well-known and powerful men and women in the nation and, to some extent, in the world. These are men and women whose faces grace the covers of national news magazines. Yet, isn't it interesting that the two non-family members I identified as the greatest individuals I have ever known have both been dead for decades, were unimportant in the world's eyes, and yet they changed and enriched my life immeasurably?

From the gospel of Luke we read: "And, behold, a certain lawyer stood up, and tempted him, saying, Master, what shall I do to inherit eternal life?" What a great question! Whatever the lawyer's intentions, isn't that a question we're all dying to know the answer to?

"He said unto him, What is written in the law? how readest thou?" Ever the teacher, Christ turns the question back and asks the student what the scriptures teach.

"And he answering said, Thou shalt love the Lord thy God with all thy heart, and with all thy soul, and will all thy strength, and with all thy mind; and thy neighbour as thyself. And he said unto him, Thou hast answered right: this do, and thou shalt live" (Luke 10:25–28).

The lawyer knew the scriptures and was able to quote perfectly the great commandment. But Christ reminded him that knowledge alone was not enough. "This do, and thou shalt live." It is not enough to know or have a testimony of the law and the truths of the gospel. If we want to gain eternal life or exaltation, we must live the law. We must go and do.

Like so many bright attorneys of my acquaintance, the lawyer couldn't resist one more attempt to get in the last word. "But he, willing to justify himself, said unto Jesus, And who is my neighbour?" (Luke 10:29). Christ's response was the wonderful parable of the good Samaritan.

So what should we take from these interchanges? Obviously the Lord doesn't judge things the way the world or even His disciples did. Success, wealth, or power are clearly unimportant in the eyes of the Lord. Even a scholar's knowledge of the scriptures and the commandments is not enough. Membership in this Church, a tithing receipt in your pocket, and even a temple recommend in your purse will not be enough to help you attain eternal life. Christ clearly taught that if we are to attain exaltation and live in the presence of the Father, something far more difficult is required. Humility and service to the least of our brethren is what the Lord asks of us. We need to go and do the Lord's business.

An article in the *Church News* told the story of a group of religious instructors taking a summer course on the life of the Savior, focusing particularly on the parables. "When the final exam time came . . . the students arrived at the classroom to find a note that the exam would be given in another building across campus. Moreover, the note said, it must be finished within the two-hour time period that was starting almost at that moment.

"The students hurried across campus. On the way they passed a little girl crying over a flat tire on her new bike. An old man hobbled painfully toward the library with a cane in one hand, spilling books from a stack he was trying to manage with the other. On a bench by the Union building sat a shabbily dressed, bearded man with a sign: 'I need money to eat. Please help me.'

"Rushing into the other classroom, the students were met by the professor, who announced they had all flunked the final exam.

"The only true test of whether they understood the Savior's life and teaching, he said, was how they treated people in need."[1]

Sisters, are we at risk of failing our own final exam? We all have very good reasons why we can't provide service. We are so busy with our families, jobs, church callings. Our means are limited. We are afraid of putting ourselves or our families in harm's way if we reach out to the downtrodden or despised in our own communities. But as I picture myself standing before my Savior, thanking Him for all that He has done for me, my own excuses begin to ring a bit hollow.

Several years ago, I was in Indonesia as part of a humanitarian expedition that was putting in a water system on the island of West Timor. While Indonesia is actually the most populous Muslim nation in the world, this particular village had been visited many years before by Seventh-Day Adventist missionaries who had converted the majority of the people in the area. On Saturday, which was the day they honored as the Sabbath, they asked members of our group if we would like to join them at their church services. Several of us readily agreed, delighted at the opportunity to worship with these truly good and humble people.

A very sweet spirit filled that humble church, constructed of cinder blocks with a corrugated tin roof. Most of the villagers themselves lived in mud brick huts, with roofs of thatched grass. These were very poor people by any standard, scratching out a living by subsistence farming. Near the end of the church service, a basket was passed among the congregation, and out of pockets and from tied handkerchiefs came a cascade of coins and an occasional bill or two. Knowing that few if any of these peasants received any kind of regular income, I was startled by the contributions. Their sole access to cash was typically what they were able to earn carrying their produce to the town, some miles away, to sell by the roadsides. During the closing hymn that followed the offering, I asked the assistant minister, who was kindly translating much of the service for me, whether the contributions went to support the pastor and the running of the congregation. "Oh no," he assured me, "we collect funds to help support an orphanage in Uganda." In my surprise, I blurted out, somewhat rudely, "But these people are so poor!" He just smiled and said, "But the orphans are so much poorer than we are."

In King Benjamin's magnificent sermon on service we read: "And now, if God, who has created you, on whom you are dependent for your lives and for all that ye have and are, doth grant unto you whatsoever ye ask that is right, . . . O then, how ye ought to impart of the substance that ye have one to another. . . . feeding the hungry, clothing the naked, visiting the sick and administering to their relief, both spiritually and temporally" (Mosiah 4:21, 26).

If we, like the Apostles, want to be great in the kingdom of heaven, or if we, like the lawyer, want to gain eternal life, we need to abide by the counsel the Savior gave to Peter, to "feed my sheep" (John 21:16). If we love Him and learn to *do*, not just know, the things of the kingdom, we will indeed find joy and glory in His service as His true disciples.

Note

1. "Viewpoint," *Church News*, 1 October 1988, 16; also James E. Faust and James P. Bell, *In the Strength of the Lord: The Life and Teachings of James E. Faust* (Salt Lake City: Deseret Book, 1999), 289–90.

SAINTS ALIVE

༺ ᗢ ༻

Nan Hunter

I once asked my good Catholic friend how a Catholic becomes a saint. She told me those nominated to be saints will have done much, sometimes even miraculous, good work, and have served long and unselfish lives—far beyond the normal. In The Church of Jesus Christ of Latter-day Saints, a person can become a Latter-day Saint of God at age eight. According to the LDS Bible Dictionary, Saints are all "those who by baptism have entered into the Christian covenant."[1] That's exciting news. There is something compelling about being called a saint and our intense desire to be with the Saints.

In 1834 Phoebe Carter, a maiden of twenty-seven years, joined the Church, and a year later left her "parents and kindred, and journeyed to Kirtland, Ohio, a distance of one thousand miles, a lone maid." She writes, "My friends marvelled at my course, as did I, but something within impelled me on. . . . [H]ad it not been for the spirit within I should have faltered at the last. . . . When the time came for my departure I dared not trust myself to say farewell, so I wrote my good-bye to each, and leaving them on my table, ran down stairs and jumped into

---

Nan Greene Hunter, a graduate of Brigham Young University in zoology, has served in various leadership positions in the Young Women and Relief Society and as music director in Sunday School and Primary. She wrote the lyrics for the hymn, "Father, This Hour Has Been One of Joy." She served with her husband, Richard A. Hunter, when he presided over the New Zealand Auckland Mission. They are the parents of eight children, and every summer Nan holds "Grandma Camp" for her twenty grandchildren. She is serving as a ward Young Women president.

the carriage. Thus I left the beloved home of childhood to link my life with the Saints of God."[2]

In May 1947 under very different circumstances, I linked my life with the Saints of God when I entered the waters of baptism and then received the Holy Ghost. At that moment, I, as did you, became a covenant saint of God. Each week as we partake of the sacrament, we covenant to remember Him that we may have His Spirit. For me that covenant—to bear the burdens of others, to serve, forgive, love, to remember to do the things the Savior would do, to be like Him—defines what it means to be a covenant saint.

Sainthood is an ongoing process, defined daily by ever-changing circumstances. Our habits and responses to the mountains of life soon determine if we scale those craggy peaks with joy, contention, or complaint. Years ago, as a young mother of eight children under the age of thirteen and a busy bishop husband, becoming a saint had to happen on the fly or not at all. Here's a sample from my journal of how my days went back then:

> This morning at five I got out of my bed
> For Tuesday's the day I always make bread.
> While the wheat was grinding, I threw in some wash
> And mended some overalls for sweet baby Josh.
> I put bread in the pans, ready to rise,
> Just as the sun kissed the bright morning skies.
> I paused for a moment, then ran up the stairs
> To wake up my eight little grumbly bears.
> I made a few beds, curled up some locks,
> Unplugged the toilet, and found Jimmy's socks.
> I ran back downstairs to get breakfast cooking,
> Thankful Betty Crocker wasn't there looking.
> I had the bread in my arms ready to bake
> When over my foot slid Michael's new snake.
> I sprang from my skin to see what was the matter
> And dropped all the dough upside down with a clatter.
> I tried to remember my new resolution,

Which was to be calm in the face of confusion,
So rather than yell as I usually do
I just took a pencil and bit it in two.
By now a smoke smell was burning my nose,
And I knew that the morning would be "one of those."
The children came running, ready for prayer,
As father strolled calmly from out of his lair.
"So is something burning?" he asked with a grin.
"It's burnt!" I replied, and that silenced him.

As often as not, my days began with similar scenes of rush and chaos. While all but the preschoolers were away at school, I'd wash, fold, scrub, read scriptures, write in my journal, garden, visit teach, and whatever else I could squeeze in—even a mall shopping spree to pick up supplies for Mutual—before carpooling from school, to baseball, ballet, piano for three, Cub Scouts, and Brownies. Dinner fits in there somewhere. I covered all that in my verse and ended with:

Then comes homework, and stories, and prayers to be said,
Drinks and the bathroom
Drinks and the bathroom
Drinks and the bathroom
And whatever else they can think of
To keep from going to bed.
At last it's 10:30 and I can't hear a peep.
I'll study my favorite, 3 Nephi 17,
But then midway through
I fall half asleep.
As I crawl to the edge of my welcoming bed,
Wondering if I'm alive or nearer to dead,
I pray, "Thank thee dear Father, tho' I'm weary and faint,
I just know by tomorrow that I'll be a saint."

It helps me to know that as a covenant Latter-day Saint I am called to serve my "fellowmen," who are my children, my siblings, our extended family, my ward members, and those I love, many of whom are friends and neighbors waiting for the gospel. And truly, on those busy days of serving the ones who mean more than life to us, we are saints.

In Romans 12, Paul offers great insight on "how to live as becometh saints."[3] He directs us specifically into helpful paths of *doing* the work of saints. When you read these principles in Romans, you will say, "Yes, I can do that." "Yes, I will do that." "Yes, I am doing that." "Paul is talking about me. I *am* a saint." Because, dear sister, you are. Let me select a few highlights from that chapter.

In verse 9 Paul says, "Let love be without dissimulation." Dissimulation implies a hidden agenda behind your love. You want something from a person, therefore you feign or pretend love to obtain a personal reward. That behavior is not the true love of a saint. In verse 10 Paul goes on to say that we are to be "kindly affectioned one to another with brotherly love." We love each other because we are members of one family. Each person we meet is far more than a mere acquaintance; all God's children are our brothers and sisters.

At the age of ten, I learned a lesson about being "kindly affectioned." Early in my life I had decided to be nice to people. I saw it as the right way, but I also thought as a young girl that even though I didn't have the costly, beautiful clothes of others and even if I wasn't as cute, that I could still belong if I could be nice. So nice I was.

In our class, one particular girl was ridiculed and teased because she was ungainly and her face was not pretty. I felt very sorry for her and didn't join in their jeers, but though I spoke to her with kindness and smiled, I never played with her or included her among my friends. One day an invitation came to her birthday party. I was reluctant to go, but my good and kind mother encouraged me to do the right thing. She wrapped a lovely present, curled my hair, directed me to wear a nice dress with my Sunday shoes, and sent me off. We lived in a humble home in Salt Lake, but when I arrived at this classmate's home I was not prepared for what I saw. Her house, set back on a busy street next to a large grocery store, the lawn unkempt, and the cement ragged, made my little house look like a palace.

I was shown into a sparsely furnished living room where preparations had been made for a celebration: some crepe paper hung from the light fixture over a table where a birthday cake sat. Sadly, I was the only person who came to that party. It is a scene I shall always remember; feelings of hurt for her come back to me even now. When this girl told me I was her only friend, I felt a deep sense of shame. If I were her only friend, then I had not been much of one. My minimal act of saying hello and refraining from verbal abuse and sneers didn't lift my actions to the level of a saint. I learned a great lesson that day. Saints are kindly affectioned. They bear other's burdens. They are wholehearted when it comes to inclusion.

Paul teaches another great lesson when he describes saints as "rejoicing in hope; patient in tribulation; continuing instant in prayer" (Romans 12:12). When we are facing trials, contention, and mountains of problems so tall and so steep we feel faint, remembering these attitudes can help us have the passion and determination to let go of despair and cleave to hope.

Many years ago we were involved in a heartbreaking business experience. I was terribly hurt by what happened, and I wallowed in self-pity and sorrow. Finally, knowing I couldn't live like this forever and not wanting to feel this way for even one more day, I tried to get a grip on myself. I studied the scriptures and prayed to know how to rejoice in hope and be patient in tribulation. I found the answer, after much study and prayer, embodied in the principle of remembering "the covenant wherewith ye have covenanted" (D&C 90:24). I promised the Lord if He would give me peace, I would strive with all my heart to remember the covenants I had made.

During that difficult time in my life, I was teaching early morning seminary. I tried to be a better teacher. I doubled my efforts to do good, serve more, smile more, love more. When the sign-up sheet came around for anything, I signed up. I looked in the neighborhood, under rocks, in rills, for anything and everyone I could serve. As I worked harder to be a covenant Saint, I began to feel the Savior take up my burden of resentment and lighten my heart.

Of course, I had my down days as well, and as the holidays approached, I could feel a heavy heart approaching with it. Finances were challenging; little fears started to creep into my mind and heart. When I saw my efforts to rejoice in hope and exercise patience begin to falter, I added fasting to my fervent prayers. I pleaded with the Lord for one small miracle—to be led to someone who really needed my help. If He would show me where to go and what to do to serve Him, I would know that the Lord loved me. That was the confirmation I needed.

One day, driving down the street on an errand, I spotted a woman I had never seen before but who I knew immediately needed some-thing. I parked the car, crossed the street, and asked, "Do you need some help?" Bursting into tears, she told me she had missed the bus that would get her to the train station on time to get to work. Recently divorced and supporting two teenage children, she was doing all she could to keep body and soul together. She was desperate. If she didn't get to work on time, she knew she would lose her job. My heart filled with joy; I knew this was my answer. Father in Heaven had sent me to help her. He did hear my prayers. He loved me and He loved her, and even though His children are as numerous as the sands of the seas and the stars in the firmament, He is acutely aware of the small details of our lives. He loves us beyond measure.

In Romans 12:13, Paul counsels: "Be eager in giving hospitality." In the true sense, hospitality is much more than setting a beautiful table and feeding people with your best china and silver. William Barclay's commentary on the book of Romans notes that William Tyndale in his New Testament translation wrote that the Christian should have a "harborous disposition" (what a magnificent adjective). Barclay then adds that "Christianity is the religion of the open hand, the open heart, and the open door."[4]

Several years ago when our last child left for college, Richard and I thought we needed to recover. So we left for the beautiful islands of Tonga to "harbor" for six weeks and to allow Richard to work on a project. We were treated with great love and hospitality. While visiting the island of Ha'a'pi, we were invited to be guests at the seminary graduation, which began with a gigantic feast. Upon tables laded with food were shelves for even more food. We ate for two hours and at seven o'clock were ushered into the chapel. From the stand, where we were asked to sit, I watched the reverence and beauty of these dear people—the girls in their white dresses, the boys in white, short-sleeved shirts, bright ties, and the traditional wraparound lava lava, all of them covered with flowered leis to their noses. We sat, and we sat, . . . and we sat some more. The music played; the Saints were quiet. Finally at about 7:45, I gently nudged the man sitting next to me and asked why the meeting hadn't started. He explained that one of the girls living on an outer island couldn't get her boat working, and the stake president had gone to the dock to wait for her to arrive. Patiently and sweetly the audience sat. Their concern was not for passing time, but for the girl. She would not be bringing them gifts when she arrived; she wasn't an important guest dignitary who would be conferring upon them crowns or honor; they gained nothing by awaiting her arrival. Their waiting spoke loudly and clearly of the love they had for her and their desire to acknowledge her accomplishments as a seminary graduate. No one complained or griped. What I saw that night was true hospitality of spirit. I hope I will always remember its pure and selfless generosity.

Paul shares much more counsel about living as a saint in Romans 12, but let me end with another poem, one more reverent in tone than my first one. I don't know who wrote it, but I have had it pasted on my fridge for years. It captures the feeling of remembering and being lifted as covenant Saints in each moment of our busy lives.

> *Dear Lord of all pots and pans and things,*
> *Tho' I've not time to be a saint*
> *By dreaming in the dawn*
> *Or storming heavens gates,*
> *Make me a saint by getting meals*
> *And washing up the plates.*

Tho' I must have Martha's hands,
I have a Mary's mind,
And as I black the shoes and boots,
Thy sandals, Lord, I find.
I think of how they trod the earth
As I scrub the floor.
Forgive this meditation, Lord,
I haven't time for more.
Thou who didst love to give men food
In room or by the sea,
Accept the service that I do,
I do it unto thee.

Notes

1. LDS Bible Dictionary, s.v. "Saint," 767–68.
2. Linda Madsen Sheffield, "A Letter from Phoebe Carter Woodruff to Mama," *BYU Studies*, 19 (Winter 1979), no. 2, 200.
3. Romans 12 headnote.
4. William Barclay, *The Letter to the Romans* (Philadelphia: Westminster Press, 1955), 180.

"The Deadly Sin of Pride"

Mary Ellen Edmunds

It was 1976, and life was good. I was thirty-six, I'd been home from my health mission to the Philippines for about two-and-a-half years, I had decided to return to the profession of nursing, and I felt good. Then, wham! I was called to go on another mission. This time to Indonesia. They had called a nurse from England who was a convert, and they needed someone "seasoned" (that means old) to go with her. We would be the first lady missionaries in Indonesia. *No thanks!* That's what I thought. *Been there, done that!* But I decided to go to the temple to see if I was right.

Never do that if you're not ready to hear the answer.

So then another idea surfaced. *"Hey!"* I started thinking, *"This is my reward for the tough missions I've already served!"* I had served several missions, I had worked on learning other languages, I'd taught at the Language Training Mission (LTM) and knew my way around. This was going to be a piece of cake! *"I'll show these younger missionaries how to do this!"* I thought.

I entered the LTM in September of that year with "all humility." . . .

There were *two* of us in the entire place learning Indonesian. My

---

Mary Ellen Edmunds, popular author, speaker, and Relief Society teacher at the Missionary Training Center in Provo, earned a bachelor's degree in nursing from Brigham Young University and has served on the faculty there. In addition to her service on the Relief Society General Board, she has been on four missions and was a director of training at the Provo Missionary Training Center. She has a fondness for the peoples of Taiwan, Hong Kong, Indonesia, and the Philippines, where she served on her missions.

companion *was* from England, yes, . . . but she grew up in Malaysia. The Indonesian language is almost exactly the same as the language of Malaysia. Not like Spanish and Portuguese—more like Spanish in Mexico compared to Spanish in Argentina. It quickly became apparent who was the "slow one" in the class. I'll give you a hint: Her initials are M. E. E. I still remember our first test. I got two things right: my name and the date.

Well, friends, the entire year and a half was sort of like that. It was hard! It was extremely challenging and humbling. And it's one of the best things I've ever done. I'm so thankful for what I learned and felt, and for those I came to love so dearly.

Early on, our mission president assigned two local companions to work with us, Darsi and Endang. One of the responsibilities he gave us was to teach them English. He said it would help them all the rest of their lives. (And, indeed, they both were able to get excellent employment later, partly because of their English skills. Endang, for example, has been teaching seminary and institute for about twenty years).

Darsi was exceedingly shy. She was tiny and quiet and frightened to be in front of others. But she began to learn English very rapidly. Within a short while, she was reading Church books and magazines along with the scriptures. Both Darsi and Endang helped me with Indonesian as well. As time went along, my language skills improved, and I became more confident and comfortable speaking.

Toward the end of my mission, I received a letter from a dear friend, Arlene Flanders. A member of the Relief Society General Board, Arlene and her husband were traveling to Asia and wanted to visit me. She said she'd love to speak to the Relief Society sisters and asked if I'd be willing to translate for her. Would I! Of course! What an incredible way to finish my mission.

Early in 1978 they came—all the way to Central Java. The day came for Sister Flanders to speak to the women, and they began gathering. Then an interesting thing happened. I suppose, as I look back, that the Spirit had been trying to contact me for quite a while, but my pride in what I was about to do had kept me from hearing. So the Spirit shouted: "Edmunds! Who should be doing what you're doing?!" This question was one I usually asked myself. Early on I had formulated it to help me not take over and "show off" instead of "showing how."

Instantly I knew the answer, even though I had a nano-second more of pride and a little tantrum. ("But I want to do this! I've been looking forward to it! This is my *last hurrah!*") I knew that Darsi was the one who should translate. I whispered to Sister Flanders, and she understood immediately. But it took some talking before Darsi agreed (and by now I was almost frantic. I knew it had to be her, not MEE). I said something silly like, "I'll be right behind you, and I'll help you if you need me." Ha!

I say Ha! because there is no way I could have done what she did. She translated into Indonesian, but when she could sense that some couldn't understand, she switched to their native language: Javanese! Even now I think of what it would have meant to me compared to what it meant for her. For me it would have been a sweet entry in my journal. "I was a *star!*" For Darsi, it was an amazing, life-changing experience. A few weeks after I had returned to the U.S., I heard that Darsi had combined a couple of doctrinal talks about welfare by President Marion G. Romney and had spoken in a district conference. Incredible!

Friends, I could go on and on with true stories of my personal struggles with the sin of pride. You don't have those struggles, do you? Does it sometimes seem like pride is the most annoying interruption in your life, jumping in when you think you're doing fine, trying to smother your little store of meekness and humility?

The author of Proverbs declares that "Pride goeth before destruction, and an haughty spirit before a fall" (Proverbs 16:18). Howard W. Hunter adds, "Surely the lessons of history ought to teach us that pride, haughtiness, self-adulation, conceit, and vanity contain all of the seeds of self-destruction for individuals, cities, or nations."[1] Then he reminds us that President Ezra Taft Benson said, "The only true test of greatness, blessedness, [and] joyfulness is how close a life can come to being like the Master, Jesus Christ."[2]

In my soul-searching I've settled on three critical reasons why pride leads to destruction:

Pride separates us (1) from God, (2) from each other, and (3) from our true selves . . . from who we really are.

Pride lures or just plain jerks us off the straight and narrow way. Can't you just feel it some days—pride trying to pry your fingers off the iron rod? Pride gives us that transitory, falsely strong sense of "Hubba-hubba, ding-ding, baby you've got everything!"

Pride is one of the seven deadly sins, with the emphasis on deadly—deadly and deadening.

In an *Ensign* article, Elder Joe J. Christensen quotes from *What Is Sin? What Is Virtue?* by Robert J. McCracken: "'If we make a listing of our sins, . . . [pride] is the one that heads the list, breeds all the rest, and does more to estrange us from our neighbors or from God than any evil we can commit. . . . [Pride] is not only the worst of the seven deadly sins; it is the parent sin, the one that leads to every other, the sin from which no one is free.'"[3] The thought that strikes me most forcefully in this quote is that pride does more to estrange us from each other and from God than any other evil we can commit!

From President Ezra Taft Benson's remarkable 1989 sermon on pride comes the following: "Most of us think of pride as self-centeredness, conceit, boastfulness, arrogance, or haughtiness. All of these are elements of the sin, but the heart, or core, is still missing.

"The central feature of pride is enmity—enmity toward God and enmity toward our fellowmen. Enmity means 'hatred toward, hostility to, or a state of opposition.' It is the power by which Satan wishes to reign over us. . . .

" . . . The proud wish God would agree with them. They aren't interested in changing their opinions to agree with God's."[4]

Elder Dallin H. Oaks describes further how pride can separate us from God and from each other: "The pride of self-satisfaction is the opposite of humility. This attitude insulates us from learning and separates us from God. . . .

" . . . A person who has the pride of self-satisfaction cannot repent, because he recognizes no shortcomings. He cannot be taught, because he recognizes no master. He cannot be helped, because *he recognizes no resource greater than his own.* . . .

"Preoccupied with self, the pride of self-satisfaction is always accompanied by an aloofness and a withdrawal from concern for others."[5]

Elder Oaks quoted Henry Fairlie, author of *The Seven Deadly Sins Today.* Listen to what Fairlie says about the ways in which pride *does* separate us from each other and eventually even separates us from who we really are: "Pride may excite us to take too much pleasure in ourselves, but it does not encourage us to take pleasure in our humanity, in what is commonly shared by all of us as social beings. The turning into ourselves has turned us away from our societies. It is a sin of neglect: it causes us to ignore others. It is a sin of aggression: it provokes us to hurt others. It is a sin of condescension: it makes us patronize others. All of these are turned against our neighbors, and when in our Pride, we do not realize how aloof we have become, and how cut off even from what in our own nature we should most deeply know and enjoy."

Fairlie concluded that self-absorption produces a "self-improvement" that "is measured only by how good one feels about oneself." In this there is only "discontent," which "is always one of the punishments of Pride."[6]

The scriptures abound with condemnations and cautions about pride. Proverbs 6:17 lists six things the Lord hates. "A proud look" heads the list!

The Lord warns us in Doctrine and Covenants 38:39, "Beware of pride, lest ye become as the Nephites of old." And in Proverbs 28:25 we read: "He that is of a proud heart stirreth up strife."

Elder Joseph B. Wirthlin has cautioned: "Pride and vanity, the opposites of humility, can destroy our spiritual health as surely as a debilitating disease can destroy our physical health."[7] Isn't that the truth? Think of the shock when you've heard that a friend has cancer or MS or some other terrible disease. But did you hear that *Edmunds has pride* and is *critically ill spiritually*? That's got to be even worse.

How does pride destroy our spiritual health? Among other things, maybe it keeps us from hearing and hearkening to the counsel of a prophet. Is it ever pride that keeps us from doing things President Hinckley has asked us to do, such as trying a little harder to be a little better,[8] freeing ourselves from the bondage of debt,[9] attending the temple as often as we can,[10] being faithful in our tithes and offerings,[11] and being more cheerful and optimistic?[12]

Does pride ever keep us from being modest and appropriate in our dress, speech, and behavior? Does pride keep us from repenting and from forgiving? Does it keep us from praying earnestly and honestly? With pride, it's who you *know*, and with meekness and humility, it's who you *are*.

So pride does separate us from God. And it does separate us from each other. I mentioned that it may also separate us from ourselves!—from our own god-like nature, our own innate goodness. It may keep us from doing what our hearts would prompt and even compel us to do.

Pride interferes with so much of what we really want in life: the precious blessings of meekness and humility; peace of soul and contentment; a sweet relationship with our Heavenly Father, the Savior, the Holy Ghost, our family, and others.

Pride may interfere with our ability to be grateful, satisfied, and content. It leads to misery and regrets. Pride may lead us to be increasingly negative, critical, pessimistic, judgmental, competitive, and contentious.

Pride makes us falsely confident, thinking we can succeed without any help from anyone, including God. C. S. Lewis said that "a proud man is always looking down on things and people: and, of course, as long as you are looking down, you cannot see something that is above you."[13]

Meekness and humility remind us we're "in process." We *are* invited to try a little harder to be a little better even when we're already pretty good.

Pride keeps us from being willing and able to submit. It takes meekness and humility to submit, but as King Benjamin has taught, that's the only way we'll ever become genuine saints and more childlike and Christlike. "For the natural man is an enemy to God, and has been from the fall of Adam, and will be, forever and ever, unless he yields to the enticings of the Holy Spirit, and putteth off the natural man and becometh a saint through the atonement of Christ the Lord, and becometh as a child, submissive, meek, humble, patient, full of love, willing to submit to all things which the Lord seeth fit to inflict upon him, even as a child doth submit to his father" (Mosiah 3:19).

C. S. Lewis believed that "There is one vice of which no man in the world is free; which every one in the world loathes when he sees it in someone else; and of which hardly any people, except Christians, ever imagine that they are guilty themselves. . . . There is no fault which makes a man more unpopular, and no fault which we are more unconscious of in ourselves. And the more we have it ourselves, the more we dislike it in others. . . . According to Christian teachers, the essential vice, the utmost evil, is Pride. . . . it was through Pride that the devil became the devil: Pride leads to every other vice."[14]

How can we avoid and overcome the sin of pride? Benjamin Franklin said that pride "is the last vice the good man gets clear of."[15] That's encouraging! In his autobiography, he elaborated: "In reality, there is, perhaps, no one of our natural passions so hard to subdue as *pride*. Disguise it, struggle with it, beat it down, stifle it, mortify it as much as one pleases, it is still alive, and will every now and then peep out and show itself; you will see it, perhaps, often in this history; for, even if I could conceive that I had compleatly overcome it, I should probably be proud of my humility."[16] As President Spencer W. Kimball noted: "When one becomes conscious of his great humility, he has already lost it."[17]

Pride is like a pop-up on the screen of our lives. It just *is*. Do you know what I mean? It sometimes gets through our filters, it sneaks through our barriers. We might catch ourselves in a meeting or lesson thinking something like "*Boring*. . . ." Or "Hello! . . ." Or "Duh! . . ." Or how about "Boy, that was a waste of my time!"

Perhaps the biggest step to avoiding and overcoming pride is the first step—recognizing it. Maybe if we were more honest with each other about our struggle with this "deadly sin," we could help each other more effectively. Here's a quote I love, attributed to Francois René de Chateau-briand: "In the days of service all things are founded; in the days of special privilege they deteriorate; and in the days of vanity they are lost."[18] One way to avoid pride is to love—to be involved in service—genuine, no-strings-attached kindness to one another. Pure love. Charity.

Another way to avoid and overcome pride is through gratitude—appreciating and expressing thanks more often and more sincerely. Elder James E. Talmage put it this way: "Gratitude is twin sister to humility; pride is a foe to both."[19]

One of the strongest impressions that came to me while preparing this essay (besides being so *proud*) is this: One of the *worst* and most damaging things about pride is that it can keep us from receiving joyfully and gracefully any commendation or praise from our Heavenly Father.

This is one of the worst consequences of allowing pride to separate us from God. There are times when He wants to say to us, "Good for you! Good job! Well done! Thank you!" And what do we do? We talk back: "Oh, You're just saying that. It wasn't that great. You and I both know it could and should have been better. I'm such a mess! If only. . . . " *Don't talk back!* Sometimes we may think it's a way to show humility and meekness, but it's pride!

What if the Savior had done that during the days of creation? He comes back after a busy day separating light from darkness, or water from dry ground, and His Father says to Him, "Well done." And instead of smiling and feeling happy, He had to talk back: "Do you think the dark is a bit too dark?" "Did we make too many stars?" "Do you think anyone will mind that the water's wet?"

That did not happen, did it. His Father said, "Well done," and they likely rejoiced together over how wonderful it all was at the end of every single period of creation.

We neither give nor receive enough positive comments from each other, and it's so often pride that keeps these good things from happening:

"Thank you for that beautiful musical number."

"The one who usually accompanies me was sick, but I guess it turned out OK."

"Thanks for the lesson."

"Oh, I ran out of time, as usual. . . . Why does Nora always have to interrupt me!"

Ezra Taft Benson: "Pride is the universal sin, the great vice. . . . Pride is a damning sin in the true sense of that word. It limits or stops progression. The proud are not easily taught. They won't change their minds to accept truths, because to do so implies they have been wrong. Pride adversely affects all our relationships. . . . Pride is the great stumbling block to Zion. I repeat: Pride *is* the great stumbling block to Zion. We must cleanse the inner vessel by conquering pride. *God will have a humble people. Either we can choose to be humble or we can be compelled to be humble.*"[20]

Wow. We can either choose to be humble—to allow our life's experiences to deepen our faith, our courage, our hope, our meekness, and our charity—or we can choose to resist change and live consumed by our pride until a day shall come when we are *compelled* to be humble. Ouch.

Moroni, at the end of the Book of Mormon, asks us to "deny [ourselves] of all ungodliness" (Moroni 10:32). Pride is ungodly. It is godly to be humble—to be teachable, forgiving, submissive, kind, peacemakers, one heart and one mind with our fellow travelers. Can we do that? Can we get a little better every day? Can we help each other to become increasingly meek and humble? More pure in heart. More faithful and true. Holier. Happier.

Jesus is the Christ, the Son of the Living God, our Savior, our Redeemer, our Advocate with the Father, and He has done all He can to help us return to our Heavenly Home. May we respond to His meekness with our own.

Notes

1. Howard W. Hunter, "Come unto Me," *Ensign*, November 1990, 18.
2. Ezra Taft Benson, "Jesus Christ—Gifts and Expectations," *Ensign*, December 1988, 2.
3. Robert J. McCracken, *What Is Sin? What Is Virtue?* (New York: Harper and Row, 1966), 11–12; quoted in Joe J. Christensen, "Resolutions," *Ensign*, December 1994, 66.
4. Ezra Taft Benson, "Beware of Pride," *Ensign*, May 1989, 4. I strongly recommend a re-reading and careful study of President Benson's message.
5. Dallin H. Oaks, *Pure in Heart* (Salt Lake City: Bookcraft, 1988), 109, 91–92; emphasis added.
6. Henry Fairlie, *The Seven Deadly Sins Today* (Washington, D.C.: New Republic Books, 1978), 45, 52; quoted in Oaks, *Pure in Heart*, 92.
7. Joseph B. Wirthlin, "The Straight and Narrow Way," *Ensign*, November 1990, 65.
8. See, for example, Gordon B. Hinckley, "We Have a Work to Do," *Ensign*, May 1995, 88.
9. See, for example, Gordon B. Hinckley, "The Condition of the Church," *Ensign*, May 2003, 6; or Gordon B. Hinckley, "Thou Shalt Not Covet, *Ensign*, March 1990, 4.
10. See, for example, Gordon B. Hinckley, "'Oh, That I Were an Angel,'" *Ensign*, May 2002, 6; or Gordon B. Hinckley, "Keeping the Temple Holy," *Ensign*, May 1990, 49–52.
11. See, for example, Gordon B. Hinckley, "Inspirational Thoughts," *Ensign*, August 1997, 6; or *Cornerstones of a Happy Home* (pamphlet, 1984), 9.
12. See, for example, Gordon B. Hinckley, "Each a Better Person," *Ensign*, November 2002, 100; or Gordon B. Hinckley, "If Thou Art Faithful," *Ensign*, November 1984, 92.
13. C. S. Lewis, *Mere Christianity* (New York: Macmillan, 1960), 111.
14. Lewis, *Mere Christianity*, 108–9.
15. Benjamin Franklin, *Poor Richard's Almanac*, 1732–57; as quoted in Oaks, *Pure in Heart*, 94.
16. *The Autobiography of Benjamin Franklin* (New York: Carlton House, 1944), 103–4; emphasis in original.
17. Spencer W. Kimball, *Teachings of Spencer W. Kimball*, edited by Edward L. Kimball (Salt Lake City: Bookcraft, 1982), 233.

18. Quoted by Vaughn J. Featherstone, *More Purity Give Me* (Salt Lake City, Deseret Book, 1991), 15.
19. James E. Talmage, *Sunday Night Talks*, 2d ed. (Salt Lake City: The Church of Jesus Christ of Latter-day Saints, 1931), 483.
20. Benson, "Beware of Pride," 6–7; emphasis added.

Rise Up, Measure Up

M. Russell Ballard

In the 2002 October general conference priesthood session, I spoke to the brethren in priesthood meeting. The subject I spoke on was "raising the bar" or "raising the standard" of preparing our sons and daughters to be missionaries. Sister Bonnie D. Parkin, general Relief Society president, and her counselors feel that the sisters of the Church should also know what I think you can do to help our youth to "rise up . . . measure up . . . and be fully prepared to serve the Lord." Because I feel so deeply about this subject and because I have an abiding conviction that you, the women of the Church, must have a vital, irreplaceable role in raising up the greatest generation of missionaries the Church has ever had, I am pleased to respond to their request.

President David O. McKay, in speaking to the subject of women's influence and responsibility, said this: "By divine decree, the women in the Church are assigned the noble mission of being exemplars and leaders to mankind in the two most worthwhile accomplishments in mortal life. First, the development of character. That is done in the home principally. Second, willingness and ability to render helpful service."[1]

One of the great scriptural stories of the Book of Mormon supports

M. Russell Ballard, the grandson of apostles Melvin J. Ballard and Hyrum Mack Smith, has been a member of the Quorum of the Twelve Apostles since 1985. He attended the University of Utah, has written several books, and has worked in various business enterprises, including automotive, real estate, and investments. He and his wife, Barbara Bowen, are the parents of seven children and the grandparents of forty-one.

President McKay's teaching that women, particularly mothers, have profound influence when it comes to developing character, building faith, and teaching children to render helpful service. I reminded the brethren in the priesthood meeting of the two thousand young men who fought valiantly against the much older and much more experienced Lamanite army. According to their leader, Helaman, "they . . . fought as if with the strength of God; . . . and with such mighty power did they fall upon the Lamanites, that they did frighten them; and for this cause did the Lamanites deliver themselves up as prisoners of war" (Alma 56:56).

These inexperienced young men were so spiritually and physically prepared and so powerful that they frightened their foes into surrendering. And although all of them were wounded in battle at one time or another, not one of them was killed (see Alma 57:25).

Helaman recorded the reason that these young men had developed such incredible faith: "Yea, they had been taught by their *mothers*, that if they did not doubt, God would deliver them.

"And they rehearsed unto me the words of their *mothers*, saying: We do not doubt our *mothers* knew it" (Alma 56:47–48; emphasis added).

My dear sisters, you have a far greater influence as mothers, grandmothers, sisters, aunts, teachers, and friends than you may realize. You have an irreplaceable and an unparalleled influence with our children and youth because you have such a natural propensity for the things of the Spirit. We are today fighting a battle that in many ways is more perilous and more fraught with danger than the battle between the Nephites and the Lamanites. Our enemy is cunning and resourceful. We fight against Lucifer, the father of all lies, the enemy of all that is good and right and holy. This contest is a battle, literally, for the souls of all mankind. With the fall of Sadaam Hussein in 2003, we saw graphic, twenty-four-hour broadcasts about a regime that was evil, unforgiving, and relentless. The supreme enemy, however, is an adversary even more evil, unforgiving, and relentless. He is taking eternal prisoners at an alarming rate, and he shows no sign of letting up.

While the leaders of the Church are deeply and profoundly grateful for the many members of the Church who are doing great things in this battle for truth and right, I must honestly tell you that it still is not enough. We look to you, the women of Zion who have such a profound impact upon our sons and daughters, to help prepare them to serve in the greatest battle of all.

Today, we need young men and women who are ready, willing, and worthy to serve in defending and building the kingdom of God. We need young men and young women who have been prepared and taught by their parents, especially their mothers, to make and keep sacred covenants. We need worthy, qualified, spiritually energized missionaries who, like Helaman's two thousand, are "exceedingly valiant for courage, and also for strength and activity" and who are "true at all times in whatsoever thing they [are] entrusted" (Alma 53:20).

I am convinced, sisters, that you are perhaps the single most significant key in bringing this to pass. Because of your nurturing nature, because you are positioned at the crossroads of our children's lives—day in and day out—because so much of what our children learn comes from your words and your actions, I appeal to you today to refocus and redouble your efforts in this marvelous cause. Our youth need to be taught by their mothers in clear, direct, specific terms the commandments of God. You can fill their hearts and minds with such strong faith in the Lord that they will not doubt. They, like the two thousand stripling warriors, need to be taught by their mothers to believe.

You may wonder how in the world you can possibly do more than you are already doing. I don't know anyone who stretches herself further than a mother; or, for that matter, a grandmother or an aunt or a leader or a teacher who cares deeply about the future and well-being of the children she loves and serves. I'm sure you have days when you wonder how you will ever cover all the bases. You can't even imagine doing any more. Perhaps you will need to find more personal time to think, study, ponder, and pray. Every parent and teacher needs to find time to "be still and know that I am God" (Psalm 46:10). The ever-increasing demand for more and more activity outside of the home needs to be rethought. Parents need time to teach their children the gospel. The review and reallocation of more family time would be a very good subject for a family council.

Sisters, take a look at your life and at the lives of the children you love. Carefully evaluate whether or not there are things you can do differently—not necessarily in terms of quantity of time, I think you're all stretched to the limit on that, but in terms of quality of teaching and focus. Your attendance and participation in Relief Society can help you learn from each other how to prioritize your time.

I invite you to look at the children and youth over whom you have unusual influence, certainly those in your home and extended family. But include others as well: the young men and women you teach or who live next door to you or who are in your ward and stake. Think about the influence you can have in helping them to understand the restored gospel, which will prepare them to serve as missionaries.

What we need more than anything else from mothers and fathers is to instill into the minds and hearts of their children an understanding of the restoration of the gospel with its doctrines and promised blessings. Sisters, please help us teach our children the message and truths of the restoration of the gospel. They need to know about the apostasy after the time of Christ and His apostles. I know of no greater favor you can do for your sons or your daughters whom you send into the mission field than to arm them with their own sure testimony of the restoration of the gospel.

Help them to know that the Book of Mormon is another testament of Jesus Christ, and that it is proof to the world that Joseph Smith is God's prophet of this, the dispensation of the fulness of times. Teach the youth of the majesty of the life and mission of the Prophet Joseph Smith. When you arm your sons and daughters with this knowledge, then they will enter the Missionary Training Center prepared to teach the message of the Restoration by the power of the Spirit.

Think about the words that described the sons of Helaman: *valiant, courageous, strong, active, true*. Ponder ways to teach those virtues to your children. We don't need spiritually weak and semi-committed young men or women in the mission field. We don't need missionaries to just take up space or fill a position; we need their whole hearts and souls. We need vibrant, thinking, passionate missionaries who know how to listen and respond to the whisperings of the Holy Spirit. This isn't a time for spiritual weaklings. We cannot send our young adults on missions to be reactivated, reformed, or to receive a testimony. We just do not have the time or the luxury of doing that. We need our youth to be filled with "faith, hope, charity and love, with an eye single to the glory of God" (D&C 4:5). If you need to understand the Restoration better yourself, then what better subject could you study and discuss together in your family home evenings?

Are you teaching your children how to listen to the voice of the Spirit? Are you teaching them how to repent and why it is so crucial for them to be strictly obedient and to live completely on the Lord's side of the moral line? Are you helping your children learn about Christ and come to have faith in Him and His teachings? Are you teaching them to listen to our prophet and to follow his counsel? Are you teaching them to fast and pray and to turn to the Lord for help when obstacles and challenges seem overwhelming to them? All of these principles and concepts are best taught in the home, both in family home evening and in the course of day-to-day living.

Sisters, begin right now, this very day, to help the children and youth that you love and with whom you have influence to be completely and fully worthy. Teach them how to keep their hearts, hands, and minds pure and unsullied from any kind of moral transgression. Teach them to avoid pornography as they would avoid the most insidious disease, for that is precisely what it is. Help them to stay away from evil on the Internet. Help them to be honest and to be good citizens. Teach them never to defile their bodies in any way. And teach them that vulgar and filthy language is unbecoming and completely unacceptable for a bearer of the priesthood or for a young woman of God. Teach both your young men and young women to honor the priesthood as the power of God on earth and never to do anything that would preclude a young man from being worthy to hold that priesthood.

Your daughters have enormous influence on our young men. Help them understand their role in this tremendously important endeavor. See that they dress modestly and project a wholesome image. They need to know that to wear provocative and revealing clothing is not pleasing to the Lord. Remind them that lasting beauty comes from within and is a reflection of faithfulness and purity of spirit.

There are few things as powerful as the influence of a righteous woman. How can our young women be expected to grow up to be women of God unless they have role models to follow? How can we expect them to dress modestly, speak with clarity and beauty, learn the gospel, prepare for motherhood, and become women of God—unless you teach them how to do it? How can we expect them to keep themselves pure and encourage the young men in their lives to do likewise, unless you model purity and reinforce that there is no happier way to live? How can we possibly hope that our young men will grow in wisdom and stature unless you, their mothers and grandmothers and friends, show them how proud you are of them as they live worthy of holding the priesthood?

Teach our youth how to work and to find joy in working hard. Those who earn a good portion of the money for their mission bring to their service a depth of commitment that will bless them in finding, teaching, and baptizing the honest in heart.

These are high standards, and these are not small requests. I understand that, but I do not apologize for them. They reflect the Lord's standards for all young men to receive the Melchizedek Priesthood and for all young men and women to enter the temple, to serve as missionaries, and to become righteous husbands and wives, fathers and mothers. There is nothing new in the requests, nothing you haven't read before. Help our youth rise up, measure up, and step up to be fully prepared to serve the Lord during this, the eleventh hour and the last time that the Lord has seen fit to call laborers into His vineyard (see D&C 33:3).

Please understand, Sisters, that the day of the "repent and go" missionary is over. The day of parents hoping to get their semi-wayward son or daughter on a mission, expecting that somehow the mission president or a righteous companion will be able to work a miracle, is also over. I hope these words do not sound too strong or uncaring. I believe completely and totally in the sweet power of repentance to change the heart and life of anyone willing to undergo that process. But I also believe, from long and hard experience, that the mission field is not the place to initiate that process.

May I share, then, ten things we can teach our youth to better prepare them for a lifetime of service

1. Teach them to understand and accept the Lord Jesus Christ, His atonement, and His love for each one of us.
2. Teach them to develop a meaningful prayer relationship with our Heavenly Father—real soul-searching, personal prayer both night and morning along with daily family prayer. (This begins at the mother and the father's knee.)
3. Teach them to give the Lord more time by studying the scriptures and gaining an in-depth understanding of the marvelous message of the restoration of the gospel through the Prophet Joseph Smith. Help them to be missionaries who match our glorious message.
4. Teach them to keep the Sabbath day holy. Help stem the drift away from keeping the Sabbath day holy through your own attitude, activities, and example as parents and adult leaders. We've got a problem with that, and you can help.
5. Teach them to work and put earnings in a savings account for a mission. This, of course, is best encouraged by parents in the home who make missionary work a priority.
6. Teach them to pay a full and honest tithe. Such teaching is underscored when parents take their children to tithing settlement and teach them from the time they are small to set aside 10 percent of all they earn and to do so joyfully.
7. Teach them to limit the amount of time spent playing computer

or electronic games. The number of kills or baskets or points one can score in a minute with a computer game will have no effect on children's ability to be a good missionary and may, in fact, dull their senses, emotions, and receptivity to the Spirit. Limit time watching television, going to movies, and watching videos. And beware—be fully aware of what our youth are watching on all kinds of media.

8. Teach them to accept responsibility for decisions, to develop self-control, and to obey God's commandments.

9. Teach them not to waste time. Focus on things that matter most, such as serving others and finding joy in the happiness of others.

10. Teach them to recognize the prompting of the Spirit and to seek the companionship of the Holy Ghost, especially in sharing the gospel and testimonies with others.

Sisters, it goes without saying that as we "raise the bar" for our sons and daughters to serve as missionaries, we are in essence raising the bar for all of us as well. If we expect more of our youth, naturally we are also expecting more of their fathers, their mothers, and others who directly influence their lives. Remember, Helaman's two thousand stripling warriors were faithful because "they had been taught to keep the commandments of God and to walk uprightly before him" (Alma 53:21). They had faith and did not doubt that God would deliver them because their *mothers* had taught them (see Alma 56:47–48). This instruction came to them principally in their homes.

Now, I have one more suggestion. Some parents feel they don't have the right to ask worthiness questions of their children. They think that is the purview of the bishop alone. Allow me to dispel that myth once and for all. Not only do you as mothers, along with your husbands as fathers, have the right to know the worthiness of your children but you have the responsibility. It is your duty to know about your children's spiritual well-being and progression. You need to monitor carefully the issues and concerns they share with you. Ask specific questions of your children regarding their worthiness and refuse to settle for anything less than specific answers.

Sisters, do not slip into the mistaken idea that you need to be a best friend or a pal to your child or the youth you are called to serve. You need to be a mother or a Church leader who teaches God's commandments and the expectations He has for His children. That means you will need to be firm yet loving in expecting your children and our youth to be obedient. There are far too many of our youth who are living by their own rules rather than the rules set by God.

I admire and respect you sisters more than I know how to completely express. You are crucial to the work as we seek to build the Lord's kingdom in these last days. I know that you are very familiar with a statement President Spencer W. Kimball made more than twenty years ago. But let me repeat it again in the context of what we have been discussing. "Much of the major growth that is coming to the Church in the last days," he prophesied, "will come because many of the good women of the world (in whom there is often such an inner sense of spirituality) will be drawn to the Church in large numbers. This will happen to the degree that the women of the Church reflect righteousness . . . in their lives and to the degree that the women of the Church are seen as distinct and different—in happy ways—from the women of the world."[2]

I couldn't agree more with President Kimball. Much of the major growth that is coming to the Church will come because of you— because you teach young men and young women to be ready, willing, and worthy to serve on missions, to know the gospel, and to go forward to teach it with power to the world. It will come because your own happy, righteous lives spill over into your children's lives as well as into the lives of others whom you will serve. It will come because your children develop respect for a woman of God with whom they've interacted personally. And it will come from your support of your husband and your Church leaders. It will come because your children see from your sterling example that the only way to be happy is to keep the commandments of God and because they learn from you how to share the joy they feel with others. It is not possible for you not to have influence, my dear sisters. The only question is how far-reaching and how righteous your influence will be.

Let us never, ever forget that this work is all about people. And no one has more influence over boys and girls, young men and young women, men and women, and families than you do. Never, ever make the mistake of underestimating the influence you are in the Church and in the world.

President Gordon B. Hinckley, whom we all love, said this in setting the standard and the pace for all of us: "We have [so much] work to do, you and I. . . . Let us roll up our sleeves and get at it, with a new commitment, putting our trust in the Lord. . . . We can do better than we have ever done before."[3]

My sisters, I hope that things I have written have not offended any of you but rather that you can feel the love, the respect, the admiration, and the concern for you that emanates from the First Presidency and the Quorum of the Twelve Apostles and other Church leaders. We ask you to join with us in the sacred work of taking the blessings of the restored gospel to the people of the earth. Each one of you is precious. Each one of you has a mission to perform in the battle for the souls of our Heavenly Father's children. There is no power or influence in the Church greater than you are to solve the challenge that has been repeatedly pled for by President Hinckley when it comes to retaining in full fellowship those who join the Church. We ask that you lead out in your roles as auxiliary leaders, assisting the bishopric, assisting the full-time missionaries, and loving into full fellowship those who find the truth and come into the Church. Let your influence and love embrace them.

May God bless you with the vision to realize who you are and what the Lord has for you to do, and may we all "rise up . . . measure up . . . and be fully prepared to serve the Lord."

Notes

1. David O. McKay, "Women's Influence and Responsibility," *Relief Society Magazine* 43, no. 12 (December 1956): 807.

2. Spencer W. Kimball, "The Role of Righteous Women," *Ensign*, November 1979, 102.
3. Gordon B. Hinckley, "We Have a Work to Do," *Ensign*, May 1995, 88.

PREPARING THE "GREATEST GENERATION OF MISSIONARIES"

꒰ꜜꜞꜜ꒱

Anne C. Pingree

Courageous examples of righteous women in the scriptures have always inspired me. I have thought often of Hannah, the faithful wife of Elkanah. Unable to bear children, Hannah was a "woman of a sorrowful spirit" who "poured out [her] soul before the Lord" in the temple, pleading for a son (1 Samuel 1:15). "The Lord remembered her" and blessed Hannah with a son (v. 19). While Samuel was yet a small boy, she returned to the temple and told Eli the priest, "I am the woman that stood . . . here, praying unto the Lord. For this child I prayed; and the Lord hath given me my petition which I asked of him: therefore also I have lent him to the Lord; as long as he liveth he shall be lent to the Lord" (1 Samuel 1:26–28).

We don't know exactly how Hannah prepared young Samuel for his life's mission. Surely Hannah felt great joy as "the child Samuel grew on, and was in favour both with the Lord, and also with men" (1 Samuel 2:26). What we do know is how Hannah responded when she left Samuel with Eli the priest: "And Hannah prayed, and said, My heart rejoiceth in the Lord. . . . There is none holy as the Lord: for there is none beside thee: neither is there any rock like our God" (1 Samuel 2:1–2).

Anne C. Pingree, the second counselor in the Relief Society general presidency, received her bachelor's degree in English from the University of Utah and has a strong interest in literacy programs. She has served previously as a Relief Society General Board member and in various stake and ward leadership positions. She served with her husband, George C. Pingree, as he presided over the Nigeria Port Harcourt Mission. They are the parents of five children and the grandparents of four.

Hannah rejoiced! Today the Lord has asked LDS women to give Him the world's "greatest generation of missionaries"[1]—young men and women who meet a higher standard of faith in and commitment to His gospel. As mothers, grandmothers, aunts, neighbors, and ward members, we have been given a sacred charge. Like Hannah, let us rejoice in this opportunity and reach for a higher standard for ourselves.

How can we help prepare our young men and women "to rise up, to measure up, and to be fully prepared to serve the Lord,"[2] not just for eighteen months or two years but for their lifelong missions in mortality? We must teach them, first, to be meticulously obedient and faithful; second, to work hard and sacrifice; and third, to be covenant makers and covenant keepers.

In his October 2002 conference address, Elder M. Russell Ballard asked us to teach our children to be "meticulously obedient and faithful."[3] "Do the simple things," he advised.[4] One sister shared with me how she and her husband reared their seven children. "We have daily family prayer and scripture study," she said. "We faithfully hold weekly family home evenings. These regular practices have been the formula for keeping our family together and on track." Simple things, practiced daily in our families, can "bring to pass much righteousness" (D&C 58:27). As Alma reminds us, "By small and simple things are great things brought to pass" (37:6).

In our homes we teach children to be disciples of Jesus Christ through simple everyday habits such as regular personal and family scripture study, individual and family prayer, service to others, and experiences in keeping the Lord's commandments. It is often in seeing that these practices occur daily that a mother's mettle is tested. For instance, what mother during the last few years hasn't been presented with challenges to the principles of modesty in dress and speech found in *For the Strength of Youth?* Church standards for our youth are high and we adults must also adhere to them with precision. I heard recently of a sister who felt great satisfaction in reaching her goal to lose weight and become more physically fit. As she improved her physique, she also changed her wardrobe, buying clothing that showed off her newly toned body. As a Young Women adviser, she wore one of her new out-fits to a joint youth activity. One of the Beehive girls said to her, "Sister Jones, if I get muscles in my arms like yours, do you think my mom will let *me* wear a top that tight?" That honest question caused this Young Women leader to rethink her wardrobe choices.[5]

Contrast the interaction between this Beehive girl and her adviser with that of a new convert and a sister missionary in another part of the world. A faithful Nigerian mother observed the modest dress of an older sister serving as a missionary in her country. She noticed that the sister missionary always wore longer, stylish skirts and short-sleeve blouses in this hot, humid region of equatorial West Africa. The Nigerian sister, a convert now serving as a Young Women president, had left behind a worldly lifestyle when she joined the Church. Now as she quietly and carefully observed the dress and demeanor of the senior missionary sister, she taught her own two daughters this same standard of behavior and modesty in dress.[6] Without ever realizing it, the sister missionary had become an influence for good in the lives of these new Church members. She did not intend to be a role model, any more than Sister Jones intended to be one for her Beehive girl. The reality is that we are *all* role models for our daughters and sons, for the young women and young men we interact with, and for each other.

As covenant women, we are blessed to know who we are and *whose* we are. We know of the sanctity of our bodies. To be meticulously faithful in dressing modestly is not to follow some arbitrary guideline; rather it is a way that we "reverence our womanhood"[7] and express our faith. Our dress in a very real way shows our understanding that our responsibilities and our covenants are directly connected to Jesus Christ and His work upon the earth. When we teach young women to be modest, when we say we value modesty, when we proclaim that we are covenant daughters of God, we *must* be meticulous in living out these doctrines, or our daughters will surely be confused.

This conversation was recently overheard in a department store where a teenage girl was shopping with her mother for a swimming suit. As the young woman pointed out bikinis she would like to try on, her mother said, "That bikini is cute, but I won't buy it for you." The frustrated teenager asked, "How can you say it's cute, then say you won't buy it for me?" Five minutes later the daughter was in the dressing room trying on one bikini after another, with her mother saying, "Your father is going to be furious with me!"

Just as Satan strives to entice mothers and daughters into following the world's standards of dress and behavior, he also seeks to ensnare young men. Internet pornography, violent video games, hard rock music, and other media practices are tools the adversary uses to dull young spirits and lead many into a life of worldliness rather than missionary service. One young man was first introduced to Internet pornography as a result of innocent curiosity. Unable to forget the images, he became addicted to pornography, which triggered feelings of guilt and depression. He said, "I kept going to church so I wouldn't upset my parents. But I knew the lifestyle I was caught up in was wrong. I noticed a change in my own countenance. . . . I became calloused and hardened. I found myself lying to my parents, my bishop, everyone around me. Inside I was going through personal turmoil and spiritual torment." The young man continued, "I humbly bowed before the Lord in tears and pleaded for strength beyond my own. Night after night I prayed, and finally I knew I had to talk to my bishop." He approached his bishop and began a long and difficult repentance process and eventually was found worthy to serve a mission.[8]

A very important part of our mission is to teach our young men to be "modern-day Joseph[s]" who flee from evil. In other words, when exposed to pornography or other destructive influences, they "leave immediately—whether by a mouse click, a channel change, or a quick exit from a friend's house."[9] Being "meticulously obedient and faithful" in the simple things like prayer and scripture study will help fortify our youth against evil and unrighteous influences and will help them have the courage to resist temptation and be obedient and faithful.

A second foundational principle that will help young men and women "rise up, measure up, and be fully prepared" to serve the Lord is to be committed to the principles of hard work, self-discipline, and sacrifice. Parents must model these principles of discipleship as they teach them to their children. One family frequently discussed missionary service, making clear the distinction between a *sacrifice* and a *blessing*. Missions were anticipated as special blessings from the Lord with opportunities for growth and service that would require careful preparation. These parents wanted their children to *want* to serve. The mother noted that for about thirteen years her three sons, assisted by their father, had four morning newspaper routes. "These routes were our city boys' cows," she said. "In other words, each morning instead of milking cows, they delivered 220 newspapers. It was time spent working *together* daily. As parents, we felt the discipline of early rising along with the responsibility of completing a task would help our sons throughout their lives. The money earned was the boys' missionary funds. They deposited the money and watched the balances grow as they calculated the amount needed for missionary service."

She continued, "We wanted our children to be obedient and faithful missionaries. We tried to prepare them spiritually, physically, emotionally, and financially. They were not sent alone, but were led; we didn't ask them to do anything that we wouldn't do ourselves." These habits of hard work and discipline not only helped three sons and a daughter to *go* on missions but they also helped one son to *stay* on his mission when adversity almost overwhelmed him. A unique language in the mission made it necessary for this missionary to be assigned for most of his time to one companion—a difficult, disobedient elder. For months the faithful missionary struggled, worked, prayed, and counseled with his leaders. The situation did not improve. His mother believes that his stability during this trying time resulted from his compelling desire to serve and succeed—lessons he had learned at home.

Ten years later, reflecting back on this difficult time, this valiant returned missionary and new father recounted how he named his son "Matthew" to remind him of the strength he found in this New Testament book. He added, "If I could have named my son Matthew 5:7, I would have . . . out of respect for the Sermon on the Mount, because that sermon means a lot to me. It first became my favorite passage of scripture when I was on my mission. I was going through a particularly challenging time when I felt I was trying as hard as I could but was still unhappy. I had been taught by my parents to 'feast upon the words of Christ, for behold, the words of Christ will tell you all things what ye should do'" (2 Nephi 32:3).

This young father continued, "I put the words of Christ to the test every day and each time the words told me what I should do." Those words and teachings in Matthew 5:7 along with the strength of his parents' teachings carried this missionary through the most difficult times of his mission.[10] Hard work and sacrifice can bless the lives of all young men and young women as they prepare for missionary service.

The third foundational principle that can help young men and women "rise up . . . measure up . . . and be fully prepared to serve the Lord" is to be "covenant makers and covenant keepers."[11] How can we do this? What does this mean to us as mothers? As we get on our knees and pray to the Lord, He will teach, guide, and direct us. The Spirit prompts the prepared. Our poignant prayers can be like those of Alma: "O Lord . . . grant unto us that we may have success in bringing them again unto thee in Christ . . . give unto us . . . power and wisdom. . . . Behold, O Lord, their souls are precious" (Alma 31:34–35).

Power and wisdom are what we need as we teach our children early about the covenants they make at baptism. We can discuss with them, pray with them, and foster understanding of the Savior and His mission. Our privilege and covenantal responsibility is to stand as His witnesses in the world. Again, simple, consistent practices will lay a strong foundation. Testimony and beliefs shared with children will help them establish a pattern of their own belief and testimony as it did with a young man named Taku.

In Japan, where less than one percent of the population claims to be Christian, Sunday is a work day, and students are expected to participate in school activities. To do otherwise brings severe discrimination and heckling. Taku, a third-year middle-school student in Saga City on the island of Kyushu, faced a dilemma trying to keep the Sabbath day holy, as his parents had taught him from his earliest years.

During the critical third year of middle school, most students attend a cram school after regular school. They study late into the evenings each day and fill their Sundays with studies and after school activities—all in preparation for end-of-the-year exams, which determine each student's future in high school and college.

Taku had reached the third year and knew he was at a critical crossroad in his life. Just after the school year started, Taku was reminded again in a talk at a district conference about the importance and the promised blessings of observing the Sabbath. Taku resolved to honor the Sabbath day, one of the simple things he had been taught to do in his home. All year Taku remained true to his goal. He did not study or participate in school activities on Sunday. Finally, the time for the dreaded tests came. Taku's parents felt he would definitely need God's help. The night before the tests, his father gave him a blessing promising his son that if he showed faith, he would pass the test. The scores came out. The Lord had indeed blessed Taku. He was one of the few who obtained entrance into the school he desired. Taku knew the Lord had blessed him beyond his normal abilities.

But this was not the end of this young man's test of faith. Upon admission to the prestigious high school, Taku found that many tests were administered on Sunday. His faith did not waiver. He went directly to his instructor and said, "As a Christian, I believe Sunday is a holy day. I do not study on Sunday and I cannot take the exams on Sunday." To his surprise and the disbelief of almost everyone else, his teacher praised Taku for his integrity and offered to allow him to take the tests on Saturday.[12] By committing to keep the Sabbath day holy, Taku learned that even in a non-Christian society that often discriminates against Christians, the Lord keeps His promises to those who are covenant makers and covenant keepers.

Of course we don't *always* receive tangible rewards for keeping the commandments and honoring our covenants. The Lord teaches each of us life's lessons in different ways. Our son Clark was a competitive high school swimmer and co-captain of a top-ranked varsity team with a long tradition of winning the state title. For many years Clark trained six days a week. He would arise at 4:30 A.M. to practice for an hour and a half before school and again for several hours following school. Early in his life, however, Clark made a decision never to practice or compete on Sunday. His coach knew of that decision and ridiculed him saying, "Clark, you'll *never* be a champion!" By the world's standards, he never was. As a senior, he did not place first in the state in his grueling 500-meter freestyle event. But in his dad's heart and mine, he was a *true* champion. Clark honored the Lord's Sabbath day and put God first in his life. He lived a life of integrity—and that's what pleases the Lord.

We know as mothers that the results of all our daily teachings—all we do regularly to help perpare our children—may come together in a moment that defines a life. Think of Enos, for instance. He wrote, "I went to hunt beasts in the forests; and the words which I had often heard my father speak concerning eternal life, and the joy of the saints, sunk deep into my heart" (Enos 1:3). As Enos was "struggling in the spirit" for many hours and pouring out his soul to the Lord for forgiveness, his faith in Christ, planted and nurtured in his soul years earlier by his father, brought about this life-changing moment, which led to the remission of his sins (Enos 1:1–10).

Defining moments don't come only to the rebellious. Thom, a seventeen-year-old Latter-day Saint attending a very large, predominantly Jewish high school in the eastern United States, was nominated for the title of "Mr. Quince Orchard," the equivalent of homecoming king. The competition for this annual male popularity contest included an interview with the contestants before a school assembly made up of thousands of people from the student body and community. Each young man was asked to identify a person in history, living or dead, whom he admired. Then the contestant was asked to share a question he would want to ask this person. Usually not at a loss for words, Thom could think of nothing to say.

"Then suddenly," he said, "it was as if someone put something into my mind and I knew what to say. Without thinking or caring about the consequences of my response," Thom said, "my mind caught hold upon Jesus and I boldly began bearing my testimony of Jesus Christ. It was as though all the things that I had ever learned from my parents, seminary teachers, and Church leaders came together in this one defining moment when I understood clearly the power of the Atonement in my life." After bearing his witness of Jesus Christ, Thom said to the large audience assembled, "I would ask Jesus this question: 'Lord, how did you have so much love for each of us that you would take upon yourself my sins and the sins of all mankind?'"

The large auditorium fell silent and the audience sat stunned as Thom finished his response. When the curtain closed, a teacher standing backstage rushed up to Thom and said, "I can't believe you did that."[13] Thom was a covenant maker and a covenant keeper as he boldly testified of Jesus Christ before nearly 5,000 nonbelievers. Two years later as a powerful, "spiritually energized"[14] missionary in the Ukraine Kiev Mission, he continued keeping his covenant to "stand as [a witness] of God at all times and in all things, and in all places" (Mosiah 18:9).

Like Hannah as she watched her son Samuel "grow on in spiritual strength" and prepare for his life's mission, we rejoice when young women and young men like Thom "rise up, . . . measure up," and become "fully prepared," as Elder Ballard has urged, to serve the Lord as his "greatest generation of missionaries."[15]

Preparing this generation for *their* missions is part of *our* mission. As adults, whether we have children of our own or not, we should teach today's young people to be meticulously obedient and faithful, to be committed to the principles of hard work, and sacrifice, and to be covenant makers and covenant keepers.

LDS women will be given increased capacity and blessings to rise to a higher standard, to the Lord's standard, as we commit to teach sons and daughters, nieces and nephews, and grandchildren to do the same. This comforting knowledge, that the Lord is ever with us as we seek Him, gives us spiritual confidence and noble purpose as mothers. As we offer to the Lord the "greatest generation of missionaries," let us rejoice. For we *know* that "there is none holy as the Lord: . . . neither is there any rock like our God" (1 Samuel 2:2).

Notes

1. M. Russell Ballard, "The Greatest Generation of Missionaries," *Ensign*, November 2002, 47.
2. Ballard, "The Greatest Generation," 48.
3. Ballard, "The Greatest Generation," 47.
4. M. Russell Ballard, Worldwide Leadership Training Broadcast, 11 January 2003.
5. Personal knowledge of author.
6. Personal letter in possession of author.
7. Susan Bednar, BYU-Idaho Six-Stake Fireside, 16 September 2001; available at www.byui.edu/Presentations/Transcripts/Devotionals/2001_09_16_Bednarsusan.htm
8. "Danger Ahead! Avoiding Pornography's Trap," *New Era*, October 2002, 34.
9. "Danger Ahead!" 34.
10. Personal letter in possession of author.
11. Ballard, "Greatest Generation," 47.
12. Personal letter in possession of author.
13. Personal letter in possession of author.
14. Ballard, "Greatest Generation," 47.
15. Ballard, "Greatest Generation," 47–48.

"The Lord Has Beheld Our Sacrifice, Come After Us"

Susan W. Tanner

About a year ago, my parents had just completed a three-year mission and were settling into a new little home nestled in the shadow of the Jordan River Temple. Standing in the midst of unpacked boxes one afternoon, my dad answered a telephone call. It was President Gordon B. Hinckley, who delightedly told Dad he had a great new assignment for him. He was calling him to be the president of the Nauvoo Temple. Our family was in shock. We hadn't thought we were going to have yet another opportunity so soon to share our parents with the rest of the Church.

Within a few weeks, my parents were gone, leaving behind unpacked belongings, new furnishings, children and grandchildren, and a family room view of the Jordan River Temple soon to be replaced by a family room view of the Nauvoo Temple. The most important thing they left behind, however, was their lifelong legacy of sacrifice and service.

Somehow the call to serve and sacrifice for Nauvoo seems appropriate. The entire early history of that city is one of sacrifice. Just as my parents left their home and many belongings behind to follow the

Susan Winder Tanner was called as the Young Women general president in October 2002. She received her bachelor's degree in humanities from Brigham Young University. She is a wife, mother, and homemaker. A former member of the Relief Society General Board, she has also served in numerous stake and ward callings. She has traveled extensively internationally with her husband, John S. Tanner, a BYU professor. They are the parents of five children and grandparents of five.

Lord's call, the early Saints left their homes and belongings as they fled from Nauvoo to trek into the unknown West.

The Saints knew they needed their temple covenants to strengthen them for the ordeal ahead—to protect them and help them endure afflictions. Hundreds flocked to the Nauvoo temple in the winter of 1846. Even after Brigham Young encouraged them to begin their exodus, they lingered. "Notwithstanding that I had announced that we would not attend to the administration of the ordinances, the House of the Lord was thronged all day, the anxiety being so great to receive," President Brigham Young reported. "I walked some distance from the Temple supposing the crowd would disperse, but on returning I found the house filled to overflowing.

"Looking upon the multitude and knowing their anxiety, as they were thirsting and hungering for the word, we continued at work diligently in the House of the Lord."[1] This tender scene of Brigham returning to administer to his anxious brothers and sisters reminds me of the Savior compassionately tarrying with the Nephite multitude (see 3 Nephi 17).

Before these early Saints left that winter, they inscribed in capital gold letters on the wall of the Assembly Hall of the temple, "THE LORD HAS BEHELD OUR SACRIFICE, COME AFTER US."[2] They had sacrificed their all to build this temple and to make these covenants. They hoped that others would follow. Covenant-making and covenant-keeping require sacrifice on our part, but in return we are richly blessed—both as communities and as individuals.

As I've thought of the faith and endurance of the early Saints, I have wondered what characterizes such people. Like the people in the City of Enoch and the people of Nephi 4, the Nauvoo Saints were a covenant-making and covenant-keeping people, happy and at peace because the love of God dwelt in their hearts. This love of God, or charity, is the transforming love *from* God, an indebted love *for* God, and love for each other *like* God loves.

A perfect society must begin with individuals working to perfect themselves. President Howard W. Hunter said, "The key to a unified

Church is a unified soul—one that is at peace with itself and not given to inner conflicts and tensions."[3] We make our baptismal and temple covenants personally and individually. And as we individually keep those covenants, we bless the societies of which we are a part.

Certainly, women can play a major role in unifying the Church and strengthening communities. Eliza R. Snow said, "It is the duty of each one of us to be a holy woman. . . . There is no sister so isolated, and her sphere so narrow but what she can do a great deal towards establishing the kingdom of God upon the earth."[4] We are women of covenant, which means we strengthen our families, bless our ward families, and build righteous communities.

Each of us has, often in our own histories, stories of righteous women who influence generations, women whose dedicated lives resound with the Nauvoo Temple phrase, "The Lord has beheld our sacrifice, come after us." My husband's third great-grandma, Elizabeth Haven Barlow, was such a woman. Her personal experiences spanned most of early Church history. Her cousins Brigham Young and Willard Richards introduced her to the gospel. After studying the Book of Mormon, she was baptized and soon left her home in Massachusetts to join the Saints in Far West, Missouri.

She, along with countless others, endured the persecutions and expulsions in Missouri and Nauvoo, commenting only, "We all felt more sorrowful at seeing Apostles leave the Church than we did over our trials and persecutions."[5] Their hearts ached for former leaders who had lost their faith. On the way west, her experiences were difficult—she bore a child as she crossed the plains; her six-year-old child was kidnapped by Indians; she struggled for survival when her husband was sent on a mission; and, ponder this, she served as Relief Society president for thirty-one years.

Her daughter wrote: "To mother the Gospel had meant everything. No sacrifice was too great." She closes her mother's biography with this promise from the Book of Revelation: "What are these which are arrayed in white robes? . . . These are they which came out of great tribulation, and have washed their robes, and made them white in the blood of the Lamb. . . . They shall hunger no more, neither [shall they] thirst . . . : and God shall wipe away all tears from their eyes" (Revelation 7:13–14, 16–17).

"The Lord has beheld [the] sacrifice" of such women, and we are invited—in fact it is our duty—to "come after [them]." President Spencer W. Kimball said of our times, "The righteous woman's strength and influence today can be tenfold what it might be in more tranquil times. She has been placed here to help to enrich, to protect, and to guard the home—which is society's basic and most noble institution. Other institutions in society may falter and even fail, but the righteous woman can help to save the home, which may be the last and only sanctuary some mortals know in the midst of storm and strife."[6] What a wonderful privilege and trust is ours as women in these latter days.

Let me conclude with a modern-day example of a very different sort of trial from what our pioneer forebears endured, yet one that shows an individual woman's power to influence her family and strengthen her community. Several years ago my dear friend's oldest daughter got married. It was perfect: loving family members, warm, Indian-summer weather, and a beautiful and happy couple. After the temple ceremony, the family took photos, had a family luncheon, and then hurried from Salt Lake to Provo to prepare for a wedding reception that evening.

About a half hour before the reception was to begin, everything was ready—everything, that is, except that the caterer hadn't arrived with tablecloths, the wedding cake, and refreshments. Helpful friends had called the caterer's business and her home and left desperate messages. Someone drove to the business, but it was all locked up. Ward friends rallied and found tablecloths for the tables and flowers for centerpieces. They bought a small cake from the grocery store, decorated it with flowers, and even offered to buy refreshments. The family declined this kind offer because by this time guests had arrived.

As people came through the line, my friend gave a simple, brief apology for the lack of refreshments, then concentrated the talk on celebrating the marriage of this wonderful young couple. Even so, the no-show caterer became quite the topic of conversation—especially among the men at the party. They joked that the bride's father had no doubt planned this fiasco to reduce expenses. But as the party went on, we learned an astonishing thing about a Mormon reception. You don't have to eat to have fun! We all had a glorious time that night focusing on the things and people who mattered most.

After most of the guests and family members had left, the caterer rushed in with an ashen face, grief-stricken that she had made such a terrible mistake. She had written down the wrong day on her calendar. Never before had she done this. My friend simply reached out and hugged her. "Don't even worry," she said. "We're just grateful you are all right. We were worried that something terrible had happened to you. We had a wonderful time tonight, so there's no harm done for either of us." My friend was not feigning love or forgiveness; she truly felt what she said.

Her example taught those of us who were there so much. Think what anger and retaliation could have cost the caterer and her business. Think what a mother's decision to celebrate the wedding rather than worry about the refreshments taught her daughter about what is important. Think what she taught all of us about the power of the pure love of God. Here are a few lines from what the caterer wrote to her two days later: "I find myself with extra time today . . . since I haven't a wedding to serve tonight as I had planned. First and foremost, once again, please accept my deepest regrets for Thursday evening. In our ten-year history, I have never created such a disaster as I did for you and your family. Words cannot express the hours of agony I have grilled myself with as I have pondered the evening and what you must have felt. I want to make some sort of restitution for these damages and I hope you will help me create that situation. . . . I am so sorry.

"I also wanted to tell you of the profound experience this has been for me from an eternal perspective. In my life, I have never been treated with such Christlike love and compassion as you did that night. Your first impulse was to embrace me, and to comfort me, when I should have been consoling you! You were not waiting with wrath and anger at my mistake, but rather with love and understanding—as I have always hoped Heavenly Father would be waiting for me. You knew, without asking, the intents of my heart. Over the years, I have dealt with petty complaints ('I didn't like the color of the punch!,' etc.). You had every justification to be angry and yet you chose a higher road. Since that night, my mind has continually returned to a central theme . . . 'as you have been forgiven go and do likewise.' My way has been kinder and gentler with my children, my husband, and my staff. When their work has fallen short of my expectations, I have looked on the intent of their hearts rather than their shortcomings. I am sorry this lesson came to me at your expense, but it is one that will be with me forever. Thank you for your loving example of the higher road."[7]

My friend's righteous actions enriched all who knew her that night. I have witnessed in the scriptures, in our history, and in our communities the influence of righteous women. Let me reiterate Eliza R. Snow's words: "It is the duty of each one of us to be a holy woman. . . . [that we may] do a great deal towards establishing the kingdom of God upon the earth."[8] Heavenly Father loves each one of us. I know this. He is counting on us and will bless us to succeed in this noble effort. With Elizabeth Barlow, with my friend, with my own parents as they headed for their latter-day mission to Nauvoo, I seem to see engraved in their lives in capital gold letters a summons for each of us: "THE LORD HAS BEHELD OUR SACRIFICE, COME AFTER US."

Notes

1. Joseph Smith, *History of The Church of Jesus Christ of Latter-day Saints*, edited by B. H. Roberts, 2d ed. rev., 7 vols. (Salt Lake City: The Church of Jesus Christ of Latter-day Saints, 1932–1951), 7:579.
2. Heidi S. Swinton, *Sacred Stone: The Temple at Nauvoo* (American Fork, Utah: Covenant Communications, 2002), 136; see also E. Cecil McGavin, *The Nauvoo Temple* (Salt Lake City: Deseret Book, 1962), 96.
3. Howard W. Hunter, "That We May Be One," *Ensign*, May 1976, 106.
4. Eliza R. Snow, "An Address," *Woman's Exponent*, 15 September 1873, 62; see also *LDS Women's Treasury: Insights and Inspiration for Today* (Salt Lake City: Deseret Book, 1997), 415.

5. Israel Barlow Family Association, *Biography of Elizabeth Haven Barlow*, reprint July 1958, 3; see also *Church History in the Fulness of Times* (Salt Lake City: The Church of Jesus Christ of Latter-day Saints, 1989), 190.

6. Spencer W. Kimball, "Privileges and Responsibilities of Sisters," *Ensign*, November 1978, 103.

7. Letter in possession of Christina Parkinson.

8. Snow, "Address," 62.

LET YOUR SPIRIT
TAKE THE LEAD

༺༂༄

Wendy L. Watson

Do you remember a popular old song that said: "You make me feel like a natural woman!"? Since we know that "the natural man is an enemy to God," what might we deduce about the "natural woman"? "The natural [woman] is an enemy to God, and has been since the fall of Adam [and Eve]" (Mosiah 3:19)—that's what an angel told King Benjamin. With that truth in mind, anytime anyone or anything makes us "feel like a natural woman," we shouldn't hang around to sing another chorus; we should flee.

A few days ago a woman called me who was feeling discouraged, distrusting, jealous, and mad. "Mad at myself," she said, for some things and someone from her past that had made her feel like a natural woman. She was mad at herself for not following through on promptings, and now she felt immobilized. "I've made outward changes in my life," she said, "but something's still wrong inside." She was feeling like a natural woman, and it felt *bad*.

Some natural things can be good: natural ingredients, natural sunlight, natural fibers. Apparently, the natural look can be fresh and refreshing, although personally, it's a look that, for years now, I've

Wendy L. Watson holds a Ph.D. in family therapy and gerontology from the University of Calgary and also holds degrees in nursing and psychology. She has spent more than two decades teaching, researching, writing, and consulting in marriage and family therapy, both nationally and internationally. Author of Purity and Passion, *she is a professor of marriage and family therapy in the School of Family Life at Brigham Young University and was chair of the BYU Women's Conference in 1999 and 2000. She has served as stake Relief Society and Primary president.*

avoided sporting in public. Yet, as potentially offensive as my *natural look* may be to others, it's my *fallen nature* that offends God. Perhaps, ultimately, this is because when I let my "natural woman" dominate me, I deny the Atonement. I either don't feel a need for the Atonement and doubt its existence, or I don't believe in its power for *me*—to help me really change my life. When I feel either of these things, the effects of the Fall are probably rising up in my life.

Sisters, the Fall was real, and the effects of the Fall are real. When Eve, and then Adam, took that courageous step that moved us forward from our premortal existence into mortality, *everything* related to this earth fell. Our natures fell. (Can't you almost hear the "thud"?) Brigham Young even taught that the earth fell out of its orbit.[1] But as for us? Well, we fell precisely into our orbit—the orbit of the Fall, which was prepared by God our Father before the foundation of the world.

Where did this magnificent Fall leave us? It left each and every one of us spiritually deprived and in grave need of power beyond any that even our most intense efforts could ever provide. We could *never* work hard enough or fast enough or long enough to free ourselves from our fallen natures. We needed a Redeemer.

Over the past thirty years as a marriage and family therapist, I've often witnessed the pain of those who need healing of the kind that can come only from the Atonement with its power to change not just *behavior* but the *behaver*—inside and out. We need the Savior. We need His atoning power. He is the Healer. He will carry us "across the gulf of misery" and pull us out of it, if necessary. There is power in the Atonement for each and every one of us.

How do you picture the power that is in the Atonement? Is it like a huge reservoir of healing water that we immerse ourselves and our life histories in and come out clean and with happy endings? One woman saw it that way. Is it like a gigantic warehouse filled with vials of oil clearly labeled with our names? Another woman saw it that way. How do you picture the power for you that's in the Atonement? It really is there, you know. . . . Or do you?

Question: How can we really believe in the Atonement? How can we access its power?

Answer: Through the companionship of the Holy Ghost.

The angel who taught King Benjamin the truth about the effects of the Fall (that the natural woman is an enemy to God), and that those effects would be permanent ("and will be forever and ever"— sounds rather permanent, doesn't it?), continued: " . . . *unless*" (and aren't we grateful for contingency plans?) "[she] yields to the enticings of the Holy Spirit, and putteth off the natural [woman] and becometh a saint through the atonement of Christ the Lord" (Mosiah 3:19; emphasis added). Our responsiveness to the Holy Ghost will help us access the Savior's atoning power, and through that power we put off the natural woman and become a saint—and gain salvation.

All-pervasive changes occur through our association with the Holy Ghost, according to the Prophet Joseph Smith. Are you ready for a whole new you? The Holy Ghost is "powerful in expanding the mind, enlightening the understanding," but *also* one's whole soul and body are influenced, the Prophet Joseph revealed, leading to "a new creation by the Holy Ghost."[2]

A *new creation!* Now that's a makeover.

Years ago there was a credit card ad that caught my attention. The marketing slogan named the credit card, then added, "Don't leave home without it." Perhaps a slogan that would focus our efforts as we seek salvation could be: "The Holy Ghost: You can't get home without him!" Because the truth is that we cannot work out our own salvation *alone*. Don't even try it. It's just not possible. We need the guidance and direction, inspiration, revelation, comforting, counseling, tutoring, testifying, ratifying, nurturing, enlightening, purifying, and sanctifying of the Holy Ghost—if we're ever going to *be* who we really are, *do* what we came here to do, and return safely home.

So where do we start? (Or start over?) How can we really cultivate our own companionship with the Holy Ghost?

Start with prayer. According to President Boyd K. Packer, "[The gift of the Holy Ghost] is awakened with prayer."[3] Pray to Heavenly

Father in the name of Jesus Christ for the companionship of the Holy Ghost. Let your Heavenly Father know that you're serious about securing the perpetual presence of the Spirit in your life, that you're willing to do whatever it takes—willing to stop doing whatever needs to be stopped, to start doing whatever needs to be started—to access the power that's in the Atonement for you, to put off the "natural woman" and let your divine nature rise up. Let Him know of your true desire to fulfill the wonderful mission for which you were sent here to earth, and then to return home to Him. We need to be relentless in seeking the Spirit, tenacious in pursuing His influence, persistent in acquiring skills to hear His voice.

Will our efforts be worth it? Elder Bruce R. McConkie said: "There is nothing as important as having the companionship of the Holy Ghost. . . . There is no price too high, no labor too onerous, no struggle too severe, no sacrifice too great, if out of it all we receive and enjoy the gift of the Holy Ghost."[4]

After praying for the companionship of the Spirit, pray for the ability to recognize how He communicates with you. It's your right and privilege to know. Don't let His presence and His promptings in your life be a best-kept secret—from you. Pray diligently to know how to tell when He is with you. Pray fervently to know how He speaks to you.

One woman said, "I feel there's such a gap between my present ability to hear the Spirit and how it should be." As we talked, she realized that, ironically, that feeling of dissatisfaction was probably prompted by the Spirit. She had just taken one step forward in recognizing how the Spirit speaks to her, in this case, through unsettled feelings.

Take a moment for a retrospective look at your life. Remember those times when you didn't know the Spirit was with you, but now looking back, you know that He was there—urging, nudging, prodding. How did He try to speak to you?

Notice those bittersweet times when you actually did know He was whispering to you, but you chose not to follow through. Again, how did He try to prompt you?

Finally, notice those wonderful times when you heard His voice and heeded. Did a short message, almost a sermon in a sentence, come to your mind? Were you prompted to remember particular words from the scriptures, from a hymn, or from your patriarchal blessing? Did a few words or phrases that someone spoke linger with you, perhaps making you feel differently than you ever had before—more peaceful, more hopeful? How did you feel? What did you feel?

President Packer said: "The voice of the Spirit is . . . a voice that is *felt* rather than heard. It is a spiritual voice that comes into the mind as a thought put into your heart."[5] Pray to have the Spirit teach you how to hear His voice.

From time to time, add fasting to these prayers and watch what happens. Just like Nephi of old, you will be "led by the Spirit not knowing beforehand the things [you] should do" (1 Nephi 4:6). One woman was guided to learn how to hear the voice of the Spirit while reading the scriptures. She was tutored to kneel in prayer, to thank her Heavenly Father for the scriptures, to request that the Spirit be with her as she read, and then to tell the Lord what she needed from the scriptures that particular day—one question she needed answered, perhaps guidance in a relationship, perhaps confirmation of a decision. She would then open her scriptures—anywhere—and begin reading. She never had to read very far—in fact, most often it was only one or two verses before the Spirit gave her the answer she was seeking. Through these daily question-and-answer sessions with the scriptures and the Spirit, her sensitivity to the whisperings of the Spirit increased—and she fell in love with the scriptures.

I have related her experience to others who then tried the same experiment; the results have been astonishing. Everything from financial problems to relationship concerns have been solved. And in the process, their ability to hear the voice of the Holy Ghost has increased.

What else can we do to hear His voice? Create an environment in which He will feel comfortable. Take out the garbage. Clear away all the debris of this world that offends the Spirit of the Lord. Check for dishonesty and disobedience—past and present. Unrepented sin acts like Velcro™ for more sin, and it repels the Holy Ghost. If there are things to clear up from your past or your present—repent! And don't miss one life-saving step. If you don't know how to repent, talk to your bishop.

Check for any contention and unforgiveness in any of your relationships. Check your language and tone of voice—and your volume.

Scrutinize your TV and web site viewing habits, videos, movies, and music. Look for "lust dust," and get out your lie detector. You'll find that even the most benign-seeming TV shows often pander to the lowest common denominator on earth, which is: the natural woman.

One wife was concerned about the video viewing habits of her husband, although from worldly standards they were very tame. Still, she was concerned. He'd already sorted through his video collection once and discarded several. Yet, she still felt troubled. So she prayed that her husband would be led to remove any videotapes that were preventing the Spirit from being in their home in full abundance. A few days later her husband came to her with a huge stack of videotapes. One hundred and two tapes to be exact. "I'm throwing all these out, honey," he said.

"Why?" she asked.

"Because a question kept coming to my mind, and I used it to screen my videotapes one more time. The question was, "Whose agenda is this supporting?"

What a powerful question, one that could be used to screen everything from videotapes to employment to recreational activities. "Whose agenda is this supporting?" (One caution about using that question: Not long after this husband tossed the videotapes that supported the adversary's agenda, he was called as bishop.)

We are counseled to dedicate our homes and then, in the spirit of the temple, to see that no unhallowed influences enter or prevail. Be aware that while you're trying to remove the adversary's influence from your homes and hearts, he'll be doing everything he can to sneak into your life. A recent TV ad for fabric softener shows a porcupine talking to a woman folding laundry: "I'm _____," the porcupine says, giving the name of the soft, cuddly bear he's trying to impersonate.

"No you're not!" replies the woman, who knows her friend, the bear, better than that.

"Yes, I am. I'm soft and cuddly," the porcupine protests, sticking his prickly quills into the clean towels he's perched on.

The woman quickly puts an end to the porcupine's lies and presence in her laundry room with two simple words firmly spoken: "Please leave." He does.

I don't know who's been coaching those marketing people but if I didn't know better, I'd guess someone had been reading Moses chapter one. That conversation parallels one between Moses and Satan, when the adversary poses as the Lord to trick Moses into worshiping him. Moses can easily tell the difference, and after being badgered by Satan, Moses finally commands, in God's name: "Depart hence, Satan," and he does (Moses 1:21).

We're taught in holy temples how to deal with the adversary. Get the adversary out of your mind, heart, home, and life. Tell him to leave. (And you don't even have to say, "Please.")

Now that we've talked about some ways to increase the presence of the Holy Ghost in your life, let's talk about what difference it would make. How would having the Holy Ghost as your constant companion change what you would be able to do, say, think, or feel? Recently, I asked eight women from ages eighteen to fifty-five to try an experiment. For five days, in their morning prayers they were to pray, with concerted effort, for the Holy Ghost to be with them that day. Then throughout the day as they encountered any difficult, tempting, or trying situation, they were to pray for, and really picture, the Spirit being right there with them. These women's experiences were amazing. They came to know for themselves—in an incredibly short time and in very tangible ways—the truth of Nephi's words: "The Holy Ghost . . . will show unto you all things what ye should do" (2 Nephi 32:5).

These women experienced an increased desire to de-junk their physical environments, a greatly reduced desire to watch TV, an increased desire to reach out to others and to follow through on commitments (to others and to themselves), and an increased desire to take care of their bodies by living the Lord's law of health more fully. (One woman noted that she started thinking much more about life and much less about food, for her a liberating change.)

These women were better able to see quickly how they could have handled a situation better (including "mothering moments" that went awry). One young mother said: "My three-year-old noticed how calmly I handled a situation that normally would aggravate me. 'Mom,' she said, 'you have *good* patience.'" A middle-aged mother and grand-mother said: "I was able to express some concerns to my husband in a way that he could really hear them. In the past, I've been either too emotional or I've soft-pedaled the whole thing, not wanting to upset him. Either way, I'm not taken seriously. This time, with the Spirit with me, I had a voice. I felt empowered—although that's not quite the right word. I had a clarity of thought and a clarity of expression that was beyond me. In fact, when I look back on the situation I think, *That wasn't me,* and yet I've never felt more myself."

The group also reported that mental focus, the ability to really study, and the desire to learn increased. In addition, their physical energy dra-matically increased because energy-draining negative emotions were gone. One said: "In the evening I actually felt like cleaning up my house, and my husband and I started running at night together. What a change from sitting exhausted with him in front of the TV and complaining about my day." Stress diminished markedly. One young mother of two children under three said: "The pace of my days changed. Everything got done, yet without my usual franticness. Everything was more peaceful, more meaningful." A shift in priorities occurred: "For our date night we chose to go to the temple instead of to a movie," one reported.

Profound changes took place in their conversation patterns. Old habits of backbiting, gossiping, and cynicism simply fell away. They found it easy to be kinder, gentler, and more patient in conversations with others. A first-year university student said: "I felt more confident with people. I listened in a different way to my friends, and I knew how to respond to those who were having problems. It was like I knew what I said was true, and so did they."

One woman experienced the Spirit helping her to know what *not* to say: "A colleague had been rather rude to me the day before, but this day, really thinking about the Spirit being with me, I didn't feel any irritation. No malice. No urge to punish him with either sarcasm or cold silence. He came to me and apologized, and I felt very calm—like I should just listen and be silent. I actually believe I was being taught how to 'be still'—inside and out—to be more Christlike, both in my actions and my feelings."

A young wife and mother said: "I was taught to be more mindful of timing when to discuss things with my husband. I now see that, in the past, I've almost set us up for failure—for being frustrated with each other—by not recognizing how important timing is." This same woman, however, also felt quite discouraged and disappointed in herself at the end of the five days. "It's been a week of ups and downs, and I have many regrets. These five days have been a huge wake-up call for me. I let my physical body, that was tired and exhausted, take over my spirit, and I discovered that my spirit really can't be as open to the influences of the Spirit when my body is in charge." This good, honest, and conscientious woman felt like she had spent her five days struggling with her "natural woman."

Let's go back to that important stumbling block on our road to salvation, the "natural woman." Even when we're not carnal, sensual, or devilish, our fallen natures have tendencies that, although they might not make us enemies to God, certainly can wreck havoc with relationships and obstruct self-understanding. Our fallen natures can lead us to be childish and self-centered, fearful, competitive, condemning, noncompassionate, easily discouraged, proud, impatient, gossipy, paranoid, argumentative, divisive, distracted, demoralized, and dishonest—just for starters.

When we put *on* our natural woman nature, many harmful things can seem "natural." It's "natural" to want to act impulsively. It's "natural" to perpetuate harmful and hurtful traditions of our parents: a woman who has seen her mother treat her father poorly will "naturally" treat her own husband the same way. "Naturally," we will fear new experiences. Naturally, we will look at past behavior to predict future actions. And it's only "natural" to want to be acknowledged for the work we've done and feel disappointed and underappreciated if it goes unrecognized. Worse yet, what distress we "naturally" feel if someone else is applauded for what *we* did! It's "natural" to want vindication when someone has hurt us, to become discouraged when we fail, to want pain to stop—now. It's "natural" to want reciprocity in our relationships (I'll scratch your back if you'll scratch mine) and to feel upset and neglected when we don't get anything in return for our "niceness" to others. And, of course, it's "natural" to ask, "Why me?" when diagnosed with cancer, or question, "What have I done wrong?" when we're single, over thirty, and childless.

But sisters, when your spirit—your *true* nature—is influenced by the Spirit, what are your responses to the very same trying situations? Faith? Courage? Love? Forgiveness? Humility? Patience? Tenacity? Kindness? Repentance? Charity? Even gratitude?

Ask yourself this question: When your spirit, power-packed with divine DNA, is accompanied by the Holy Ghost, what happens as you face difficult situations?

The answer is: absolutely wonderful things that always defy and surpass this world's understandings and predictions—and even our own.

Therefore, when we catch ourselves kindly excusing a behavior, either our own or a friend's, by starting out a sentence with: "Well, it's only natural to . . . , " we should stop and ask ourselves: "By saying this, am I unwittingly fostering the 'natural woman' in myself or in my friend? Might I unintentionally be opposing my own, or my friend's, efforts to work with the Spirit to put off the natural woman and let our true divine nature surface?"

I've thought a lot about a statement made by Brigham Young concerning how to manage tempting or trying situations. He said: "Stop and let the spirit, which God has put into your tabernacles, take the lead."[6] I love that. Stop and *let* your spirit—complete with its divinely inherited DNA—take the lead. Let your spirit, under the direction of the Holy Ghost, respond to the situation.

Think about that for a moment: What would you be drawn to do if you really followed the practice of letting your spirit take the lead? How would you manage the mundane? How would you handle the next crisis? (There will always be another one, you know.) How would you respond to the very next tempting or trying situation—if you truly let your divine nature rather than natural impulse lead out?

Become a "natural-woman detective" in your own life (not in others' lives; that would just be another natural-woman thing to do). "Angels above us *are* silent notes taking,"[7] and perhaps some are even running celestial video recorders. When you're in the midst of a difficult situation, imagine angels taping the sequence and asking each other, "Will we be labeling this episode as 'Natural Woman Takes Over' or 'Divine Nature Takes the Lead'?"

I believe that for many of us our divine natures are getting restless—very restless! Perhaps it's because the clock is ticking on our mortal probation. Within each of us are superb spiritual gifts that are longing to be set free. It's time to establish an ever-closer companionship with the Holy Ghost. He can personally tutor each of us how to access the power in the Atonement. It's time—and past time—to put off the natural woman and to let our divine nature take the lead.

Notes

1. Brigham Young, *Journal of Discourses*, 26 vols. (London: Latter-day Saints' Book Depot, 1854–86), 17:143.
2. *Teachings of the Prophet Joseph Smith*, sel. Joseph Fielding Smith (Salt Lake City: Deseret Book, 1976), 149.
3. Boyd K. Packer, "The Cloven Tongues of Fire," *Ensign*, May 2000, 9.
4. Bruce R. McConkie, *A New Witness for the Articles of Faith* (Salt Lake City: Deseret Book, 1985), 253.
5. Packer, "Cloven Tongues of Fire," 9; emphasis in original.
6. *Discourses of Brigham Young*, sel. John A. Widtsoe (Salt Lake City: Deseret Book, 1954), 70.
7. "Do What Is Right," *Hymns of The Church of Jesus Christ of Latter-day Saints* (Salt Lake City: The Church of Jesus Christ of Latter-day Saints, 1985), no. 237; emphasis added.

INDEX